BY WILLIAM EVERSON

## VERSE

These Are the Ravens (1935)
San Joaquin (1939)
The Masculine Dead (1942)
The Waldport Poems (1944)
War Elegies (1944)
The Residual Years (1944)
Poems MCMXLII (1945)
The Residual Years (1948)
A Privacy of Speech (1949)
Triptych for the Living (1951)
An Age Insurgent (1959)
The Crooked Lines of God (1959)
The Year's Declension (1961)
The Hazards of Holiness (1962)
The Poet Is Dead (1964)
The Blowing of the Seed (1966)
Single Source (1966)
The Rose of Solitude (1967)
In the Fictive Wish (1967)
A Canticle to the Waterbirds (1968)
The Springing of the Blade (1968)
The Residual Years (1968)
The City Does Not Die (1969)
The Last Crusade (1969)
Who Is She that Looketh Forth as the Morning (1972)
Tendril in the Mesh (1973)
Black Hills (1973)
Man-Fate (1974)
River-Root/A Syzygy (1976)
The Mate-Flight of Eagles (1977)
Rattlesnake August (1978)
The Veritable Years (1978)
The Masks of Drought (1980)
Eastward the Armies (1980)
Renegade Christmas (1981)
The High Embrace (1985)
In Media Res (1985)
Mexican Standoff (1989)
The Engendering Flood (1990)

## PROSE

Robinson Jeffers: Fragments of an Older Fury (1968)
Archetype West: The Pacific Coast as a Literary Region (1976)
Earth Poetry (1980)
Birth of a Poet (1982)
Writing the Waterbirds (1983)
The Excesses of God (1988)
Prodigious Thrust (1996)

# WILLIAM EVERSON

# PRODIGIOUS THRUST

### AFTERWORD BY
### ALLAN CAMPO

BLACK SPARROW PRESS
SANTA ROSA 1996

```
PS
3509
.V65
Z62
1996
```

PRODIGIOUS THRUST. Copyright © 1996 by Jude William Everson Literary Estate.

AFTERWORD Copyright © 1996 by Allan Campo.

All rights reserved. Printed in the United States of America. No part of this publication may be used or reproduced, stored in a retrieval system, or transmitted, in any form or by any means, electronic, mechanical, photocopying, recording or otherwise, without written permission from the publisher except in the case of brief quotations embodied in critical articles and reviews. For information address Black Sparrow Press, 24 Tenth Street, Santa Rosa, CA 95401.

### ACKNOWLEDGMENTS

The quotation used on the half-title page (p. 23) turned up among my notes, but I have not been able to ascertain its source. Certain of my own poems herein were first published in *The Catholic Worker* and *Timbrel And Choir*: and the section from Part One called "Printer" appeared in the *California Book Club Quarterly*. "The Sphinx" was originally published in *Residual Years* (1968) and "Part Two" was originally published in *Earth Poetry* (1980). To these publications acknowledgment is gratefully tendered. It is also fitting that I should publicly thank the Guggenheim Memorial Foundation, whose assistance enabled most of this poetry, as well as much more to be written.

—William Everson (Brother Antoninus)

Typeset via Microsoft Word and True Type by Roxanne Bartlett, Jason Rainey, Letitia Martwick, Diana Dorsett, Judith Shears, and Bill Hotchkiss and rendered in Souvienne with University Ornate heads. Text editing by Allan Campo, Bill Hotchkiss, and Judith Shears.

Black Sparrow Press books are printed on acid-free paper.

**LIBRARY OF CONGRESS CATALOGING-IN-PUBLICATION DATA**
Everson, William, 1912–1994
    Prodigious thrust / William Everson ; afterword by Allan Campo.
      p.  cm.
    ISBN 1-57423-007-7 (pbk.: alk. paper) — ISBN 1-57423-008-5 (cloth trade: alk. paper) — ISBN 1-57423-009-3 (deluxe cloth: alk. paper)
    1. Everson, William, 1912–1994—Biography.  2. Poets, American—20th century—Biography.  3. Catholic converts—California—Biography.
4. Dominicans—California—Biography.  5. Spiritual life—Catholic Church.
6. Christian biography—California.  I. Title.
PS3509.V65Z62    1996
811'.52—dc20                                        96-21543
[B]                                                                    CIP

# JANUA CAELI

...*a little cry, the Babe's, that only,*
*To keep the human pledge and match the human woe,*
*That little sound, unsleeved, in the air's raw magnitude,*
*From the brute cave, where the mountain*
*Shook in its flawed stone: that tiny sound.*

*And she who had not quailed to meet the angel's gaze*
*Put forth her hand, and touched the tranquil*
*Brows of that glory.*

# TABLE OF CONTENTS

Preliminary Notes to Allan Campo,
    from Brother Antoninus, March 15, 1963 ................... 9
Author's Foreword to *Prodigious Thrust*, (October 30, 1992) ....... 13
Author's Preface (July 2, 1956) ...................................................... 19
Part One: THE UNIFYING FORCE ............................................... 25
Part Two: FROM THE DEPTHS OF A VOID ............................... 67
Part Three: THE FORCES OF THE PANG ................................... 97
    Triptych for the Living
        i: The Uncouth ................................................................. 112
        ii: The Coming ................................................................. 126
        iii: The Wise ...................................................................... 132
Part Four: THE FALLING OF THE GRAIN ................................ 135
        i: Toward Solstice ............................................................. 164
        ii: At the Edge .................................................................. 169
        iii: A Game of Cards ........................................................ 204
        iv: The Quittance of the Wound ..................................... 210
        v: The Crowning of the Queen ...................................... 216
        vi: In the Ripeness of the Weed ..................................... 220
        vii: The Burning Book ...................................................... 268
        viii: From the Summer of the Flesh ................................ 273
        ix: Past Solstice ................................................................. 292
        x: Advent ........................................................................... 294
Epilogue: I BEG FOR DELIVERANCE ......................................... 297

*In Situ*: The Making of *Prodigious Thrust*,
    by Allan Campo ...................................................................... 305
*Notes* ............................................................................................ 324

# Preliminary Notes to Allan Campo

*The first letter was handwritten on stationery of Saint Albert's College (Dominican House of Studies for the Province of the Holy Name, 6172 Chabot Road, Oakland 18, California). The second letter, dated the same, was typed on plain paper.*

---

Dear Al:

The enclosed letter explains itself. It is to be placed in the MS of *Thrust* between the Acknowledgment page and the Table of Contents.
Received your letter and will answer soon.
Great trip in New York.
Am going to take vows.
Yrs
    Antoninus

March 15, 1963

---

Allan Campo
6010 1/2 Brynhurst Ave.
Los Angeles 43, Calif.

March 15, 1963

Dear Al:

I returned from New York to find the typescript of *Thrust*. I could not resist the appeal of the fresh, clean, white pages, and yesterday I plunged in. I read it right through.
I must confess I was stunned. I had not looked at it for years, and suddenly to find myself immersed in this outgrown child of my brain was an astonishing experience. Episode after episode which I had forgotten rose before my eyes. Everywhere unqualified assertions confronted me, rebuking me with a self-righteousness which I remembered only too well, but which, encountered in the flesh, embarrassed me more painfully than I ever expected. The strait-laced rectitude coupled with the towering sensuality staggered me, and the astounding, unreflecting tendentiousness exasperated me no end. As you know, it is not that my faith has in any way lessened, but that my attitude toward its tenets has tempered and gained breadth.
But the style! Lord, how that book ploughs on through! It is fantastic—surely one of the strangest creations in the Church's long line of eccentricities. As I began to read I thanked my stars that I had not been able to publish it at the time; but now that I have finished it, I really regret that it is not in print. A great many things about my development would be made clear. It has a strength, an incredible strength, that overcomes all its deficiencies, even the clumsiness of the poor Third Part. I have earned, with my poems, a measure of fame, but nothing compared to what this book would have brought me.
And I am relieved about one thing: my conscience is clear in regard to Mary. I feel that there is no essential violation of taste, that she does emerge as a person of great dignity and transcendent worth. I understand the feelings that moved her to prevent publication, and I dare say the world sides with her. ... If she could only

have risen to the occasion and verified everything I had spoken of her, proved, in her greatness of spirit, the claim I made for her....

And yet of course this is not the whole story. Ortega in his book on love says that it is the highest instinct of the man to bring the sum of his experience to the world, which, if he fails to do, makes him feel he is betraying his deepest responsibility; whereas it is the highest instinct of the woman to protect from public gaze the inmost secrets of herself. This is the archetype which divides us. How many women, outraged, have destroyed the great visionary work of genius their lovers brought to them, fondly expecting they would be only too glad to pass it on to the world?

...

It seems to me that the book stands chiefly as a witness to the religious attitude at one level of its development, and does this with astonishing power, with great transforming beauty. And I say such things well aware that, coming from me, they may nullify the judgment. Chronologically it stands between *The Crooked Lines of God* and *The Hazards of Holiness*. In *The Hazards of Holiness* we see burned away the tendentiousness and self-righteousness that was the chief determining element in *Prodigious Thrust*. The final poem in *Hazards*, "In Savage Wastes," stands at the opposite polarity from *Thrust*. It is my own answer to myself, my own rebuke to the aggressive righteousness that strapped my mind, and of which poor [James] Dickey got the final rumblings in that ludicrous exchange in *Sewanee Review* [#D 17 & #D 18 in Scarecrow *Bibliography*]. Good riddance. Let it go. But is it not strange that a spiritual defect of that kind can be the chief element in what is, surely, an astonishing literary creation?

Tendentiousness is perhaps the most condemned feature in the critical program of our time. Our age seeks the pure aesthetic; it is anti-polemical, anti-programmatic, almost anti-subject matter. For us, propagation is propaganda, and we loathe it. But yet there is a certain genre, actually a very powerful genre, which is the direct product of tendentiousness. A certain compelling torsion is inconceivable without it, and we see it at its greatest in Claudel. He never passed beyond it, so that in the end his tendentiousness achieved a maturity and seasoned efficacy which *Thrust* never touches. But *Thrust* has something Claudel himself could never approximate either, and that is its American spirit. It seems to me a product of American Puritanism, in the same sense *Lord Weary's Castle* is. And the tendentiousness of the early Lowell, made possible by his puritan past and his dogmatic Catholic adhesion—a struggling rhetorical wrestling, achieving out of its anguish and labor a consummate expression he could never touch again—finds a kind of prose counterpart in *Thrust*. Lowell solved the problem of his Puritanism by renouncing the Church and writing *Life Studies*. I solved it by the depth-probe via Jung and writing *Hazards of Holiness*. Lowell lost his Puritanism all right, but he lost everything else with it. He certainly lost his stature as an artist, for when he chose one polarity to the exclusion of the other, he erased the field of tension within him upon which the drama of an art is enacted, and no matter how much his friends praise his later work, it has lost its life. But what I really want to say is that regardless of our solution, these early works are something neither he nor I could ever recreate, not even if we wanted to, which is out of the question. And I look on *Thrust* and smile with wonder, but the wonder is all the same one of gratitude, as Lowell must look back on *Lord Weary's Castle*, embarrassed by its strictures, but awed by its undeniable power.

    Well, enough. Let me thank you again and again for the long hours of typing from my smudged and faded carbon. I cannot say I regret that I let you do it, for I have the fruits, but I know it was an imposition on your time, self-imposed but nonetheless real, that nothing can repay. But I do thank you.

    Give my regards to all in Los Angeles. I would hope to see you soon but I do not know when that will be possible. Everywhere my readings are proliferating this spring, so that I have little time. As I grope out into new areas of awareness, I am chastened by the knowledge of all the imperfect levels behind me, so ignorant of the real spiritual problems a man must go through, but so earnestly expressed. Of all these, or among these, surely *Prodigious Thrust* is most revealing.

    Yours,
        Brother Antoninus

# Author's Foreword
## to *Prodigious Thrust*

RELIGIOUS CONVERSION IS PERHAPS the greatest moment in human experience. I say perhaps because other peak experiences all have their advocates, and the subjective criteria become confusing. I make this claim on the basis that, in terms of impact, the conversion experience follows the spiritual model of the archetypal sex act, a universal myth celebrating the encounter between the Lover and his Beloved.

Thus the symbolism is true to expectation. The experience launches the soul out on a quest that dwarfs the paradigmatic model, leaving the psyche in disarray, akin to the madness of the lunatic and the lover, the poet and the mystic, not to mention the lascivious exuberance of the sacred whore. All are bounds-breaking: the ecstasy of the flesh and the rapture of the spirit. Each is true to the intrepid demand of a proclivity gauged on extinction, the annulment of relationship in the extremes of volition. Religious conversion is the centering of insuperable divinity into the most fragile interstices of created being. It should come as no surprise, then, to learn that I found my God in the bed of a fallen woman, one who taught me the secrets of a passion beyond the reaches of mentation; in fact the admonition evokes the irresistible rejoinder: "He would!" But the poet-mystic turns a cool ear to the rebuff, serene in the plenitude of [the] making forces of life.

In this intrepid stance the Lover seizes the Beloved in an embrace that compresses all being in its matchless comprehension, drugged with a stupefying symbiosis redolent of [word(s) missing]. [I] make such conjectures because this book must subsist by virtue of that attribution or fail utterly.

***

Fred Rizzo, who had written his doctoral thesis on my poetry at the University of Oklahoma, published in *The Denver Quarterly* an article entitled "Brother Antoninus: Vates of Radical Catholicism." I had permitted him access to the manuscript of *Prodigious Thrust*, and he commented on it as follows:

> Everson's narration of the encounter with the woman who would lead him to his conversion reveals the ambivalent directions—sensuality, Puritanism, Eros and Agape, to name some of the extremes—in what Unamuno would describe as "a man of flesh and blood." And as such, though the narration is fraught with contradictions and many tyrannical assertions, when one considers it in terms of Everson's earlier and later development, it is nonetheless a moving narration of his quest for meaning.

Actually, what is at issue here is the matter of attitude. Rizzo was writing in the wake of Vatican II, the most sweeping cultural revision in the history of the Church. But I had written a decade earlier during the pontificate of Pius XII, who ran a very tight ship, standing as the epitome of conscious control from the top down. Moreover, I undertook the awesome task of revisioning the classical consensus as to the incompatibility between sensuality and mystical contemplation. (Converts rush in where theologians fear to tread!) I did this by retaining the abiding religious discourse hallowed by centuries of polemically trenchant rhetoric so repugnant to the visionaries of Vatican II. But now the Church is steadily moving back to recover its ancient norms of expression, and exaltation is once again coming into favor. It is my hope that my convert's unblushing naïveté, contradictory and tyrannical though it may be, will gain acceptance among perceptive readers on the lookout for significant trends.

It was only to be expected, then, that after baptism I would attempt the recovery of so crucial a moment in the evolution of my life. But I could not deny the relevance of the negative element in the prevailing positive dimensions of the experience. I sought to body forth the disconcerting contrarieties of actual experience, foregoing the spirit's thirst for ideality in the interest of the actual.

***

I began my account in 1952, shortly after entering the Dominican Order. I was fully forty years old and at the top of my powers. My major effort of this period was the printing of my handpress edition of *The Novum Psalterium Pii Xii*, the first fundamental printing of this great opus since the time of the primitive [sic—era of Gutenberg] Church. But I was having difficulty in mounting it as a project, bedeviled by many untoward delays, so that the writing of *Thrust* emerged to absorb my thirst for creative release. When I think of this book and the *Psalter* going forward together, neck and neck, so to speak, it blows my mind, but as I say, I was at the peak of my powers and made a good showing before I was compelled to relinquish both projects in that ineluctable spiritual aridity known as the Dark Night of the Soul.

When I first began writing my conversion story, I asked my wife, to whom my conversion was accountable, if she would peruse the work as it progressed, but she demurred, saying she would defer to the wisdom of the Order as [to] the work's publishability, so I launched out in full stretch, and, chapter by chapter, narrated the story of my life as I had lived it. But when I submitted it to the Fathers, I was told she must see it and approve of it for publication because Catholic moral theology holds that one cannot disclose the sins of another without that person's permission. I therefore placed *Prodigious Thrust* in her hands and awaited her reply.

It was not long in coming and it was painful. She said she could not countenance the notoriety that publication would entail. Furthermore I had made her a saint, and she felt the attribution was untenable. The monastic censors checked it out, but, given the prior judgment on moral grounds, offered no report, effectively forestalling publication.

Then Father Victor White, the eminent English theologian who taught at the West Coast Dominican House of Studies that year, read the book and was enthusiastic. He approached the incumbent provincial and fired him up regarding the significance of what I had written, then sought out my wife to persuade her to permit its publication. He gave it the highest praise, comparing it to St. Augustine's *Confessions* and used other glowing examples to convince her, but to no avail. At first staggered by these glowing attributions, she came to question his estimates, conjuring up doubt and finding objections, prone to fears and misgivings, apprehensive of the impending denouement, were the book to appear, revoking the measure of that certitude which had carried her despite all resistance back to the Church, she clung to her stance of categorical refusal. Victor White, due to his open espousal of the psychology of C.G. Jung, was not without his enemies in the conservative wing of the Order. He was cautioned to adopt a modicum of discretion. My superiors in turn bade me moderate my efforts, putting the matter on hold. This I reluctantly did. Victor White returned to England, and the matter seemed closed.

Then in the Autumn of 1955, Frank Sheed, the renowned Catholic theologian and publisher, wrote to me saying that recently in San Francisco one of his salesman had learned through the grapevine of my autobiography, and Sheed asked if he might see it. My hopes soared: it seemed a new angle that might prove fruitful. Such was Sheed's prestige that my superiors did not object, and I posted the manuscript.

The result was sensational. A telegram arrived inviting me to fly back to New York at the publisher's expense. Permission was granted, and the week following Thanksgiving I found myself on my first airplane flight going East. In the big city I was wined and dined and made much of. Frank Sheed said he believed he could produce a version acceptable to my wife as well as myself. With that understanding I signed a contract and returned home to California.

But before leaving I had made a profound error in judgment. Apprehensive of air transport with its sensational crashes, I had written [my wife Mary] a poignant letter disclosing my opportunity, assuring her of my love, and beseeching her prayers for my safety, hopeful that Frank Sheed's reputation would reassure her with the credibility effort. I returned to find that exactly the opposite of my intention was the resounding result. ... The predictable outcome was a marked deterioration of our relationship.... Frank Sheed...had suffered a fall during street-preaching and [the manuscript] languished pending his recovery. He finally flew to England, taking the manuscript and editing it according to his conception of the work's potential. He called in Victor White, who read what he had written and reacted negatively, but it was nothing compared to my reaction. I was outraged. Sheed cut the living guts from my book, eviscerated it, plexus and groin, the libido and the soul. I cast myself down and wept at the livid atrocity, swearing I would never again suffer such indignity in the interest of expedience. As for my wife, she stood her ground....

At the profound shift in values from the conservative Fifties to the radical Sixties, the lurid corpse of *Prodigious Thrust* lay unread but not forgotten, its auspicious rhetoric confirming its heritage in the immutable past. But when the revolutionary onslaught of Vatican II erupted in the vitals of the stunned Church, I thanked my stars my book had not been issued. I was aware of Thomas Merton's embarrassment before his best-selling conversion story of the Forties, *The Seven Story Mountain,* which in retrospect seemed hopelessly naïve and uncritical, left gasping for breath by the cyclone of Vatican II. As I say, it left me thanking my stars that *Thrust* had been spared such ignominy before it surfaced.

So I turned my back on my book, leaving it unacknowledged, an orphan. Under the impress of the period, my attitude underwent a profound transformation: though I deplored the jettisoning of the Church's contemplative norms in favor of social action, the new spirit did excite me to celebrating the acclaimed modernization of the ancient hegemony. I sensed a similar softening of attitude in the perspective of my wife, and I boldly featured [Part Two], "From the Depths of a Void," in a collection of essays called *Earth Poetry,* and it went unchallenged....

William Everson
    Santa Cruz, California
    October 30, 1992

# Author's Preface

ALTHOUGH THIS WORK WAS YEARS aborning, it never achieved its shape, remains a kind of bloody stump, a painful truncation. Its first part, which was meant to prefigure the long growth of vocation in an unwritten second book, cannot be balanced by the abrupt "Epilogue" now serving as termination. Moreover, the episodic nature of treatment throughout—a characteristic natural to the poet but fatal to the narrator—delivers it up to an inherent lack of unity no juxtapositioning can overcome, so that the line of development proceeds by loose association rather than conscious plan. Finally, what was conceived as essentially a book of poetry supported by an autobiographical context, came, through the incorporation of so many digressions, to swell out of all proportion, until the poems survive only as a kind of archipelago awash in an ocean of prose.

However, beneath these disjunctive elements resides a basic integrating factor, and that is its point of view. The book was written in a monastery,* and that fact informs its whole character. Monasticism is the perfect mode of Christian integration, and in this book a man, having undertaken the monastic life, seems to recapitulate his relevant past in terms of its unifying context. In so doing he assumes its qualities of withdrawal and quietude as prime determinants against which the recapitulation may be engaged, and if he dredges up elements not traditional to the substance of monastic reflection, his justification can only be that the monastery was made to engage the actual shape of men's hearts as the world delivers them up to it, and nothing less. This book registers the torsion between the extremes of monastic and secular tendency, a man's struggle to synthesize the evocative simplicity of the one with the wounded sensibility of the other, the struggle to bring a chaotic past and unitive ideal into an immediate equation, and secure through their engagement a true triumph and a clear emergence.

Of course it fails. I have said the quietude and withdrawal of monasticism have been used as determinants against which to gauge the past. But not only is present day monasticism, in its state of rapid transition, too unresolved to represent the final crystallization it should ideally provide, but the writer's practice of it has not been sufficiently mature to utilize the very considerable degree of detachment it has actually retained. This conjoined deficiency blurs the focus, and accounts for the great areas of irresolution, and the terrible willfulness of attitude, which leave their stain indelibly upon these pages, making of the book a radically different thing than one might expect from the cloister, and the very truncation witnesses to the extremity of torsion achieved. It was, obviously, written too soon. Many years will have to go by before such a triumph and such an emergence are possible.

Nonetheless, monasticism, hearted as it is upon the sacramental reality, and especially Dominican monasticism, with its prime theological orientation, has been an extraordinarily stabilizing force in the writer's life, and such integration as the book possesses must be attributed directly to it. He can truly say that it could not have emerged from any other context, would have come forth a radically different thing. And it is this which brings us back, despite the deficiencies, to the unifying factor that binds the elements together.

We begin, then, upon the way of conversion, which precedes the way of rectification, and we seek to establish the threshold of the spiritual life, establish it in all its cruciality, the prelude to purgation and salvation. In so doing, the whole cauterizing process must emerge into the forefront of the consciousness again, and the suffering-out must be undergone at the acute level of retrospection. This requires a corresponding degree of exposure, and I hope that I have not exaggerated its anguish and its truth. But in the decision to issue so naked an account what I cannot evade is the pain it will bring to one whose life I have not spared but whose sanctity I revere, and yet I proceed on the strength of factors quite apart from any pain or any pleasure it may cause either her or myself. If it is demanded of me what right I have to do this, I can only say that the facts of our lives impinge upon issues larger than we, issues very much alive today, and which ought to be met today, not fifty years hence after a comfortable interval of time has so softened the impact of reality as to make all issues innocuous. For the Christian there is nothing, really, to conceal, aware as he is that what is now done in secret will be shouted from the housetops—though I concede I do not know how one may presume to anticipate that event. Otherwise it is mostly a matter of one's attitude, what one is willing to yield; a matter, shall we say, of taste. Is it not at the level of taste that the dreadful wound may be contained in an act of exquisite fitness, subsumed in the mercy of our human love, and healed in the depths of the divine compassion?

And if my words, volcanic, sear new wounds too deep for her to bear, inundating with fire an area of soul already painful beyond all penance, I can only pray that they may increase in her the holiness her own pain for me confirmed. But I do so in fear and trembling, and I ask the almighty God to forgive me for appropriating so brutally the office of her sanctification, knowing that every iota of egoism accruing in my act will be most ruthlessly appraised.

Brother Antoninus, O.P.

Feast of the Visitation, July 2, 1956
College of St. Albert the Great
Oakland, California

---

*The Dominicans have always spoken of their houses as *convents*, and their life as *conventual*, but history plays tricks with words. A convent has become simply a house for female religious. I have, therefore, in the teeth of Dominican tradition, adopted the terms *monastery*, *monastic*, and *monasticism*, as the only really vital ones in use today which grasp the essential meaning of a common life separated from the world.

# PRODIGIOUS THRUST

*"The whole of creation desires to pass out of itself, to renounce itself, because it is incomplete and will never rest until it rests in Him. Exasperated by its deficiency it is moved to self-denial in a prodigious thrust toward the perfect."*

# Part One

# THE UNIFYING FORCE

*For I am the least of the apostles, who am not worthy to be called an apostle, because I persecuted the church of God. But by the grace of God I am what I am, and His grace in me hath not been void.*

                                          Saint Paul

IT IS DEEP NIGHT, AUTUMN, 1953. In the cloister garth the herbs, boxwood and ivy and the lank selal, wrapped in the thick, warmth-retaining darkness of their autumnal foliage, reach out their limbs to draw the last vigor of the year, and from their secretive pores they yield that indefinable odor of the season, half-wild, interrogative and mysterious as the whispering of time, to question and inform the dark, the mingling testimonial of the profferance of seed. The monastery, shrouded in the depths of its recollection, gathers into focus the diffuse consciousness of its correlated lives. It is a Dominican House of Studies, and I, a Lay Brother, contingent to that study but not engaged in it, pause in my rounds to taste a moment the translucent night, grateful for its goodness, its wise regardful stars.

And standing among these autumn-laden herbs I let my mind lift over the monastery roof, slate-steep, jutted with gables and the high-flung cross; lift over the oaks outside; lift over the endless avenues lacing the narrow shelf of earth between the molded hills and the eastern edge of the Bay. Westward the lights of San Francisco dapple the tranquil shore. I see them every night from my cell high in the monastery, a myriad glitter, uncountable. Northward the Sacramento, draining the inland valley and the immense watershed beyond, spends itself in the Bay, crossed and recrossed by its taut bridges arching their lanes of traffic high in the voiding night.

Beyond reclines the Pacific, swart, resistant, unquenchable to the mind, and deeper than man yet knows. Beside it, hugging the Bay like a harlot clasping a sleeper, the city murmurs its insolent provocation, hectic under its flotsam lights, its water-woven mists, flushed with the fantastic vision it holds of its own uniqueness, restlessly stirring the hunger of its unfulfillable wish.

And the great secular age, the strident and profane creation of free thought and humanistic sufficiency, lifts itself up to its sanguinary consummation, more shrill and intense than any which preceded it, more corrupt because more complacent, more vulnerable because more complex, vitiated by more grandiose dreams, cutting itself off from the earth by the institution of the machine as the great civilizations of the past cut themselves off by the institution of slavery; and in the cutting losing more and more of its interior unity, that frail ghost of its Christian past, utterly fragmenting; and as the fragmentation sets in, striving, as invariably occurs, for the purely mechanical unity of enforcement: Caesar's necessitous expedient. Everywhere the torque toward mere mechanical unity intensifies; the passivity of the East solidifying into the terrible blood-stained emphasis of economic collectivism; the activism of the West narrowing into the insane intensity of technological concentration, each in its over-simplification scanting the vision of a transcendent God etched on the heart of man.

The night, like a condor's wing, vast and unruffled, holds over the monastery. From a side door the Novice Lay Brothers emerge into the cloister and make their way round toward the chapel for their evening prayers. They whisper. I see only the white sides of their tunics blur between the arches, their black scapulars one with the gloom. They will kneel in the denser dark of the chapel and say the Rosary, their voices rising and falling in liquid accents. They are very young, and have tasted almost nothing of the implacable war of that world; but it will come to them, as it comes always to the innocence of life, clarifying it, obtruding upon the rapture of its vision the necessity of choice, temptation and faith grappling together in the interstices of the being, the world's battle plunged into the very deepnesses of the soul. They are not aware. The peace of the cloister, the peace of the monastery hangs huge and unruffled, hovering the dark.

And I lift up my eyes to the rows of windows where, each in his cell, the young clerics lean above their texts, bringing their minds to bear upon the mystery of knowledge unresolved. They too are young, these Student Brothers, but more formed now, and growing into the deep integration of manhood. Soon they will be priests. For seven years they give themselves to the absorption and mastery of knowledge, and the deep formation of prayer; the formation of the liturgy and the common life, and the contemplative's unceasing commitment; and for the rest of their lives they will spend it. If they are true Dominicans they will die exhausted, expunged of the ineluctable burden of truth; will die on that line where the violence of the world and the violence of God engage each other, to be transformed by that violence into the vast tranquillity of Heaven.

And faintly, off there in the city, I hear the hour-stroke of the carillon high in the distant Campanile. The University is closing down its lights for the night, its students trailing off into the eucalyptus darkness, boy with girl, books bunched under their arms, lingering. Its professors swing down from the great library stacks to waiting automobiles, wheel toward home in the Berkeley hills and a book by an autumnal fireside to round out the long day of their knowledge. A good life, and a useful one, and for many deeply enviable. But I, musing in my cloister, who had only to move through the life of secular learning to find it not whole, have turned in here to a deeper integration. But yet the University is there, with its own validity, and its own vision of the Truth; and insofar as it is true we also are bound to it. For though the Franciscans, whom I envy, take by instinct to the wilderness, the Dominicans have always planted their houses by the great centers of learning. Who remembers now the days when the Friars dominated the intellectual life of Europe, St. Thomas and St. Albert delivering from behind the most renowned lecterns in the world? They are quite vanished. And almost as a direct consequence of that neglect (I mean the repudiation of the God-centered man from the halls of learning), on a hill over the Campanile bulks the dome of the cyclotron, that womb of the Bomb, the weapon of the man-eating atom. Are we bound as well to *that*? Indeed we are. That is our time, our century. The monastery was conceived as counter to the actual world, the world as it exists, in whatever century, and it cannot relinquish its function.

And in the cloister dark, in the monastic solitude, possessed of that comprehension, I ponder the leaf-fall, summer's lingering devolution, ponder the fall of seed, the fall of life, ponder the disjunctured human violence, and the mind's flight beyond. And suddenly, over the cloister wall, like a kind of fatal confirmation, shrill and intense as the screech of an unclean demon, floats the high wail of a siren. Off there, in the tangled web of the city, an ambulance is threading its way down the long arterial to some congested intersection, where disaster perches on the twisted steel, over the smashed glass and the running blood. And there flashes across my mind, made lurid now by a cumulative terror, the vision of those mute bystanders huddled in fascination about a spot on the asphalt, a focal area of concentrated pain. And the mind gags on revulsion, confronted with the city's ugly enormous abstractness, where human value dies in the mass and is made nothing, the intense episode seen merely as one of the vast organism's local agonies, no more than some spasmodic clot of reaction, an automatic reflex twitching a ganglion.

But the heart fights free. What suffers out there on the asphalt is the anguish of a soul, shorn of its bodily amplitude, and face to face with death. It is hard enough to pray for an age, much less the ganglion's abstract reaction, the jerk of a tortured nerve, but a *soul* draws prayer like a magnet draws iron. And under his scapular the heart of the friar grapples the invocation and finds its mode, is delivered up to it, the whole grasp of his function. In the heart of the Christian, pain and the individual anguish find their torturous center, and he draws it into himself in that act of willed approximation which is the thing he is sent to do, his act of worth, perhaps his deepest usefulness. In his heart's own torment, the world's anguish is taken up and finds its hospital, its rehabilitation, the act of mercy and comprehension, which is his prayer.

Now the siren tracks down its destination, and its wail hangs hushed. And before it begins again, back on the merciful homeflight, the monastery draws upon itself its immemorial silence, its deep ingesting peace. The herbs, boxwood and ivy and the lank selal, drink of their sustenance, drink of the earth's bestowal, and the air's clean gift. The hour, spent now, dissolves into its aftermath, and the night glides on.

# FRIAR

I AM A DOMINICAN LAY BROTHER. One called, however, by actual status, a *donatus*, or *tertiary*, the designation of those who, usually because of some canonical impediment, may not make solemn vows. The Benedictines speak of us as *oblates*, and I like that. Its meaning is unmistakably sacramental: the oblation of the whole being, the consummate yielding of the total self as transcendental gift. But if *donatus* conjures up rather the hedging equivocation of a mere contribution, the irony is that it may well be nearer the truth. However, true oblation or mere donation, either way the technicality is the same. The Constitutions provide that the *donatus* be clothed in the habit of the Lay Brother and enrolled in the Third Order, that secular wing of the Dominican synthesis, begun as an affiliated association of lay people, and since expanded into a kind of catch-all, wherein every element contingent upon the Order may find its disposition, from Fraternities and Congregations, to an occasional secular priest and the ubiquitous *donatus*. For the latter, indeed, it is the final ambiguity. He lives *with* the First Order, but is *of* the Third; he rarely sees the Third Order, but is inseparable from the First. This is the tight-rope on which he teeters down time.

For Time, which seals the regular religious to his finality, is hardly a friend to the *donatus*. It is in time that his acuteness of balance must be maintained, and it whets its edge as it goes. The liberty he enjoys, the freedom to leave on the instant, has in it the hidden liability all freedom entails. The uncommitted man is thrown back constantly on his changing interior state: if he fails it will be his own instability that will betray him. In his days of darkness, days that are of the very essence of the religious life, his soul cries out for liberation, and there is nothing to hold him in check. One thing only in the religious life makes its renunciation intelligible, and that is the sublimity of the vows. These alone guarantee to the religious that what he has renounced will find its uttermost compensation; these alone fortify him against the recalcitrant forces which rack the inner man, and the demons which assail him with temptation from without. Against the deep inclinations of the body and the luxury-loving mind cloying on delight the *donatus*, vowless, has utterly no weapon, no hold on any psychological certitude. He subsists by the sheer sustaining force of grace, a force unseen and unfelt; whereas the vowed religious achieves in his act of fealty a spiritual commitment and a psychological stability which put him beyond all question: he *knows* what God expects of him, and in that knowledge is his peace.

Perhaps for this reason the *donatus* constitutes the most indefinite element in any monastery, and in a sense the most particular. Certainly he is the least enviable. For though he is obviously *of* the community, yet, as we saw, in an absolute sense he is not; though at one level he does live the religious life, at the deepest level he does not. He performs, indeed, everything a true religious performs, but not in the context of the same interior conditions, which makes all the difference. His assent is never final. Though it is made over and over in every act, it never touches the absolute. The Order cannot really count on him, and not being able to count on him can never really use him to the full. There is always something he is able to hold back, and which it can never touch, can never *activate*. He remains an enigma, the one man with a reservation in a context of utter obediential relinquishment. You see him in choir night after night, until you take him as much for granted as the statues in their niches, but one morning his stall stands empty. He has quietly packed his bag and left. Perhaps you never hear of him again.

Usually he does not stay long. Almost always he is an older man, as often as not a convert with a botched marriage behind him, or some born Catholic whose wife has died. "Their wives," observed an old Lay Brother with wry insight, "are either *bad* or *buried*." What he meant was that the true vocation really lay elsewhere, that this was merely an alternative, something forced, as it were, by fate, which is why it rarely works out. He generally lacks the motivation to keep faced up to the appalling grind of community life. There is no true interior stability, and he finds his old habits, his old independent attitudes too powerfully entrenched to survive beyond the first months of initial enthusiasm. Because he comes late to the life he suffers excruciatingly through trials which a regular religious takes in the normal trend of youthful adjustment. And though the superiors are more indulgent toward him, both out of natural sympathy for his difficulties and the lesser commitment of his state in the Order, still, it is usually only a matter of time. He may make the life a veritable hell on earth for those around him before he capitulates and departs. "Your *tertiary* is the real vocation-tester," the same old Lay Brother observed. "If you can stand up under the gaff of one of those poor souls breaking into the life, you can stand up under anything."

On the other hand the *donatus* sometimes makes an exemplary religious, performing spontaneously what others do only under absolute obedience. But no matter how well he integrates, there is always that separateness about him, an interior quality never quite eradicable from his attitudes, a lack of final relinquishment fixed under an inherent commitment. It may show in nothing more than a word or a gesture, but all the same it is there, and because it exists as a definite *lack*, he never escapes his problem. He may seem to, if things go well with him, and he feels secure in his well-being; but let them change for the worse, as they inevitably must in the religious life, and then begins for him the time of dreadful temptation. His imagination presents the manifold good he might be doing elsewhere, more deeply fulfilled in himself and more consequential in his work for the betterment of men, while everything at hand seems stale and ineffectual. This is the thing that sets him apart; he is the supremely temptable man.

And of course there are more apparent distinctions. Even by placement he is subtly removed, set off down at the tail of the line. This is proper, because for him there can be no advance. The religious, as he ages in the life, and the older friars die or are sent elsewhere, advances stall by stall up the line of the choir, with new men coming in below him, until he too has lived out his span, and passes away, and the gap closes; his stall is filled by another, and the office goes on. But not the *donatus*. The young postulant Lay Brothers coming in are temporarily stationed below him, but as soon as they survive that period of first appraisal, accept the scapular and enter the Novitiate, they pass him up. And there he stands, at the foot of the line again, hunched and grizzled beyond the pink boyish faces, for all the world like one of those grown men in a rural school who sometimes decide late in life they want a little learning, and old as they are come to class for a winter when the farmwork is slack, and sit there, bashful and perplexed, among the staring children.

But ambiguous as his position is, the *donatus* can still persist, and the monastic life at any level is a very great glory. Moreover, he can make the liabilities inherent in his state operate toward his sanctification. His very insecurity may become a perfecting element if he uses it with resolve. Exposed to the vagaries of spirit, the restless blowing winds of his soul, he learns to endure them in the full poignancy of their demand, knowing himself deeper and deeper, the fickleness that is his human nature revealed by the crossfire, which is the stability of the monastery riddling the instability of his wayward heart in its flight through life.

He knows he has at least advanced into the Church as deeply as he himself can go. It has been a painful transition at his age and from his background, but when he survives it he discovers the worth of it in his own soul, and what it means, though he is mostly unable to say it. It is all gain, that much is certain. For if he serves the Order till his death he can never repay a fraction of the sum received (whoever returns physical work for spiritual gain is never out of debt), and finds it sufficient to live the Lay Brother's life, doing such tasks as are assigned. So I. Having been both writer and craftsman, poet and printer, these arts indeed I continue to practice. There is a fundamental Dominican principle: *develop the talents*, and all the immolation of the self is never meant to be their neglect. But yet it is actually the contemplative life, the deep interior life of the monastery, which is the commitment keeping me here. Entered now into my third year in the Order, my fifth in the Church, I look back down the staggering progression of heart and soul that has brought me where I am.

Someone has said it takes eight years in the Faith to shape a Catholic mind. I wonder if for me eighty will suffice, after the stubborn habits of my indecisive life, and those multiple crimes-of-the-infinite, my sins, have scored like glaciers my being, leaving upon it the crude gouges of their ancient trek. Yet here I find myself, past midpoint, in the heart of my old animosity, the Church, living a Rule which for seven and a half centuries has shaped in sanctity those who have professed it, living it among men dedicated to the highest truths to which the human soul is capable of aspiring.

And though as Lay Brother I am not assigned to formal study, certainly the influx of truth in these years dissolved the taut constriction of attitude which from the beginning was my focus in the Church. I entered the Order like a clenched fist. My spirit was knotted upon an intensity of commitment to which I directed my entire force. In that intensity, like many a *donatus*, I have fallen time and again on abject defeat, have been the painful exacerbation of those around me, whose charity sustained me through my violations, whose forgiveness absolved me in my guilt. I sought to make raw purposiveness my whole sustenance, a thing which is not possible. But gradually that benignant spirit thawed my knuckled heart, and as I drank of its deep springs, and learned to trust the resilience of its poise, letting the influx of grace rather than the obduration of my will or the breathless anxiousness of my concern govern the means I was to take, gradually the pervasive charm that is the fruit of the religious life flowed in to me. I learned to stand in an equipoise I had never known before.

For it is *Veritas*, Truth, which is the essence of this vision, and it needs no anxious adjustment. It sleeps uncontained at the heart of things, unmarred by all their cleavages, and its mode is utterly sweet. The sweetness of that truth flows into the crannies of the tormented soul, a soul shaken by all the doubts of natural existence, allaying them, tempering the pitched anxiety and the morbid self-concern. Pride itself, most stubborn of all entrenchments, dissolves before that sweetness, and learns to reckon toward a deeper end. In the heart of this vocation an equipoise obtains, counterbalanced across the confusion of epochs, and that poise itself perfects.

To have found, in so brief a compass, not only the Church but the vocation within it, involves a compression too intense for cool appraisal; and if, in that intensity, one celebrates the particular state above the general one, let the inversion be discounted, and set down simply to the flush of arrival. For obviously the soil germinates the flower, the vocation grows from the conversion, and is a realization, a true fruition. As in the natural order one attains to creative manhood by virtue of being born into the world, so in the supernatural order one attains to the religious life by virtue of being "born" into the Church. When you enter the Church you enter the City of God; when you enter an Order you enter Her very citadel.

For the Orders may each be called pillars of the great interior structure, cornerstoned by the bishoprics and peaked by the Papal crown. The Dominicans, as an element, are an Order of theologians, and into their hands the Church has, in a manner of speaking, entrusted Her divine truths. These the Order most watchfully regards, but the reservation is here important. It is as if in a family a given son takes naturally to a particular task, so that with time it comes to be considered his specialty. Not that others may not perform it with diligence and care, trustworthiness and indeed brilliance; but simply that in the working-out this son accepts it with a special concern, and it becomes, in a way, his own.

For the Orders have a great deal more in common than they have in opposition, a fact emphasized by those who have shared more than one, and who tell us that the joy and peace each radiates and thinks of as its own is in reality the common heritage of religious life, which is essentially the intensely lived life of the Church. They bewail the divisions, the local prides, which often characterize the relations between the various families. As an eminent Dominican has said: "Saintly religious, however much they love their religious institute, as is proper, never place their own Order above others for they realize that since these, too, bear the approbation of the Church, they are gardens of delight to the Saviour."

Sectarianism in spiritual matters is indeed distasteful, but it must be confessed that it is natural to the novice. Prone to its exaggerations, if he is a convert as well he is doubly liable. And for the older members, who have fulfilled themselves in their apostolate and possess that ease which enables them to take their own accomplishments for granted, his attitudinizing is patently ludicrous. Just as the successful and talented scion of a great family wears his dignity with genial assurance, serenely above the obvious insecurities of the *nouveau riche* who ape him, so do they wear with unconscious ease the famous habit of their Order.

But the novice, the convert, is like an orphan, who in his extraordinary good fortune has been adopted into a great House, and at last belongs, and discovers himself in its greatness. In the framework of that greatness his own true worth emerges, and he sees himself as a new being, magically transformed by the greatness of the thing which has lifted him out of his callow limitation. And in his very great gratitude, born of that very great discovery, he proclaims the nobility of the thing that has transformed him, and sings its virtues, its singularities and its distinctions; so that the elders are amused and somewhat embarrassed, and look imploringly at their guest with that gesture of helpless commiseration with which one excuses the exaggerations of striplings, fools and enthusiasts.

But the excess has one great merit: it militates against that deadly uniformity which the magnitude of the modern apostolate has clamped upon the religious institutes. Benedictine and Dominican and Franciscan and Jesuit tend to merge indistinguishably together, the same work breeding the same attitudes and reactions, so that it falls to the incoming generations more and more to discover, salute and foster the unique impulse that brought each Order into being. It is in this sense that the celebration of the individuality of an Order becomes not sectarianism but legitimate distinction, and as distinction, valuable, the demarcation of a heritage not to be squandered away in an innocuous uniformity, but clarified and cherished.

For certainly the distinctions exist, and there is no gainsaying it. In the great life of the Church there are many spiritual emphases, and when a man has thrown himself totally into the spiritual ascent, these particularities loom large. The prevailing spirituality is one in which the Dominican finds himself often quite ill at ease. "I would rather feel compunction," says *The Imitation of Christ*, "than know how to define it," a remark which has been setting Dominican teeth on edge for five hundred years. The Friar Preacher identifies it immediately as an observation which, once lodged in the consciousness of a people, is capable of doing insidious damage (as it has), and very little good (as it has not). It is for this reason that he often feels himself apart from the enthusiasms of his generation, and unable to lend himself to the consolations of a solidarity based on such complacencies.

I remember once, before my entry, while still in that questing indetermination before a vocation crystallizes, I was speaking with a man who had taken his training under another Order, and on the subject of the Dominicans he was respectful but diffident. He felt they are too ambivalent to be really effective. Committed as they are to that categorical scholastic distinction between the active and contemplative lives, they are caught in a fatal oscillation between the double role of apostle and monk, the victims, you might say, of their historical origin between the medieval and the modern worlds. As apostles they are shackled by their monastic observances; as monks they are vitiated and scattered by their exterior apostolate. Just as the Benedictines have survived by specializing in scholarship, so the Dominicans have survived by specializing in theology—professionals, to be sure, with all the connotations of the word, but, alas, neither apostles nor monks. Actually, it fell to the modern Orders at the dawn of the contemporary world to perfect a spirituality of the apostolate beyond the old distinctions, and rescue the Church from the fatal ambiguity in which the ancient Orders had left Her. Not that these are now valueless—far from it; they have their specialties, and in any case they witness to the Church's universality; but it is a pity that with the world going to pieces they cling to that narrow traditionalism which is one of the unmistakable marks of the truly moribund.

Take, he instanced, the Dominicans and their liturgy. They make much of having retained their own Rite, as if that were a virtue, instead of recognizing it as simply one more element to keep them introverted, aloof from the real unifying forces in the Church. Worse, they have a kind of segregation policy in regard to their Houses of Studies, rarely sending their men to train in the great secular universities, which more than anything else gives them that peculiar insularity of theirs, so that even their professional work emerges somehow off key, swaddled in a methodology quite out of touch with current perspectives.

I smile now at the caricature, though one would be unwise to underestimate, in certain instances, the perceptiveness of the objection. But the division between contemplation and action is not mere scholastic subtlety; it is grounded in the human intellect itself, as Aristotle discerned. The Dominican life is not founded upon a fitful oscillation between monasticism and apostolicity. Rather it is conceived as rising out of the well-springs of a contemplative totality, moving by sheer force of the divine infusion toward an irresistible release, and ultimate expenditure of the full bestowal born of those deeps. The Dominican monastery ought to function as a kind of powerful heart, ingesting and expanding in the pulse of a profound movement, a diastole and systole that draws in and breathes out that mysterious force, the vibration of the divine throb, the fully augmented pang of knowledge and love that is the essence of the mystical life.

As to the so-called Dominican insularity, the great Thomistic truths were purchased at too painful a cost, across the defections of too many centuries, to dilute in the cross-waters of every turbulent generation. For the Dominican, if the truth is to radiate, it cannot be graded down to some admixture of prevailing acceptabilities. When your heritage is valuable, you hold to it and it preserves you. In the value of its heritage the Order itself becomes a kind of monastery, conserving within the walls of its tradition and its observances the truth it is committed to protect. It does not fear the charge of being obsolescent, for it knows that the Truth can never become obsolete, can never be other than vital, fresh, lively and young; and that it is the movement of that Truth itself which, deeply received, expands and transforms the agent, and through that transformation penetrates the spiritual darkness which engulfs the world.

Hence its resolution of what is perhaps the Church's most crucial interior problem, the balancing of the active and contemplative elements, constitutes, not the accused liability, but the very essence of its characteristic spiritual poise. For it has managed to contain an issue which, historically, fractured again and again the structure of religious life: the apostolic element gradually forsaking contemplation to terminate in outright laxity or mere activism; the contemplative element in desperation forcing a secession to undertake a new synthesis around recovered ascetic norms. The Dominicans met this problem by perfecting the art of dispensation, while retaining the statutory immediacy of primitive legislation, and by coalescing around an interior unity based upon prime theological considerations rather than upon assiduously cultivated psychological techniques. And though it has had its corruptions and its reforms, it has accommodated them within its own resilient context, and has staved off the bane of schism.

But as the age advanced, the cost became increasingly prohibitive. For although the Order was indeed conceived in terms of the "mixed" or apostolic life, which achieves its superiority only by virtue of a contemplative fullness overflowing into action, the technique of dispensation stipulated that in the event of conflict between the monastic and apostolic requirements, the monastic, or contemplative, must yield—a provision astute enough in the Thirteenth Century, when Christendom was dying from sheer rigidity, but today, when activism triumphs as a universal hysteria, when the whole world, East as well as West, is disintegrating from a profound deficiency of contemplative values, the mandate of dispensation merely hastens the collapse. It is from this perspective that the Dominican constitutions, famous for their ability to keep "up to date," may become fatally outmoded: there is nothing in them to enforce the preservation of contemplative fullness. Dispensation, the accelerator which dissolved the rigidity of medieval monasticism, has no corresponding brake to check the activist plunge. Confronted with a thyroid age, the Friars may descend from an apostolic Order to a merely active one in a matter of years.

For such is the compelling demand of the world that the contemplative element is always the first to wither; and when it does, the root of the active life itself goes dry. This is the vicious circle the Church has come to know so well. Among the Dominicans too the active element has had its hey-day, and withered and gone dry, and all that original apostolic zeal that shook Europe out of its grossness and its physical torpor, and woke it to the vision of the luminous intelligibility of Christ, became gradually assimilated into the general pastoral ministry, to survive, often enough, as no more than a kind of anomalous variation on the solid work of the secular clergy; or, more likely, the teacher prevailed over either the apostle or the contemplative, and the Friar became in many cases simply a pedagogue behind a desk.

There is not an Order today, at least in America, that does not suffer in some degree from this liability. And it is because so universal a manifestation reflects a deficiency in the whole spiritual atmosphere that the matter finds its relevance here in an introduction to a conversion. The monastic life is the Christian life, the life of spiritual perfection; and the maintenance of that perfection is the maintenance of the Christian ethos, the Christian actuality. Whatever strikes at the heart of the monastery strikes at the heart of the Church. Whatever strikes at the spirituality of the monk or friar strikes at the spirituality of the Christian, the Catholic. Monastic indifferentism is the mark of a spiritual disease, and when the monasteries lose their function, the Church is losing Hers; She is not living in Her wholeness. As in a physical organism some deep digestive deficiency reveals itself in more generalized disorders, so the activism of the monk becomes the secularism of the people; and his secularism becomes their sin. What is legitimate indulgence, even necessary indulgence in them, becomes in him a kind of betrayal.

And it is out of this felt deficiency, this hunger, this sense of *lack* in her very vitals, that the Church now begins to recover Her ancient norms, seeking to bring the interior organic cohesion into full movement, deep response. The Spirit breathes through Her anew, ever new. And in the breath of this spirit the instinct of the Order, like a great underground river that may sink from sight but never go dry, gathers up its native potentialities, the substance of its true conservatism, its powerful ingesting characteristic. It is a characteristic saved from rigidity by an irrepressible informality of attitude, and a kind of aristocratic poise, which springs only out of a true freedom of soul; and it has emerged in the present century in full artesian vigor, to join the intellectual apostolate which in Europe is one of the marks of Catholic resurgence, the quickening spiritual life of Western Man. Now, with the general recovery of contemplative life, the Order draws down upon its rich monastic heritage, to implement and fulfill the powerful apostolic thrust. Whether or not it is possible in the extremely activistic Protestant culture of America to fully achieve this recovery remains to be seen. There are those who doubt it. There are those, indeed, who do not think it worth the try. But we have it on no less an authority than the Holy See that it is an attempt which can be no longer delayed.

For Rome has made it unmistakably clear that the contemporary dangers of naturalism must be fought by a return in each institute to its primitive spirit, its basic constitutions, and its unique apostolate. Adaptation must apply only to accidentals and apostolic techniques, never to the fundamental elements of religious life. If the Orders lose their distinctiveness, they lose their very reason for being, their right to an autonomous existence. "Renew your primitive spirit or die!" is the challenge of Rome to the Religious Orders in the Twentieth Century.* For the Dominicans that constitutes a challenge to balance its activity with a recovery of strict monastic observance, a zeal for the integrity of the cloister, a reassertion of its tradition of profound mortification, an aloofness from the preoccupations of worldly entertainment—in short, a recovery of the ancient contemplative norms that have always vitalized its creative roots.

For the Dominican apostolate can be hearted upon nothing else than the deeply regarding, infinitely reposeful contemplative act, its whole certitude. Only from truly unsearchable depth will rise the famed *contemplata aliis tradere*, the giving to others what has been realized in the deeps of that regard, the sublime apostolic function which in its grandeur salutes the summits of episcopal perfection itself, and is the supreme ministry of the Christian life. But this can be only as overflow. To overflow is to have been filled; to be filled is to be wholly taken up in, steeped, consummated in the thing received. Activity is its end, indeed, but only its end. Activity is the final, the supreme gesture, a kind of pure and quintessential fruit pointing up the towering sky-lifted tree of contemplation. As such was the Order conceived. To this end its whole character was established, most carefully gauged, ensuring its disposition to the infusion of grace in the primacy of the contemplative act, which must fill it or it becomes an emptiness, a hollow gourd.

And standing here in the cloister-garth, I, raw and unready, half-shaped and hardly more, open my heart again, groping to find those powerful forces around which the Order has forever integrated, that they might make me a true Catholic, a true Dominican, achieving the whole synthesis of mind and heart, body and soul, the spiritual and the physical, which is the center of the realist vision. It is a synthesis made specific in the work of St. Thomas Aquinas, whose name I am not qualified to invoke because I am not trained in his method, but whose Order I share, and in the sharing should be made a more deeply-integrated Christian than any other spiritual emphasis could make of me. Behind him stands the figure of the founder, who in his person typifies concretely that synthesis as it is typified abstractly in the *Summa*. For if St. Thomas gave us the book, St. Dominic gave us the Order, the womb within which the book found its rich gestation, and through which its knowledge must be reborn into every generation to enlighten the world.

St. Thomas brought to the Order perhaps the most consummate speculative genius the world has known, but the Order brought to St. Thomas a perfect context for intellectual fulfillment. For it must never be forgotten that his genius was truly realized in context, the lack of which has caused the great minds of the secular world to be so often vitiated and wasted. It was in the spirit of his founder, and in the equipoise of a Dominican contemplative, that St. Thomas achieved the balance of judgment, the exquisite perceptive insight, and the calm harmony of touch that set the high watermark of speculative thought in these two thousand years of the Church. The great interior forces that shaped St. Thomas remain, if they are but actualized, to shape the Dominican today. Insofar as he recovers the superb proportionate balance enjoyed in that beginning, they become his singular heritage.

For as with every organism, the specialization of its life is gauged toward its unique end. All the Orders exemplify in their function the whole charity of Christ, but each does it in its particular way. The strictly cloistered contemplatives live His hiddenness, His silence, His watchfulness. As the Cistercian has phrased it:

> Those who be vowed lie buried in the cloister or the hermitage,
> The speechless Trappist, or the grey, granite Carthusian,
> The quiet Carmelite, the barefoot Clare,
> Planted in the night of contemplation,
> Sealed in the dark and waiting to be born.

The brown Franciscan lives His patience and humility; the Benedictine lives His slow labor and His chant; the Jesuit lives His dynamism, His blazing audacity. All the Orders fill out His love, merge His love into Man's life on earth, Christ's own earthly life of love. The Dominican too lives these loves of Christ but not in such fullness of emphasis. What he does live is His thought. It is in the life of the intellect of Christ that the great contemplative act becomes for the Dominican, too, unceasing. And in this ceaselessness the Order is rooted in permanence.

Deep in the night, deep in the darkness, deep in the autumnal mystery, in the depths of the year, its gathering death, the leaf is banished unto the earth, glides toward its private finality, its absolute relinquishment. It has lived out its opportunity and takes the brief way down. And alone in the cloistering dark I taste the encroachment of the year, and ponder the lapsing trace of its death that floats to my nostril. Who should savor this mystery more deeply than we? Over and over our liturgy deals with it. Day by day we pray for our dead, our hearts are fastened forward where they are, off there, in their aftertime, and where, soon now, we will find them. In the total vision, in the contemplative's gaze, this life and the next merge in an inviolate synthesis, fused in the inseparable oneness of reality. And in that oneness all somehow meet: the living and the dead, the blessed and the damned, the angels and the demons, each in the deft appropriateness that is God's unreckonable will inhabit the mighty panorama of things as He conceives them. In that fleet vision which is our endless instant of consciousness we regard the mystery of the stupendous Fact. Swept up in the agonizing arc that is the contemplative's trajectory toward God, we gaze and gaze, and drink of our fulfillment. In the cloister dark, in the monastic solitude, the limb lets down the leaf. Back there our lives are disposed in the flawless rectitude of His ordainment, and all our fears are hushed.

---

\* "Religious and Modern Needs," Jordan Aumann, *Review for Religious*, July 15, 1954.

# PRINTER

AND THE NIGHT HUSHED IN THE INSTINCT of its newness, flawless with the filled perfection of autumn, hangs and gains depth. Far over the city the sky turns on the pivotal north, the giant constellations fingering their blind immortal way across the vista of our lives. Somewhere in the oaks outside, the night-loving owl quavers his soft salute, the declaration of his contingency, his oath of utter dependence. The mate's response, in her own intense vocabulary, the language of never-ending quest and the syllable of all wonder, comes back across me, and I taste the linger of its implication, and know thereby the instance of my self. Now from the dormitory door a priest has come into the cloister, moving down the quadrangle, rustling between the rhythmic line of the arches. In the close darkness I follow his passage by the light rattle of his rosary slung from the belt. One of the *lectors*, I surmise, making toward the library. He will verify there some precise theological detail which the books of his own full shelves have not provided, bring to completion, doubtless, the notes for tomorrow's lecture which he has been preparing.

Now he has gained the library door, and as he enters I see beyond him, there in the lighted interior, the great bank of leather-backed volumes that is Migne's *Patrologia*, massive and formidable in its ranked impregnability as some Great Wall of China of the realm of books. It is one of the monuments of Catholic book production, two hundred and twenty volumes of the Latin Fathers alone, hundreds of thousands of double-columned, densely compacted pages, pages which contain the fruit of a millennium of Christian speculation, from Tertullian in the Second Century to Innocent the III in the Thirteenth. It is, typographically speaking, an unlovely work. More than that, it is a positively hideous one, woefully brought into being at the very nadir of typographical debasement, and stands as a monumental indictment of raw Nineteenth Century industrialism. But in the sheer magnitude of its accomplishment it represents a staggering achievement; and its usefulness, from the point of view of the scholar, is inestimable. If it is not actually the center, or core, of a monastic library, it is certainly fundamental to the base of one.

The core is unquestionably Holy Writ, and that lies deeper in, back in the tall stacks, where the many volumes of Scripture are kept. The Twentieth Century has given the Church editions which are marvels of precise scholarship, but none which can match in grandeur of concept and execution the great *Complutensian Polyglot*, the most famous book of the Sixteenth Century. In contradistinction to Migne's degenerate typography this "rarest of the polyglots" is one of the paragons of the printer's craft. Completed in 1517 in Alcala, Spain, it was the twenty-year project of the great Cardinal Ximenez, and it was the wonder of its day. Updike, whose classic work *Printing Types* cannot be accused of hyperbole, has this to say of it: "It cost Ximenez 50,000 gold ducats, today considerably over a million dollars. The magnitude of the task, the efficiency of the plan, the even quality of the execution, make the beholder pause. It was a splendid conception, and it was splendidly carried out."

That splendor, it is true, was only achieved through the plunder of the New World, but men have plundered before and since who never adapted their spoil to such magnificent uses as did Sixteenth Century Spain. Moreover, behind the plunderers came the reconcilers, the missioners and friars, who healed with the gift of Faith the terrible gash of the *conquistadores*. It was they who implanted upon the new earth the undying heritage of Catholic culture. That heritage is still here, eloquent in our place names, rooted in the California past, something that has penetrated into the substance of thought and modified our attitudes. The wealth of Spanish books on the shelves of this monastery is not the least sign of that patrimony.

For few things contain and impart the immediacy of cultural impress so evocatively as books, and not only through their ideas. A book is an artifact, and every age establishes upon the basic functional structure its own particular stamp. To the intelligent printer, who perceives in the constitution of a book quite as much as in its contained ideas the qualities of its time, a library of considerable accumulation reveals like the slow siltbeds of geological deposit the mutation of attitude that went into it. Typographical style, no less than vegetative variation, goes through its cycle of conception, evolution and decadence, supplanted in time by some crossbreed or throw-back, to become so obsolete that what was once scanned by quick-eyed scholars with astonishing rapidity becomes, to a later generation, conditioned to wholly other perspectives, virtually unreadable.

In this regard I think of the Incunabula there on the library shelves, and how their very typography witnesses, quite as vividly as the ideas they contain, to the terrific disparity between our age and theirs. The format, for instance, of the *Opera Omnia* of St. Antoninus, printed in Venice in 1481, hardly twenty years after the death of the saint, attests quite as substantially to the quality of his faith, in its order, solidity and beauty, as anything he wrote. He was perhaps the last great medieval mind, and it has been said that nothing but the natural reluctance to stir up jealousy among the Orders prevents his elevation to the rank of Doctor of the Church. Be that as it may, his book, in its very format, does bear the impress of his attitude, in its theological certitude, the factor of faith, and its grandeur of assumption. And though his spirit does indeed live on among us, it is no longer possible for that spirit and mentality to fuse, as they once could, into the physicality of our books.

And it is in the vision of the book, and my great need to make the book, soul and body, be one, that I turn now my mind to the morrow's work, and remember that before I sleep I must descend into the cellarage where the pressroom is, and for the final time turn the sheets of handmade paper I damped a half week ago, so that in the morning the stock will emerge flattened and true, as soft and pliant and unsullied as newborn life, utterly receptive, fit for all the exactitude the handpress can bring to it.

It is truly monumental, the handpress, and it has the endurance and stability of monastic life itself, but my relationship to it has been anything but that. I was, when I first acquired it, out there in the world, a man wild with unresolved impulses, maddened with a frustrated eroticism, vitiated by conceit and false ambition, and sick with all the irresolute woes that haunt contemporary existence; and the working-out of that irresolution is a process which, significantly enough, has run parallel to my relationship with the handpress itself.

When I first established it, after the War, I cast about for something to call it which would crystallize my hopes and intentions, something both poetic and apposite, and I decided upon The Equinox Press. Not only were the equinoxes my favorite seasons, especially the autumnal, but the name symbolized vividly the ideal of balance, the natural leveling point between the extremes of the solstices. It caught up in my mind the humanist goal I had set for myself: to live a life of equipoise and moderation in the context of pure nature. The handpress was seen as a means to self-fulfillment; my aim was to write my books, print them and bind them, and at last distribute them; to forge forward through book after book, until across the span of my life I should have created a spiritual and typographical edifice to serve as the mark of an integration which the diversity of modern life has made almost impossible. That edifice would be The Equinox Press. In it I would attain what I considered to be my natural destiny as a creative man: the realization of the whole complex of instinct and intelligence, insight and intuition, which constitute the artist's goal, the supreme end of life.

My first book from the press, *A Privacy of Speech*, was, then, the work of a humanist. And though it was a flawed book, it was nonetheless a consummate attempt at perfection, perfection for its own sake, the sake of sheer attainment, which was the end of self-realization. But when I entered the Church my values, the whole emphasis of my mind, underwent a rapid and profound alteration. I left behind the vision of the end as purely natural balance, and struck out for the end as supernatural extremity, the absolute attainment beyond all the limited attainments of life. I laid aside the humanist work upon which I had been engaged, and left the equipoise of that old life to help feed the poor in a Catholic Worker House of Hospitality in Oakland, moving the handpress with me. As I took up the first of the conversion poetry then ready to print I changed the name from Equinox to Seraphim, and issued my second book, *Triptych for the Living*, printing from uncial type in the apostolic format of the Early Church.

In 1951 I entered the Order, and once more moved the press, hoisting its heavy parts up four stories to the monastery loft. Again I changed names, this time from Seraphim to St. Albert's, and set about in search of some substantial project outside my own writing to make a step forward from the books I had done. I decided to attempt the first fundamental printing of the celebrated new translation of the *Psalter*, the *Novum Psalterium PII XII*, which only within the decade had been given to the Church.

The *Psalter*, which is of course the book of Psalms from the *Bible*, is largely the work of King David, a man terrible in his sins and terrible in his contrition, who, more intensely than any other poet, set down the mysteries of the relationship between God and the soul. In the ten intervening centuries between his time and that of Christ the Psalms had become the choir worship of the Hebrews. Jesus cried from the cross their breath-taking anguish: *Eli, Eli, lamma sabacthani!* In the Christian era desert anchorites began to chant the whole of them every day. Translated into Latin in the Second Century they became incorporated in the Church's rudimentary rites, and retaining that centrality with the full expansion of the liturgy through the

Middle Ages to the present, they have always been the very voice of the Church at prayer. As arranged in the Breviary, the *Psalter* is the formal requirement of every priest and every cleric over the grade of sub-deacon. Hour after hour, all day long, from each monastery and convent in every Christian city of the earth, that intonation rises, and is taken up and relayed by the cloistered contemplatives through the night, so that it eternally ascends, a vast upwelling of the human heart, a mighty invocation to God. No poetry on earth has ever surpassed the *Psalter* in nobility of utterance, nor dealt with such intensity of man's exaltation in God's fulfillment, nor the deep abjection of his Fall.

The deficiencies of the Old Latin translation were, however, apparent from the beginning, but so deeply set was its integration into the liturgy that it could not be displaced. Even the great prestige of St. Jerome, to whom we owe the Vulgate itself, was not wholly sufficient to replace it; only his second revision, made about the year 387 A.D., and called the *Gallican Psalter*, was accepted, while his own superior rendering from the Hebrew, known as the *Psalterium juxta Hebraeos Hieronymi*, could not supersede a text which, once having been learned by generations of priests and monks, was not readily relinquished. At last, in our own time, the present Pontiff ordered a complete retranslation. "Made from the most recent critical edition of the Hebrew Masoretic text, supplemented and corrected by thorough recourse to the best ancient versions, the Septuagint, the Peshitta or Syriac version, the Old Latin, the Vulgate, and St. Jerome's own translation from the Hebrew, it provides a Latin text of the Psalms which takes us back to the Hebrew of the second or third centuries B.C., and which is said to be the best available with our present knowledge." This work appeared in a scholarly edition in 1945, and was soon reprinted in the small liturgical editions intended for private recitation. But it yet awaits complete realization in a superior format.

For it is a text which sooner or later must receive superlative treatment. Scholars may debate its merits, but from the printer's point of view, it is the opportunity of the age: for the first time in nearly two millennia the *Psalter* has appeared in a new official text. We are, furthermore, in the very decade which marks the quincentennial of the invention of printing, and almost every year finds some commemorative acknowledgment. And it was the *Psalter* which was, most fittingly, the first book after the *Bible* to be rendered into type. That was the honor of Johann Fust and Peter Schoeffer, of whom Douglas MacMurtrie has written:

> These two made the year 1457 stand out as one of the most conspicuous landmarks in all the five centuries of typographic history by producing the first edition of their famous *Psalter*—a book which is a never-failing source of amazement and an object of almost idolatrous admiration to all amateurs of early printing.

What more fitting a thing, then, than to issue the first folio printing of the new text on the very year of the fifth centennial of so important a book?

Thinking about it, in my first days in the monastery, filled with the zeal of entry, that flush of first enlightenment, I determined, were the Order willing, to undertake this work. I was not unaware of my limitations. There ought to be brought to bear upon it the full versatility of our accomplished world. It ought to receive the combined talents of the most perceptive craftsmen of Christendom, and emerge as the fitting statement of an age which knew how to value essentials. It should rise out of the oldest, most hallowed places of the Old World, out of Rome itself, become a perfect flower of ancient Christian culture. It was certainly no task for an obscure handpressman, set down in a new monastery on the periphery of Christendom, perched on the last rim of the farthest westward migrations; no task to be begun without resources, ill-equipped, virtually unstaffed, and no way of being sure that if once begun it could ever be finished—years of hard labor, and who could tell what kind of years, in a century of wars which few may survive? Was this not a presumption, a fool's dream? Indeed, the natural man in me replied, better never begin, better live the life of the monastery, knowing the peace of the cell, absorbed in the writings of saints and the mystics. Better keep the peace of the cloister and not sweat after these vain fleetings, wisps of ambition and pride.

But yet I felt that I had been given the vision of a great book, and somehow I could not turn from it. And when my superiors expressed their warm approval, I saw that it was time to go resolutely forward. In the high state of my enthusiasm it seemed as if I had been lifted out of my ignorance, led to the handpress and instructed in its craft, brought to the monastery where I might work, and then given the work. When I began to design those pages they moved together with unpredictable ease. It was as if the confluence of the natural processes had found one of those rare intersections where everything converges to make something judicious and true, something unmistakable and right.

This, then, was the manner in which I began the printing of the *Psalter*. It was a dream, a valid dream, certainly, but one not without a large admixture of self-consciousness and pride. It took the first two and a half years to reduce that pride from my heart, and this was done by the onslaught of a series of reversals that seemed intent on my annihilation. I discovered that great endeavors are not achieved in great dreams only. To print a crown folio of three hundred pages is quite another thing than the thin quartos I had heretofore attempted. Each sheet goes through the press twice as many times, and that, I learned, is not a job for one unassisted man; but having learned it, I could not turn back. Difficulty after difficulty arose to confront me. The extremes of temperature in the monastery loft made uniform damp-paper presswork impossible, and after a year's frustration the press was once again dismantled and lowered to smaller but more evenly heated quarters in the basement. Yet still the techniques which I had applied to the quartos proved inadequate when adapted to the folio, and long before these problems were solved a shortage of Lay Brothers had developed in the monastery, so that my original estimate as to working time had to be severely curtailed; for the essential functions of the house must be maintained, and that is Lay Brother's work. Worse than any of this, I had counted on reasonable uniformity in the handmade paper I was buying from New York as it was required, for I had not the funds to purchase a whole shipment at once, as I prudently would have liked. But now I encountered a series of thinner reams, and in consequence had to find money, and commission a special making from England to match the paper I had used, and this took precious months. Yet even so, these were not the major trials. Surmounting them was the excruciating adjustment of a convert of forty years [of age] to the interior purgations of the religious life, a process mysterious and profound, to be starkly experienced, but hardly to be described.

For it is only as a contemplative that the printer achieves true detachment from the challenging concerns that surround his craft, and which so frequently blight his work. There is in all great printing, as in all great art, the contemplative element, the mark of an absolute repose, a finality beyond the confluence of pressures by which it was born; but because the challenge of the world is so great, there is often much else as well. As a contemplative, the printer will ponder the quintessence of the work he is achieving, and will patiently protect its purity from all impinging forces, seeking not perfection itself, the end of merely human attainment, but *revelation*, the obscure beatitude hidden in the essence of all God-given things, which, if he is a religious as well, he seeks first in the direct oneness of prime contemplation, and as a printer he seeks in the judicious ordering of the complexities of his craft. It is not often possible of attainment, even in the monastery: the claims of the world are too great, the limitations of life too incalculable, the furtive revelation slips ever away; God reveals Himself only as He pleases, and only to those of the most childlike simplicity, or of the most heroic discipline. But even so, it is his endeavor, his *search*, that gives the contemplative printer his unique vocation.

But it is not a search made in isolation. In these matters, as in all the great things of life, what is sought yields not so much to the intensity of our demand as to the general context of our lives. Thus, the whole aim of the monastery is to establish the environment, the context of prayer and devotion that will enable the spirit, unobstructed, to attain to its true end and final rest: union with God.

It is a context intense but simple, a life concentrated but serene. It begins for me at five in the morning when I rise and put on the black scapular of the Lay Brother, and go down as Sacristan to make the final preparations for the great devotional activity which opens our day. The night before, I laid out all the vestments in the color of the Feast, for there are many priests, and each will say Mass, which means many altars, and there are various others at convenient places about the monastery. Going down early, I set out the great golden chalices, placing the unconsecrated hosts upon the patens, and arrange them each under the burse and chalice veil. There is then the wine and the water to be poured into the cruets and placed beside the altars, and when this is done, a few minutes of meditation in the quietude of the chapel, before the community, which rises at five-thirty, descends to begin the Great Devotion. For an hour and a half the emphasis of the monastery is concentrated wholly upon the Divine Worship. It begins with the chanting of the Hours of Prime and Terce, divided by a half-hour of silent meditation, and culminates finally in the Solemn Conventual Mass, the supreme event in the daily monastic life. The Order has, as I have said, retained its own Rite direct from the Thirteenth Century, and in the Gregorian Chant of the Mass, in the intoned recitation of the Choral Office, day upon day the interior disposition of the house is established in the primacy of the spiritual ascent. This recitation is resumed at intervals in the various Hours, and becomes the contemplative's great conditioning element, the thing he breathes, the deep, fulfilled, very basic, very intense and masculine intonation, the up-pouring of the whole aspiration in the need of God.

Following Mass, we file into the Refectory for breakfast, and after that, for the better part of an hour, I put up the vestments that I had laid out the night before, placing them carefully away in the broad flat drawers of the sacristy. I then return to my cell to make my bed, shave, and prepare for the work of the day. And finally I descend to the basement where the massive handpress abides, and at last take up the tasks of printing: setting the type, damping the paper, rolling out the ink on the wide hand-roller, or working the carefully damped sheets on the press. At eleven-thirty we go again into the Chapel for the chanting of Sext and Nons; then to dinner, the full meal of the day. We eat in silence, listening to what is read aloud. After dinner we return to chapel and chant Vespers. There follows a period of recreation, when we may walk in the garden under redwoods and tall eucalyptus trees, beside the creek called Temescal, which winds through the grounds before it disappears into the city. By one-thirty we have returned to work again, and at five we wash up and prepare for the evening liturgy. We enter chapel at five-thirty for Compline, which is the last Hour of the liturgical day and was meant to be sung just before retiring. But since Orders engaged in active work no longer rise at midnight to sing Matins, these, with Lauds, are "anticipated," chanted the evening before, a fact which requires the redisposition of the entire liturgy. After Compline there is supper, followed by recitation of the Rosary, and the main recreation period, an hour in duration, where we mingle together, each category to itself however, whether Priests or Student Brothers or Lay Brothers. As for me, this time is combined with my daily stint as Porter, answering the door bell and the telephone. From seven-thirty to nine, unless I am night porter, I take up my sacristy work, laying out the vestments; and what time I have left I give to spiritual reading. At nine-fifteen the community goes into chapel for the final time to chant Matins and Lauds, and at ten-thirty retires; but one may secure permission to make a late vigil in the solitude and deep reflection of the chapel, which is, indeed, the crown, the final consummation of a full day; for here, in this depth of darkness, one ties back to his morning's Mass, and between these great and holy times, binds up all the concerns of his life.

So much then for the basic schedule. Against it fluxes the ceaseless onslaught of the unexpected: program changes, sick Lay Brothers whose work must be assumed, errands to be run for the needs of the house, minor operational emergencies, sudden visitors or telephone calls, moments of inexplicable exhaustion in which one can do nothing but collapse upon a bench: all the consequences inextricably involved in community life, which is simply family life, as common, as demanding, and as happy. And you learn to live expecting nothing, surprised at nothing. To fight fiercely to maintain one's own inviolate schedule is, in monastic life as in family life everywhere, eventually to go mad.

This then is the context in which the monastic printer works, and into his soul goes the spirit of God and the Godly point of view. There is not enough time, working alone, to make much of a showing on a big book like the *Novum Psalterium*, say some six hours out of an eighteen hour day. And this dichotomy is what quelled me in my first two years, for I was swept up in my own ambitions and anxieties. I had committed myself to great projects and they had not materialized, and I flung myself desperately upon the handpress, and only exhausted myself until I sickened. Then I fattened, became gross and puffy in a vain bid for energy; but my weakness was not my physique, it was my anxiety. I had not discovered the secret of the life.

For the deception of the monastic life is this: it is far more exhausting to worship than it is to work. Eight hours of work is normal, but even a few hours of concentrated prayer, of deep interior commitment, is, especially in the unformed novice, quite enervating. One must be trained to it. It takes years to learn the subtle deliberate pace of the monastery; you have constantly to relinquish, renounce the confusing claims of your own desires, strip yourself of your own attachments and passions, let yourself be governed by the true interior climate of the monastic life, a climate of prayer and meditation sustained in the sublime conditioning of that immortal Chant. Taken across the liturgical year, from Advent to Advent, the Chant of the Liturgy has been described as the greatest monument of music the world possesses. For those outside, it is a rarity on phonograph recordings; for us it is our very own, the lyric of our life; it is the song we sing.

As printer and contemplative, then, one begins to regard his work in a wholly different light, seeing his pages as he never saw them before, gazing deep into the interrelations of type and paper, ink and impression, and the stilled balance of the pages: letting the full quietude of his mind, governed as it is to such imponderable influences, slowly assimilate the rich contingency of the printed page. Always before there had been that hectic element in his insight which was the sure sign of his anxiety, his overweening concern. Now he places each letter in the composing stick. or pulls each sheet on the handpress with a kind of relaxed detachment, and regards what he has done in the knowledge that it is God who has done it; and since God has done it, he finds his joy in that utter fact, a joy detached from his passion and his will. Thus months go by. Years have gone by, will go by. He has lost the illusion of accomplishing anything. He looks at his pages and is serene before their imperfections. The worst he reprints, but not frantically, for whether one prints or reprints is now largely the same.

And how can I refrain from saluting once more the handpress! For it is in its term that the attempt of the contemplative and that of the printer approach one another. Pull by pull, its elemental deliberation permits the full ordering of the depth of one's consideration brought to the problem of printing. Pull by pull, it establishes the method of creativity gauged to the pulse of a man. And a religious, a monk or friar, may find in it those ancient proclivities which have made the monastic life so basic a thing in the Western World. Here lies the true power of the press, about which we hear so much, and which we have come almost to despise: the specious propaganda of the spewing newspapers of the world. But I suppose there is a place for everything, and I have found mine.

And when God desires the completion of the *Novum Psalterium* it will then be completed, in this I am secure. And when it is completed, there will doubtless be another, hard on its heels. Already I see, shaping in the lofts of my mind, the project of printing the great Vulgate, a life's work; not, I hope, in the highblown enthusiasm of my earlier ambition, but simply because no greater book can be conceived, no more elemental text attempted—a decision, however, not to be made until all work in hand is ended.

But what will never end is the great interior life of the Order. When my bones are dust and the handpress a rust stain in the earth, that solemn majestic processional, the liturgical life of the Church in the seasonal life of man, will be going on. The Dominican Order is not very old; only seven hundred years. But soon it will be a thousand; soon, very soon, another thousand. To have formed part of it, as contemplative and printer, to have governed to its pace, been shaped by its spirit, enriched and fulfilled in its matchless joy, is to have been given the final realization of the craftsman's life, a life in which the two vocations are made indissolubly one.

# POET

AND ONCE AGAIN I LET MY GAZE probe into the close darkness of the garden, and taste with my nostrils the gifts of its beneficent herbs. High and deep lifts the night, hanging above the small lemon trees, the privet hedges and the ivied plots. I can see the stars shiver in the small earth-bound sky of the garden pool, where a stone dryad clasps in his childish arms the shape of an upwriggling fish, and I am grateful that the obscuration of the dark relieves me from considering again its dulcet figuration. The entire garden is conceived in the pattern, if hardly the perfection, of the Italian Renaissance, and in my sojourn here it has filled me with distinct repugnance. From the first I judged it more fit for the resorts of that world out there than for the very heart of a Dominican monastery. In a cloister I wanted nothing more for vegetation than the long-bladed cactus that grows in the desert. I wanted it set in otherwise denuded earth, with one of those unforgettable Spanish crucifixes dominating the center. I wanted everything here to evoke, call up and project, yes, cry out the passion and death of our Lord Christ Jesus, King and Redeemer of men, that we might be called hourly to our own passion, that death of self, that redemption of the interior man, in the eternal crucifixion which is the life of man in God.

It is this attitude, doubtless, which confirms me as the complete rigorist, an attitude accountable, I am told, in terms of my particular past, and forgiven with it, but with the very forgiveness discounted and ignored. How, I wonder sardonically, does one defend oneself against an epithet? Are these "born Catholics" so omniscient that their most complacent opinion approximates the authority of an infallible definition? This Irish-American clerical mentality, stabilized in a convenient *modus vivendi* with middle-class respectability, does it, perchance, constitute the august Magisterium of the Church? I spit upon the ground, disgusted, and turn aside.

And having yielded this much I cannot check myself, and suddenly my heart convulses in an upsurge of blistering pride and resentment, that leaves me choked in a spasm of dangerous contempt. It is the pathetic liability of the *donatus*: unstable, rootless, unattached, essentially unbelonging. And then the anger leaches away into pure self-pity, and I am spent in the hopeless sequence of uncheckable emotion, riddled and confused. Where has all my vaunted monastic certitude fled to, I, an utter anachronism, with my fake medieval attitudinizing in a modern cloister? I recall how one of our parish priests, returned to the monastery for the annual retreat, cocked a thumb my way as I stalked hooded about the chapel and asked, *sotto voce*, "Whom have we here, pray tell, Ephraim the Deacon?" I suck in my breath, all badgered sensibility, and hug my sides.

But about me the monastery, withdrawn and unwitnessing, keeps its peace, and makes no comment. That immemorial silence, ancient with the contemplative wisdom of two thousand Christian years, maintains the free simplicity of its mode. The monastic life has witnessed many such outbursts as mine in its long past and made no judgment, knowing its slow silence will heal all, knowing its peace will prevail after the imperfect lives of every generation of monks and friars that it sees nourished and fulfilled and laid in the earth, are gone. And I perceive that the monastery is in fact not so much a physical object, a structure or dwelling place, but rather a *condition*, a spiritual perspective, an attitude, a transcendent motive, beyond all the temporal appurtenances of its material composition, so that we bring to it, each of us, our individual conformation, and are each transformed.

And I, wretched rigorist, shake myself, and wonder how so nebulous a thing as a man's past can make so great a difference between him and his Brothers. What is it I see that they do not? What is it they accept that I cannot? Things, to them, are more or less as they should be; but I, emerged from my past, renounced all that, renounced it once and for all at great cost; and the knowledge of renunciation envelopes me, and I ask myself piteously if I gave up so much to rest in so temperate an equation. The past is dead. But if the past is dead indeed, what lives on? What compelling memory infects the roots of the being, and shapes the man to its bias, twisting the receptivity of the new to the hard deformation of the old? What curse foredooms the mind to its unconscious rigorism (if rigorism it be), and in the definition invalidates the value, makes a falseness of the true?

That past! That past! "It is memory that prophesies, prophecy that remembers!" And in the memory's muscular engagement the spent years surge across me, and all those violations, the hysterical acts of a soul fractured with conceit, with error, and the misjudging mind, perch vultured on my shoulder. And in their aftermath I turn my thought to the rough draft of that indeterminate book, which is all memory, the story of the *thrust*, where it lies now, on the table in my cell, earnestly begun, but far indeed from finished. It is the story of a conversion, a conversion as manifested in the poetry it occasioned. The conversion has been accomplished, and for all its consequences and its excruciating choices, it lies behind me in the indefinable contour of past event. Nothing remains now to show but the poetry, and what is that? Something of the energy is contained there, but also something of the shapelessness, something persisting in the mystery of form, the mystery which blankets and obscures the outline of its temporality, but somehow releases the abiding energy, the force, and the inherent motive that made the act what it was.

And I am taken back in my mind to that other autumn, when all the latent consequence was drawing to a head. It was Advent, 1948, and the time drew down to the winter solstice. I was writing out the last poems of *The Residual Years*, that long chronicle of my guilts, my old allegiances and my deep betrayals. I had begun it fifteen years before, a few tentative pages of verse established out of the needs of early manhood, and then built poem by poem over the decade and a half of war and peace that held the centering quest of my life. Publishing it at first as I could, in slim sheaves, under various titles, I was largely unaware of what was shaping, but I gradually gained a sense of its continuity; until at last these collections were gathered up and issued under the final generic name, to form a kind of comprehensive edition, not complete in itself, and with much to come, but yet the looming bones of the thing apparent enough.
*The Residual Years*, then, is a work of slow accumulation, but what for me emerges out of the flight of time is the blood-line in it, the ancient Viking heritage of my father, that quintessential Nordic sorrow, mood of the fens, of the fjords, and the remorseless Arctic sea, which shaped in pain the spirit of his people, and which all the blaze of California sun could not in me extinguish. For it is in fact only the earth-emphasis, the mood of primal and latter-day
paganism, paganism which, no matter in what century it appears, late or soon, evokes out of man only his ultimate futility, and the blind, unhoping quest for his fulfillment. It is the sign of *Wyrd*, the

ancient Scandinavian concept of implacable destiny. Under that sign I had written:

> Do you not doubt, being lonely of heart,
> And bleakly alive on a wrinkling world,
> The fate that so forces?
> Men doubling on death deny with their eyes
> The joy that drew them....

This was its theme, the heart of that saga, chanted over and over, the long ground-swell of *The Residual Years*.

And back and forth, modulating the ground-swell, the other influences rose and fell away, and wrought upon it their transient figuration. There was the baffling complex of familial issue and unfulfillment: my father, the restless Norwegian musician, one who might almost be called a latter-day wandering *scald*, a man of strange and thwarted genius, closed in a forbidding mixture of compulsive rages and matchless personal integrity, savage agnosticism and unbending civic rectitude; and over against him the modulating Celtic softness of my mother, fundamentally religious, intelligent, poetic, affectionate; between them creating an imbalance that filled the soul of their son with throttled intensity, but tempering it as well in a context of earnest sincerity, a social responsibility and the purposiveness of truly Christian ideals. It is the unconscious struggle between *Wyrd* and Christ that tightens the pitch of *The Residual Years*.

And there is also that other ambivalence, the long frustration with her whom I found in adolescence, clung to, and made in time a marriage; a marriage that broke in the long ruination of the war, through which as an Objector I endured its years of denial, and joined the heart of that loss to the great unfulfillment until it seemed to make of it one prolonged moan, the caught breath and the outgone sigh of deprivation, the overtone and the undertone, the long threnody of *The Residual Years*.

And last, and most consequential, the final years with her, who, born Catholic, married in the Church and fallen from the Church, yet made with me the second mating, and gave me to know what a fuller maturation of earthly love could mean; who, with a kind of holy fierceness born of her own fierce inward need, clarified the twisted ambivalence and doubt that had become my heart, and out of that clarification brought me to the threshold of the Faith.

All this is there, in *The Residual Years*, and that autumn of 1948 I was writing out its closing pages. The time was not far off when, in the catharsis of a new perspective, I would be revulsed from this book and all its effects, repudiating it as I repudiated the whole earth-rooted, sin-gnarled tree of my past. But now I see that for all its confusion it is indeed true to those states of soul out of which it was written, and to that extent partakes of the unquenchable variety of life.

For in a work of deliberate impurity, the powers of expression are made to serve unworthy ends, either from malice or, more commonly, out of a disordered heart seeking gratification at the cost of the real. *The Residual Years* springs out of that disorder, but it does not seek gratification at such cost. Christ said: Every idle word that men shall speak they shall account for in the day of judgment. In *The Residual Years* there are no idle words. There is no attempt to entertain, to stimulate or to divert. The whole purpose of its language is to approximate the anguish or the intensity out of which it sprang, to be true to the actual state in which the generating impulse is sourced.

For it is in the very genuineness of its exposure that a work is enabled to be both repellent and true, and hence, depending upon the state of the beholder, relevant. As when St. Catherine of Siena, a maiden of inexpressible purity, was made to suffer the vision of the copulating demons in order that she might be "tested," in order that she might comprehend an extremity of the actual in terms of the singleness of her own soul, and in order that that singleness might be intensified in the crucible of the real. There the problem is seen in its greatness because the artist was God. But the human artist can only expose the thing he is, and out of his individuality his very imperfections and the color of his corruptness emerge on the litmus paper of his art; as we see even in Scripture, where the corruptibility of the human instrument of expression is everywhere intermingled with the sublimest truths.

But what have these asides to do with the corrupt honesty of *The Residual Years*? I can write now as a Catholic, but that book is in no sense a Catholic book. God, in His inscrutable wisdom, did not cause me to be born into a Catholic home, where I might learn to celebrate the single truth from the beginning. Rather He set me adrift in a weltering world, at a time and among a people in whom the religious sense was not so much rudimentary as vitiated, stunted by centuries of misbelief and unreason; and He set me to work out my salvation in mysterious and uncouth ways, and He saw my searching, the multiplication of my sins, and He watched me set down in the measure of poetry the expiation of those fugacious states of soul that proved the error of my purpose, and that could not last.

But if it cannot in truth be called a Catholic book, it can with confidence be declared a pre-Catholic one. In its painful search for centrality, all its effort shapes to the one end, and its poems, like fossils, stratified in its pages, testify to that attempt. Those poems will give way in time to these, the ash of the residual years is but the ingredient out of which the thrust is to be engendered, an attempt which will, I hope, more truly merit the definition; but at the level of poetry as at the level of the flesh, my present and my past are yoked together in the single continuum of my life, the unity of existence and of art. Every poem I have written, profane or sacred, subsists in the denseness of its own expression and is unmistakable, after every iota of the action itself has been swept away. I sort them again in my mind, each one a lens that gives me to gaze back into the crucible of violence out of which it was made, as we behold the diamond, sum of the titanic pressures that made it be. And because I see contained there, like a glint in a cut stone, so much of what I was and am no longer, I seek to know it in its nature; to know it, that I may better know the thing I am.

For the form is somehow the soul of the thing, and certifies its uniqueness, which we recover and establish within ourselves, taking us into the instance of every created thing, be it poem or person, bird or beast, as we always seek the soul of the creature in the profoundness of its shape. We see the grizzly and the elk, the rattlesnake and the skunk, each in its unduplicable configuration, as our only insight into the mystery out of which it springs. What is the law beneath the lawlessness that keeps them all in being, as it keeps the tough unorthodox poem, as explicit as the ring-tailed cat, as irrefrangible as the beaver?

*Veritas.* The divine commitment! The poet's unceasing quest! The august truth in things, for which our search leads us compellingly on; the preponderant truth in things so vibrant and absorbing there that we may almost be said to lose ourselves in them, lost to ourselves in contemplation. Wherever we gaze, our soul is seized in inexplicable wonder at the radiance which burns in the fabric of existence. The poet cries out in the anguish of his awareness, cries out in the intensity of his struck heart. The philosopher regards the intricacy of being, entranced by a complicity which takes him inexorably to its cause. The contemplative, lost in his rapture, is lifted into an area where nothing else obtains but the exquisite gaze of the soul in its God. *Veritas!* The enormous existent freedom that makes the truth within and the truth without web back to the remote impulsion behind it all, the final Invincible Principle! The poet's cry, the philosopher's intellective quest, the contemplative's speechless gaze of love, all these salute the reposeful majesty of a perfection too great ever to be grasped, too wonderful to be withstood.

For God, by His knowledge, is the cause of things, and their staggering diversity of form springs from the manifold means by which they reflect the imponderable Essence. The Divine Nature is communicable according to likeness, and the being that each thing has in itself is drawn as a copy from Him. This is the reason a natural form can be called "a godlike thing." God leaves His stamp adhering in its very reality, and we glimpse that aspect of Him there, not the enveloping impact of direct exposure, but an off-given beatitude, the trace of Himself left in the created thing, the sign of His aspect, which is in fact its only intelligibility.

And the soul of man being more like God than anything he apprehends, this likeness cries out to the vast Likeness beyond them, and fills to overflowing, and his soul seeks that Likeness, and the likeness is its love. For love is a unifying force, and it is this force which establishes the tension between the likenesses, causing the beatitude of the soul to salute the beatitude in things, and seek the vaster Beatitude beyond. God creates the spinning universe out of the vastness of His love, by His act of love maintaining it in contingency, filling it with the projected tension of His energizing spirit, shot through the substance of all things, His love, His will, the tremendous faculty that makes us what we are.

And the poet cries out of his nakedness in the totality of this force, seeking to fuse it into the blindness of his soul. And the irresolution of all created things vibrates through the structure of the poem, as all things vibrate in the processes of change, entrapped in matter, caught in the flux of becoming, thrusted forward into the instantaneity of being, revealing constantly the edges of the vast shapelessness into which they forever stand in peril of subsiding, and which forever mocks them. Only in the absolute simplicity of God, pure Spirit, the Act beyond all acts, is the ultimate perfection of form achieved.

A poem, then, ought to be written in the inviolate adhesion to the mastery of this consummate force, this unifying love. Such a poem will delve beneath the urbanity of its age, and source itself in those areas of soul where the complication may truly be said to set in, where the resistances are crying out, no longer spoken from a casual concern, but seated where the language adheres to the impulse, takes on definition, measure, and weight. Generally speaking, the age of urbanity is not interested in this adherence at all; it is interested only in diversion, the superficiality of transitory attitudes, and it is these which constitute its fashions. The poetry, however, which resides beneath the by-play of fashion is the poetry which endures. From one point of view the whole course of English verse might be seen as a long process of merely technical variation upon the basic *prime matter* of its speech. Older than the insouciance of the Renaissance, older than the Norman Conquest and the deceptive softness of its French forms, outside even the Roman Dominion and the logical abstractness of its Latin, persists the old alliterative Anglo-Saxon line, compacting within its syllabic density the powerful resources of the tongue. It is the Beowulf beat, and it is immortal.

It is immortal because it is the ancient root of our eloquence. Eloquence is consequentiality achieved in approximation, the deep movement of response and fulfillment, the inner order. What impels is the love, the fierce and unifying force. For in its act of synthesis a poem is a marriage, the bodying forth of the masculine and feminine attributes, the potency and the receptivity, twain in one flesh; a marriage in the making, achieved in terms of the glimpsed beatitude, shaped out of the love behind the resistances, but with the tension contained there, fixed in the process of being overcome. A poem without the sense of this resistance, this formlessness in the act of its finding words, is not in the final sense poetry at all, though it may be very good verse.

But there is always that other source of formlessness, and it may never be escaped: the fallen intellect numb behind the senses, the inability of the man to grasp the truth given him, a screening out of the light; and the insufficient ability to render the truth he has grasped, an abject failure to conform—each a formlessness, some lack of realization in the uttered poem. These deficiencies are the real shadow in it, a shadow that is also cast over the whole of man's creation: the knowledge of his limitation, the knowledge that it is himself shutting out the light. It is here that chaos, the formlessness, takes its great toll. When we find in a poem this limitation at its least, the shadow contained at what we sense to be the point of absolute reduction, then we feel the awe and the revelation, the knowledge of the true in the perfection of the love, which is the godliness we seek. We call that poem great.

To achieve this reduction the poet goes to the point in himself at which the shadow begins, and he grapples with it. In adolescence he grappled with it in ways which were a total mystery to him. Other poetry had taken him there, and he had grappled in such a way, and the grappling had somehow become a marriage. Now he has himself been drawn to that point, and there has been a grappling, and a marriage, and the darkness in himself is somewhat reduced. But he learns very slowly what may well be grappled and what may not, what the mating is and what it is not. These elements become the instruments of his intelligence, and his pen is the instrument of his will, as he himself is the instrument of the Divine Will.

He comes to realize that this grappling in the self at the point of darkness is the deepest and most consequential activity of his life, though not necessarily at the level of language; for in the spiritual and the moral lives he must also learn to achieve such a grappling. But as a poet his medium is language, and it is in terms of the special nature of language that he must learn to make his uses. As a poet his concern will be the meaning in language that is itself, its own marriage; for it is in language that he must make it. The marriage cannot be divorced from the substance it is made in.

But language is preponderantly temporal. A poem is contained movement; it establishes itself momentarily in time, and everything it does it has to do in the actuality of its unfolding. It can be returned to, yes, but the unfolding must be re-begun. It is the process, the procession, which is the poem, nothing else, proceeding forward into the knowledge of what it might become, ingesting its ingredients as it proceeds, establishing the form of itself as it goes, the order of itself in terms of the meaning it is making, the intensive instantaneous synthesis. The procedure is the poem, the love. Love is the marriage, the state which exists beyond mutual attraction, the true join. To miss this is like missing a grace, a God-givenness, that we were meant to have. God causes poems to be made so that He might be known in ways absolutely without duplication—which is why they are all different, must each be begun afresh, almost as if none had been written before.

This book is a book about a conversion, and to render that conversion meaningful, it has been written in prose, but that is not the heart of it. It is neither the heart of it nor the best of it, for the poetry, simply by virtue of its species alone, is the greater thing, as the most degenerate man remains a greater thing than the most magnificent beast, integrated to a higher function despite his particular deficiencies. Poetry conjoins heart and mind in an act of focal integration. It is the primitivism of the heart refined in the medium of the mind, a fusion made in the marriage of language, the love of the primitive heart and the civilized mind in their marriage, which is the poem, the state beyond mutual attraction. It is the eternal grappling, truth to truth, sucked in by the draw truths have for each other, the grappling of the primitive heart and the civilized mind at the shadow of darkness lying between them and which they overcome by love, a marriage, made in the blaze of insight through a singular act, an act in language of utter uniqueness, which has always been called a poem.

An act of uniqueness, yes, but not of isolation. As the priest at the Preface of the Mass, beginning that wonderful utterance, is not speaking of himself, is not communicating his uniqueness of impulse to the congregation, but rather is voicing the whole up-longing of the Church temporal, both present and absent, both the living and the dead, even those in Heaven who await the moment when their dissevered selves may finally be joined before God, so too the poet seizes and thrusts up the substance of our deepest want. With him also we participate in the total human aspiration. With him, in the act of his poem, we salute the crowning majesty of Divine Being. The voice of the poet is the articulation of what the deep dumb psyche of common mind has been ingesting, and now pours forth. It provides that polarity by which a generation achieves its hushed fulfillment, its unspoken realization, and it is in this that its greatness is measured among men.

Thus a poem may be quite mistaken in its conclusions, and may yet fulfill something so fundamental to the pathos of our time, so densely mingled in the very atmosphere which all our lives we have breathed, that it is difficult to imagine even the most withdrawn religious being able to read it unshaken by the impact of lost humanity that sighs there. Hence it is that a poem of wrong ideas may be more conclusive than a poem of right ones, in that it may correspond more closely to the wrongness of our hearts, and be somehow more relevant to us, than the other does to the rightness of our hearts—if it is not, as well, a very compelling poem.

But the poem both right and rich draws down into our hearts for the rightness that is there, and amplifies it, so that the wrongness is shaken and defeated, and that is the true join, the perfect marriage. For it obtains where our hearts are healed as well as hit, made whole, quenched in the beyondness outside our understanding, the ineffable and consummate grace that transforms as it ripens, and in the ripeness restores.

But where is the rightness, where the richness? The poet lifts up his head and, in the hush of his heart, looks down on the page he has lately profaned with his words, and all he has so vehemently written is seen under that backward glance as but a further imperfection on the long disorder of his life, and which in the clarity of such revealment stands forth as the callowest insufficiency. The words poured out in the tall impetus of conviction are seen to be but as dust, the dead wood of enfeebled attempt. Looking down on speech so urgently placed as to have seemed the very stuff of revelation, he is appalled at the insensitivity, the spiritual gaucheries, that stood to his hand; and in this anguish he understands indeed how there is no truth like silence, and is again anguished that the silence has not been kept. His book, which was to have been the ascending line of his perfection, merges indivisibly into the corruptness of his past, only a little less a disfiguration against the luminous purity of the truth.

But yet he sees further that in the back track of his life this too must be established. For as he once lived out his sins, so must he now live out his imperfections, so must he live out his deficiencies. And these score time as those did, leaving too their trace, the record of his incompleteness; and so become his book.

And now the darkness is probed by the single note of a bell. It is time for the chanting of Matins and Lauds. Up in the *Studentate* the young friars are forming their twin lines; and so I can see through the narrow windows, descending the switchback of the stairs, the hood over the head, and the white scapular dancing before and behind, floating out from the movement of the feet, which gives the light and buoyant tread that somehow catches up the indefinable blitheness, the gaiety of the Order; and as they descend, they intone between them the *De Profundis*, that ancient, unsurpassable Psalm; so that the delight of life and the poignancy of death, the unflinching concentration on essentials which is the centrality of the Dominican vision, float down as I stand in the cloister, here in the autumnal shrubbery, with the season, in its speechless manifestation, pervading its quality in the advancing night.

Now the chapel lights go on, and from the other side of the house the priests are coming in, in ones and twos, dropping the hood back as they emerge into the cloister, and saluting each other gravely before they too disappear into the chapel. Inside, by now, all have taken their places, facing each other in the two banked rows of the oakwood choir stalls; and they kneel there, and in the hush of an expectancy hung on the verge of a magnificent articulation, they await the bell that will begin them once more upon the centuries-old *recitative* that is the Choral Office, in which the contemplative restores in the Divine Chant the focus of soul that is the life of the spirit in God. I look up into the unsearchable witness of the night. The stars repose there, sustained in a vastness beyond comprehension. It is almost time for the bell. I move to join them, and as I pass out of the cloister-garth and into the hushed interior of the chapel, I leave the night to its whisper.

# Part Two

# FROM THE DEPTHS OF A VOID

*I propose now to set down my past wickedness and the carnal corruptions of my soul, not for love of them but that I may love Thee, O my God. I do it for love of Thy love, passing again in the bitterness of remembrance over my most evil ways, that Thou mayest thereby grow ever lovelier to me.*

Saint Augustine

*God gave you no rest. You found yourself in that state where the inner self is shackled, which is like an agony of the mind, and with which Jesus is accustomed to being preceded.*

Jacques Maritain to Jean Cocteau

I KNEW HER BEFORE I MET HER. Years earlier a mutual friend gave me a drawing she had made, and I kept it on the wall. And now I think back upon that drawing, how it gazed for so long into the details of my life before she herself entered it, prefiguring her presence there, waiting with the infinite patience of all inanimate things for time to catch up.

When I came down from the Northwest after the War she...[had some contacts with] the circle of artists and poets shifting between the University in Berkeley and the studios and cafes of San Francisco [and was a friend to Robert Duncan]. I knew she was estranged from her husband, as I too was estranged, so that whenever I met her I looked at her with an interest that was more than curiosity. She was beautiful, but her face held the trace of that gauntness which shadows the countenance in deep spiritual suffering; nor did she give any evidence of being interested in men. She seemed deep within herself, sad, searching through suffering. She was friendly enough, and not remote; but yet her attention would soon fail, and one would notice that she had withdrawn once more into herself. [I was told]...that after her separation she had...[become more and more preoccupied with the Catholicism of her childhood. This had reawakened when she worked in the Kaiser shipyards during W.W. II. What had aroused her interest was reading the life of St. Ignatius of Loyola before she designed a program for the launching of the *S.S. Loyola Victory*].\*

That was the summer of 1946. After a few weeks in the city I went up-coast to the superb redwood country of the Sonoma hills where a writer friend and his wife had a farm called Treesbank, named, I believe, after something out of Dr. Johnson. And in fact all the associations there were primarily literary; even the animals about the place bore literary names, a pleasant enough custom, but one not immune to an occasional misgiving. For since we slaughtered our own veal, it was inevitable that at mealtime we should be brought to consider the pervious nature of all literary glory, as before our eyes the hocks of D. H. Lawrence gave way to the chops of Marcel Proust. I began thus a good life of friendship, compatibility, and hard work, there in that soft pastoral landscape, beautifully feminine and appealing, grave with evening fog in the creek beds, its knolls worn by aeons of seaborn rains, lush in springtime, wonderfully tawny in summer, lapsing with autumn into a deep quiescence. The deer lived like wraiths in the redwood canyons, and broad-winged hawks kept the sky. We hauled hay, milked cows, held long literary discussions out in the tranquil orchard, picking early apples.

I had purchased the handpress in San Francisco, and we made the first move now, setting it up in an abandoned apple-drying shed that I began to refurbish, and in that somnolent landscape, on a choice farm among congenial friends, I hoped to work out my sufficient existence, writing and printing, to transcend at last the reverses of a painful past. It was not to be. In the Fall of the year this woman came on a visit, and we both knew it for the hour of recognition. A week later in San Francisco we met again at the

---

\* Bracketed notations supplied by Mary Fabilli, 1/4/95.

coming-out party of a new poet, and afterward I saw her home. That night, in her bed, after the fashion of pagans, we pledged our troth.

And what can one say for the world that twenty centuries after the Son of God, two who are brought together to pledge a pact of love still pledge it in no other way? What is the vicious heritage that has shorn man and woman from any ritual of flesh? When I had first spoken to her, that weekend before, up there in the magical hinterland, under the witchery of November and the sharp-set stars, we had danced our dance of recognition. It was no saraband. But when we looked in each other's eyes, and knew each other, I had asked her, with the directness of a man whose suffering has cut through all the layers of conventionality, to share that night my cover. She had refused. Yet it was not the outraged refusal of a Christian woman offended in the depths of conscience. No, between two such ones as we, so archaic a reaction would have been patently studied.
Were she to refuse, I expected it to be the regardful declination of a modern woman, a refusal connoting nothing more final than that she is, at present, not willing. Neither of us, I would have thought, considered it as a moral problem—action entered morality only if someone were injured, and here there was no one to injure, but rather two hurts to be healed. Outside the basic therapy involved, to accept or decline was a matter of aesthetic taste, one's sense of the appropriate, or, more fundamentally, simply whether or not one wanted to. I had come too far for the cheap concerns of seduction, and she herself would have despised them. I had asked her simply, out of what I was, a man once-married who knows his needs. I would expect her to decline as simply and as directly, a once-married woman who knows as much, but who does not give herself so freely. That is not the way it was. She had said something different: "I cannot." And then she had touched my arm, and smiled a smile of such reassurance that I could not mistake her goodwill. "I do like you very much," she said, "but I cannot."
What did she mean? As I shambled morosely off to my single cover, out in the apple dryer under the redwood tree, with the fog filling the creek bed below, and that lugubrious bull named Chaucer rattling his chain by the water faucet, this was the question I asked

myself. Then I remembered the trace of that Catholic recovery I had heard mentioned, and surmised the thing therein making all the difference, by which an unattached woman showed such regard—and yet could not. I determined to forget her.

I could not forget her. I had to level off somehow the little that had been established between us. I had sensed something too fraught with consequence to be so easily dispelled, and in the following week I wrote a poem. I remember it now, for it was like no poem that I had ever written, touched with a deeper, more muted music, and it was this poem that I carried with me, folded in my pocket, as I traveled down to San Francisco through the autumnal landscape; and there at that gathering, in the crowd of so many people, I gave it to her. Watching as she read it, I saw that the week had left too its mark on her, and she thanked me in a voice nervous with tension, her face drawn and taut, telling me nothing so much as the blind heart on the brink of its known capitulation, beating in the breast, beating upon an eventuality which a little will could easily forestall, but no will was left; there was no belief; there was no conviction beyond the eyes and what the eyes said; no final truth in the heart beyond what the heart said, and the heart was wrong. The heart beat on the edge of a prodigious collapse which I, being no Christian at all, could barely surmise.

The poem I gave her I called "The Sphinx," that I might in its cadence touch the depths of a mystery the clue to which I had to know.

### The Sphinx

All day my mind has fixed upon your face
That drew me in the dance and was alone,
Saddened with a sorrow of its own.
And round that carven image wreathed a wraith
As rain is wreathed across the graven stone.

The years between us like twin rivers ran;
The dance you danced was on a nether shore.
Our bodies gestured but could do no more.
Like mutes we looked across that double span;
The years drew out their desultory roar.

Now in the dance's afterbeat I tread

> Stiff with constraint and shuffle out its pace.
> The sandy rivers merge about your face;
> As round the monolith the rampant dead
> Drain to their dim and unrevealing place.

It was all the ritual I was capable of, my cry of life out of my old death, driving me on to a deeper death, that was my ignorance. And as we later walked through the midnight streets of San Francisco, and took the long bridge over to the other shore, I was aware of all the multitudinous minutiae haunting the air around a woman who has once told a man she certainly cannot, and has since persuaded herself in spite of it that she is going to. And so the troth pledged was the Flesh-Troth, as old as all paganism, as old as all death, as terrible as death and its past, as locked and chained and death-driven as the past itself; the troth of animal man who out of his recklessness pledges toward his own stupration and turns to take up his wage.

There was tragedy here, personal, deep, and most fearful, as there is in all sin, but that did not complete the breadth of it. The fullness of tragedy lay more deeply down, infinitely wider than these miserables who now fell across that snare; it was the tragedy that in this century there had been lost somehow the ritual of restraint, the heritage of forbearance. Somehow had been lost the knowledge of what one ought to believe and ought not to do. Deeper than faith had been lost the knowledge: knowledge of man, spiritual man, and given instead only knowledge of material man, elemental, naked and dispossessed, hungry, whimpering for assuagement and a shardful of love. There was among neither ourselves nor our friends hardly the semblance of a stabilizing convention, here in the raw West, the naked and unlived-in land, where time had yet to set its heel in the substance of man's sorrow; where all the old answers had somehow to be painfully refound, each by each, alone; no long collective consciousness, the social intuition green and unseasoned, and the formalisms of other places and other peoples no longer adequate, good for nothing now but to be smashed in the search for synthesis. Children of such an age, what knowledge was there to teach us better? What creed to check such ruin?

I found work in the city, and moved the handpress down from up-coast, and we tried to live the life of good pagans. As artists we espoused the conventions of artists, and deemed that sufficient an excuse to justify our neglect. We were both badly hurt in our hearts, and full of guilt, and desperately in need of each other, and our love was one of wild intensity. We had each been rejected by mates who had left us for other partners, and the agony of rejection is like the agony of hell. There was in those early days too much to live out, too much repudiation howling for a compensatory good to be concerned with anything else than the maul of assuagement, but that was not made to last. And when it began to go, and the day arrived when we had to face ourselves, and discover who we were and what we had bargained for, it soon became apparent that the problem of religion more than anything else would be the fundamental issue between us. To me it was no great matter, but to her it was the very heart of the matter, and she began in her distress to grope back toward the little light she had so ruthlessly wasted.

For even though she had followed me into the labyrinth, after standing once perilously half free, she began now almost furtively each Sunday to go to Mass. Nor was this the obscure need which may keep a fallen-away in spite of all bodily defection week after week coming back to the Church, a sort of inherent super-stability, as if all the one-way pull of the body could never quite drag the heart. No, this was more complex. For though in the hell of her divorce she had sensed again the healing power of the Church, at the onrush of physical love she had succumbed to the bodily summons, its short-term surging offer, its insistent deceit; and when it had spent itself she found of course the deceit revealed, no surcease at all, only another man, his terrible finite insufficiency. She had given up God for a physical man and was back in Hell, wrapped with him in the stifling jointure of those damned souls who twist year-long on their immortal agony, and find no peace.

So this turning of her face back toward the Church was not the support of an old bond retained but a hope reawakened, the pull of a most tender quest, the tenuous draw of recovery, of something mysterious resensed from a remote Catholic past; the awareness of one who has stood a bare moment on the verge of rebirth and in a trice resolutely walked into the maw of annihilation, drawn by some interior demand that annuls in the violation of the body what the heart can never get at; but for all that must mutely return, steal like a thief through the great doors, and gaze and gaze at what has been destroyed, and wonder how the pieces will ever be brought together again, now that these pacts with such voracious devils have been signed and handed over.

This to me was strange. But what is more strange is that I myself began to go with her. Not out of inclination, believe me; this was not my worship; I saw no fidelity here; I hated this religion. For to your pure transcendentalist, denying on principle the efficacy of any concrete religious act, the liturgy of the Church, when he meets it, stuns him with all the impact of the obscene. This rite, this cabalistic profanation is the nearest thing he has encountered to demon-worship—the debasement of the human intelligence to crude superstition, the appalling inversion of man's highest use prostituted in these sinister gestures. He is like a saint at a Black Mass. His gorge rises; he has to get out, to break away, return under the open sky where the light falls out of the incontaminate blue, where the growing things exist in their green goodness, and the earth-life flows without check.

No, it was a fidelity to her alone that drew me, since she had to go there, to find her peace, in the manner of Catholics. Such was my need that I was willing to share the burden of her pain even to this, even in despite of such profanations as these. As a Catholic will sometimes violate his God for a woman, so did I violate mine, so did I smother my own conscience. For I had learned one lesson. I knew that what I had previously lost I had lost through false principle, the principle of my individual autonomy, a self-filled heart choked with its own concerns, who had never the humble grace really to share another's secrets, really assume another's needs, and hence was repudiated. I had to lose to learn. So I let her take her secret there, and in time went beside her, to show at last that I could leave unchallenged a need I myself could not fathom, could only, in my heart of hearts, abhor.

Actually, when she first left me to go, it struck into my soul as something other, a real threat, a desertion of me and my whole way of life, a desertion I could not endure, so that after a time I began to go also, and though it was almost unbearable for me to enter that church, still I made myself comply; the deeper insecurity drove me. Later I went because she asked me to, because she needed to have me there beside her, and it was, by then, a reassurance for me to give her what solace I could, who had caused her so much spiritual misery in those difficult days. But even after the latent apprehension had gone, and under her guidance I began to see the significance of the ritualistic act (to see the reality, I might say, of ritual as *approximation*), there remained other difficulties, at other levels. We lived in a middle-class parish, the parishioners of which were conventional Americans, and there is nothing remarkable in that; but to such a one as I, estranged from contemporary life by a profound cleavage of values, and nursing a deep-rooted contempt for all the effects of modern civilization—to such a one, everything about a middle-class American church can move to nothing but repugnance.

Later, after Baptism, I was to live in the poorest parish of Oakland, where the parishioners were largely of direct foreign extraction. In these people, for whom convention had not yet become a stultifying thing because it had been unable to crystallize in material possessions, I could truly delight. It would have been easier for me had I been able to make my orientation there. Could I but have seen the Mexican women, once I had come to some comprehension of ritual, clasping their rosaries, their heads shrouded under their dark shawls, drop down at the back of the church and make on their knees that long marvelous approachment to the Source, I would surely have understood. But that was not to be the full nature of my testing. Not only was I brought to the Church in the face of its liturgy, which affronted me on one level, but I was brought to Her in the face of something even worse: middle class mediocrity. I say worse because in the liturgy I could see at least some residual intensity, however perverse; but this other thing, as I judged it in the lives of the people about me, was mere stultifying convention, the herd-instinct oppressing by sheer complacency. From the latter point of view my problem was not that of identifying with the dirty and disheveled, as it is said to be for the Protestant when confronted by that unmistakable Old World odor of the Church, but rather with the fashionable, the modish woman or the bustling business man; not to see Christ in the poor, for which I would have no trouble, but to see Him in the bourgeois, whom I despised. Each time I entered our parish church the impact of these two estrangements, the cross-cut of this mixed ambivalent revulsion, was the positive reaction that shut me out. And it was only by a kind of inurement that I was able to overcome what I must call the *shamefacedness* of being seen in such a place at all.

But certainly it must have been more than inurement. Had it been nothing else I could never have gone beyond. For through all this time the virtually insuperable problems of a second marriage were being slowly resolved. We were joined only in that most ubiquitous of marital compacts, the disconsolate sanction of the Common Law—disconsolate because so fiercely proud and lonely, the intrepid defiance of those who make their own laws and break their own hearts. Lonely because isolated, shut off from the benediction of God and men. Proud because hurt, the hurt that no longer cares, that hits back at the social fabric because life had not brought all that had been hoped. A union based on this kind of hurt, this kind of pride, is a union doomed to anguish.

However, hope is a great healer, and so is trust, and as time grew between us so did the trust. We came, across our temperamental gulfs, to understand each other, and to love in a more deeply resolute way than the flashing appeal which had brought us together. These things gave soundness and strength, and out of the stability of strength one is enabled to make a truer appraisal of the great claims of the Church.

But more than this, my ancient prejudices were being steadily dispelled. Not, as I say, by anything I saw in the parish church, but rather because I could not in truth support them. For it is the nature of prejudice that it has no foundation in fact. I was living with a Catholic, a fallen one to be sure, but one who had long since begun the bitter way back; and it is precisely by such intimate association that the Christian point of view, the *perspective* of faith is most readily established, as day by day the old misconceptions are patiently dispelled. Those, however, who resented the new influence upon me, regarded it quite otherwise. She would openly, before the most hostile, defend the Faith and its fundamentals, and in doing so it was inevitable that she should suffer the condemnation, peculiarly scornful because peculiarly just, reserved for those who talk the one thing but live another, named as no better than the supercilious gossips who, snug in their own stagnant sins, make a point of piety and heap umbrage on the impenitent. This she endured. Nor is there scarcely a seeker who ever found faith but must for a time serve out that chagrin. Rare indeed is the one brought through on the instant, as was St. Paul, struck down from his horse this side Damascus. But rather must one live for a while torn in two, his flesh in the tentacles of an old attachment, but his heart half-free, and struggling freer.

So certain had she become, it is likely she would by then have been safely returned, save for that disruptive adventure which was my advent into the gathering focus of her life. For her family, praying that she return, my emergence must have come as a veritable calamity. It is a terrible thing to ponder the hidden intentions of God. How can it be that we were brought together to throw sin against sin before we found faith? Did it require her sin to achieve my faith? God forbid. But this I believe: God may well join two weaknesses to make a single strength. Given two sinners, fastened in their sin and confirmed in it, they may yet, through the terrible instrumentality of that sin, find somehow its cancellation. As in genetics two agents of mixed clouded character will, if joined, thrust forth a lucid positive in the glad ratio of Mendel's law. Faith is the elusive recessive hidden beneath the flamboyance of the dominant, that has only to find itself in another to then emerge, pure and serene, like the blazing blue eyes in a whole family of hazels.

For her struggle toward God, deflected by me, was not annulled by me, though I made my attempts. Rather under the anxieties of such an adjustment it intensified. She attacked without mercy the loosely formulated ethic of my own impeachable orientation. A man of deep evasions, I learned to dread her redoubtable certitude, her excoriating facts, as the sickling dreads the potent ministrations of the physician; and when, driven to the wall, I turned in truculence and smashed the closing web of truths that hemmed me round, in those defeats she fled, and found her refuge in one or another of the mystifying practices she had recovered from her Catholic past.

I would come into a room and find her huddled in a corner, bent over her *Bible*, her brows knit in an intensity of concentration that invincibly shut me out. Or again she would retire to another part of the house, and soon I would hear the Gregorian Chant of the Benedictine monks which she had on phonograph recordings—the majestic, incontrovertible finality of a music that made all my values appear utterly superficial. I had the feeling she was surrounding herself in it, like the walls of a nunnery, drawing down into it deeper and deeper, with the fearful urgency of one who, for the duration of that music, has somehow escaped Hell.

Often at night, after our desperate confusion, she would get down beside the bed and pray, the black torrent of her hair plunged straight down her back. I had seen men pray like that. During the war, in the camp of Objectors, the pious ones, the holy joes, would also pray beside their beds; it was with a pained amusement that we others regarded them. But this was something that had moved into my life in a way I could not laugh aside. This was the woman who loved me with such fierceness that the whole of my past became a thing of tameness: she of such sublime creative gifts, of such forthrightness, that I never ceased in my astonishment at the wonder of her, the spirit of her and the mind, and that most marvelous soul—

to see her thus in her agony, crouched down in my sight, given over to such a total up-thrust of the heart—this, for me, was an unbearable thing. It left me cringing and alarmed in the enormous vacuum of myself. It left me in the whole knowledge of my limitless ignorance.

But, as I have said, in the two years of our adjustment all this had softened, had given way to a blessed surcease, and the fierceness became a fondness. Between our desultory clashes we kept the truce of those whose needs outrun their spites, the truce in which their stinging cuts are closed. The love of such a woman, which appears to exist in direct ratio to her exacerbation, bears that capacity to cauterize in fire the very wounds she has inflicted, which is its engrossing recompense, the cost of its purchase. It is as if she possesses some erotic phoenix of the spirit which re-arises out of its lacerations to drink the liquor of its wounds. I had been used to Northern women, patient and adaptive, creatures of forbearance and reserve, shaped, as was I, to the inhibitive Protestant reticence of those cooler climes, whose slow-kindling indignation rarely found itself in any more overt acts than peeves and sulks—but this blood was Latin. In her, moreover, the Truth lived on as deeply as that apostolic two-edged sword cleaving even to the division of soul and body, and her guilts ran fearful and deep. For let us have no illusions. Passion masking guilt has the awful characteristic of stripping through all the pleated integuments hiding the heart of things, hurling its victim in that imbalance between the extremes of violence. I find it no matter of amazement when sociologists record that on the chart of promiscuity the incidence of Catholics runs higher than the sects. Luther's leveling indistinctions do not exist to throw them back upon the secondary stability of merely conventional behavior. These are the ones in whom the knowledge of choice gnaws like the everlasting worm. Their smallest acts are staked against damnation, and in the powerful instant of temptation they drive their guiltful bargains to the deeps.

For if the Church is truly the church of the saints, She is also the church of sinners, and by the same token. The grandeur of the choice breaks either way, though the rest of the world has largely lost all sense of the distinction. I, unbaptized and ignorant, lay in my sins, but because of my ignorance could apprehend them only confusedly in their results. She, baptized and enlightened, lay too in hers, but because of her knowledge could apprehend them most lucidly in their cause. That was the enormous gulf between us, the vast barrier we never could cross. We lay together in our shocking sins, but all the flattened parallelism of our flesh, our shameful nudeness and the fitful lust that most pitifully twitched our wretchedness, could not traverse the insuperable division that shut us apart, each from the other. I, a pagan, lay like a ravenous animal mauling its prey, and could not know why. She, a Catholic, lay like a burned angel, in the immense privacy of her guilt, and knew utterly why.

O preponderant mystery! O unsearchable witness of God! I learned the Faith of one who drove her bargain to the posts of Hell, but the pang of whose guilt was greater—that was her piercing grace. I learned [the] Faith from one of God's unspeakable magdalenes who seem made to witness to this awesome fact: that in all their intensity they are incapable of plunging themselves deeper than He can lift them high. And did, and has, and does, as I myself am the proof. I am a man who was borne out of the Inferno on the cruciform of an uplifted woman—I, who sought to use my man's strength and my man's lust only to keep her there.

But the fierceness found its fondness, and the fondness had its hope. In the autumn of 1948, I read St. Augustine's *Confessions*. It was a book I might have encountered earlier with nothing more than admiration, but because of the ripening of my life, it was made, when I came to it, my own book. Not only did I perceive my soul there, but it let me see something of the true stature of this baffling belief that had challenged my old incertitude: those elusive elements that are almost the last things to come to you, the mysticism and the mind. In St. Augustine the Faith became for me what I most desperately needed—a man's religion; but it was a thing that had as yet no correlation in my own life. I could see it in the book; I could not see it in the Church. I began to seek to find the mysticism of the book, and it was this that brought me more and more willingly into the churches. I still had no comprehension of the Mass; it remained a thing closed to me. I went, as I say, because she went, because she told me the mysticism was there, in the mystery of the Mass. I hoped to find what she had found, what the book had promised.

And it came about that we decided to attend midnight Mass, that Christmas of 1948, in the Cathedral across the Bay, the first Christmas since the disorders of the war years that this custom was resumed. The nuns had prepared the Crib to one side of the sanctuary, with fir trees banked about a miniature stable. And as I sat in that familiar estrangement of feeling which had never left me in the Catholic churches, there came to me the resinous scent of the fir trees. It cut across everything else my senses had to contend with in that place, there in the heart of the great alien city, far from my early home and the reassuring simplicity of my old life. That scent was the only thing I could seize on with anything like true realization, but this time it did not raise in me the passion of rebellion it certainly would once have done. Now out of the greatness of my need I sensed in it something of a verification, a kind of indeterminate warrant that I need not fear, were I to come to the Christ, that He would exact the dreaded renunciation of my natural world. On the contrary it was His, His own, of His making, for me to take, by which I might be brought to know the complexity of the means that are His. It was there in the Cathedral, mixed in a faint odor of incense, like a tantalization, wooing me to probe back behind the facade of appearances, the externals of things in which His might is couched, to seek for the reality that lay behind them all.

I could look with my eyes to the place from which I knew the scent was coming, the somnolent odor of forests, and I saw in the miniature stable the several statuettes, and I recognized there the figures of the shepherds. As shepherds, as Orientals, they had no relation to anything authentic in my life, save perhaps the Christmases of long ago and the yearning suspenses of childhood. What was all this to me, I reflected, as I often did before these things in my puzzlement, what was all this to me who had never so much as seen a shepherd? But hold. That scent in the air, it was taking me back into a past where something powerful and obscure was being enacted again within me; and searching there I saw the correlation. It was the sheepherders. Who were they? Dark Basques or Mexicans, watching their flocks on the great flats west of Fresno, or taking their way into the foothills and slopes of the sierra, or coming down again in autumn to graze the edges of vineyard country. And then those Navajos I had seen long ago, out there on the high New Mexican mesa, their impenetrable faces grouped around that campfire, staring without motion into the embers while the old prospector told us of their lore.

And suddenly, traced back on the long scent of the fir branches, I saw the sheepherder in the shepherd, and the shepherd came alive. And the meaning of the Incarnation, the meaning of the Birth, in terms of the sheepherder, as I remembered him, began to widen within me. In the folklore of the West the sheepherder is certainly of all types the most low. Half-crazed, it is thought, with solitude, and hence impenetrably ignorant, unfit for any more likely employment and in consequence depraved, he has become, in the obscene humor of the smoking room, a kind of minor rural god of the vice of sodomy. I too had relished this sort of vile humor, but nevertheless I had never lost my respect for his dignity, and for the occupation that took him straight to the heart of the wilderness which I, in boyhood and in manhood, had virtually worshiped.

I remembered an incident from my high school years in which a number of us were gathered together before class. It was coming near the end of the term, and the upperclassmen were talking of their plans: some to go on to the University, some to take such local employment as was available, or some to return to their fathers' farms and work out a measure of security. Suddenly, in a moment of silence, something within me found focus and I blurted out: "I want to go to Nevada and herd sheep!" It must have come out of an impulse of tremendous earnestness, one of those spontaneous declarations which strike below the inconsequential level of the thought in which it is cast, and the longing of a soul is seen in its nakedness, when all its pathetic deficiencies are swept away, and its whole desire for freedom and withdrawal, nature, and the vast sweetness of universal God, are seized up and declared, so that all who hear it are struck by the vividness of that disclosure, astounded as it erupts into the mundane context, so naive, so unpremeditated, so ludicrous and so droll. The effect was uproarious. I was left blushing in the exposure of what I had said, flattered no doubt to have made a hit, but alarmed and shaken by the disparity between the ideals which I and these others cherished.

So there was truly a deep and powerful bond between us, the sheepherder and me, though I had forgotten him. What I saw now was that he stood on the verge of the Mystery. For some obscure reason, hidden within the frame of the Event, he had been touched, and I sensed that the demarcation was not merely fortuitous. But what was the thing that made him so eminently liable, gave him that unconscious candidacy for the Divine? Was it mere ignorance? It could hardly be innocence, standing there in the complicity of his earthly sins, as inveterate as Adam and as culpable as Cain. Was it simply that he was as common as dirt, the "perdurable fellahin," prime specimen of the Great Unwashed? In a churchful of Solid Citizens he was as incongruous as a sheepdog at a dance, and the sympathetic incongruity of mind and manner yoked us together. In the essence of his utter simplicity, his total lack of pretension, he stood there, ripe with the odor of sheepdung and juniper twigs, mutton grease and fir resin, and I recognized him. When a few days later I came to write *The Uncouth*, that was the underlying force of it, seated in such ancient affinities, making it what it is.

But there was more at work here than the genesis of a single poem. For one thing, that night saw the fashioning of a bridge, a mode of transference from the involvement of the past to the requirement of the future. There is a time when, after the logical structure of the Faith has been perceived, its truth acceded to, its use affirmed; when the insufficiency of one's past is wholly realized, and the sufficiency of the Church has been gradually discerned—still, there remains a final blankness of those areas of association which make in the mind the living thing a religion must be, and until this blankness is spanned it is not possible to shape the deep assent a whole faith requires. And it was the odor of the fir, the memory of sheepdung and mutton grease, cutting across the closed interior air of the Cathedral, that transformed the shepherd into the sheepherder, and brought me with him to my knees at the Crib. In the choosing of the sheepherder I too would be chosen, and in this choosing, this bringing, this bridging, would be dispelled the old anxiety I spoke of, the fear that the acknowledgment of the Christ, who somehow had remained in my imagination as a kind of sacerdotal decoration, a roofed-over church-god, would deprive me of that fullness of religious response relative purely to Earth, the natural kingdom and the great sustaining Cosmos, the only religion I had ever had. For it had been pantheism, mistaking effect for cause, rather than atheism, asserting effect without cause, which had all those years secured my adherence.

In a time of powerful materialist emphasis I had become a pantheist because my spiritual hunger had to find an absolute on which it could center, and because the material sum of things was the only God in which I considered it possible to believe. Without an absolute my very existence, the utter manifestation of things, was incomprehensible, and one other than their totality would not suffice. I did not claim to have worked out my position with care: I hardly concerned myself at all with formal philosophy. I was too distrustful of the rational faculty for that. With William James I could say: "Reality—life, experience, concreteness, immediacy, use what words you will—exceeds our logic, overflows and surrounds it.... A man's *vision* is the great fact about him."

My vision, then, was my one great fact. It seemed to me that reality could indeed be appraised through the sequence of cognitive acts, but only instant by instant, each instant unique and hence essentially unverifiable, with the complex of being manifesting itself as nothing more than a kind of divine concatenation, like adjacent photographs on the reel of a motion picture, having only a proximate relationship. Everything therefore was stretched through an enormous framework of relativity, in which the leaf that fell in the forest and the sigh of my own outspent breath were each existentially related, the totality of which must needs be the only tenable absolute. The act of worship was the act of recognition, no more. One might cry out to the God, but that cry was itself simply one more element in the great design, one more element in the undecipherable pattern that disposed all things.

In this view substance was but the concomitant of tension, the signature of purpose and counter-purpose, made between them when they met, as the whirlpool is the sign born of two meeting waters. But these tides were themselves only aspects of a greater reality, the vast Inclusiveness, that kept them both in being. In a universe of total motion, form could exist only by virtue of repetition. Purpose and counter-purpose were the means by which the God, the energy, might manifest Itself by participating in Itself, design realized in resistance. Substance was achieved in repetition that form might show forth, an ingredient created out of the God's own tension, for Its own manifestation, as a man snaps his fingers, tonal form sprung from the frictive action, the effecting of an effect. There was thus no evil, in any positive sense; I was not a dualist. Consciousness was the illuminate byplay engendered between the purposes, an element in the abstract design, capable of apprehending them and the chaos in which they were engaged, catching them up and amplifying them in a new modality, another variation. Pleasure, health, enlightenment, intellection, all these were the simple attestation to the dominant purpose. Pain, injury, discomfort, anxiety, fear, all these were the invincible witness of the subdominant counter-purpose, and their term was destruction, the cost of the tension, the penalty of design. Morality was the implicit valuation by which this participation and this avoidance were recognized, but it had no absolute. Nor could there be sin, metaphysical violation; there could only be error, the unreckonable mischance haunting the cleavage at the heart of all things.

And the whole of the universe had but one proclivity: to be consumed—formed and destroyed, formed and destroyed, endlessly. Thus sex: the divine power exploding out of the tissue of being, the male-flesh, seeking the counter-thrusting ground, driven like a shaft into the vascular orifice, their orgasm the uncontainable volcanic force breaking its own way out; birth an inscrutability, a smudge of the blind power clotted like a chance infection in the entrails of the female and sucked up into creaturehood. So too with the creative psychic act, a glint struck off the dynamic core, fragment of the divine preponderance burning like a jewel in the plasm of the brain; man's whole meaning, brain and plexus, twin polarities, radiating each its own pulsation of the uncheckable energy, two gouts of the supreme majestic force, locked together in a terrible oscillation, flashing back and forth between them the fitful signals of their hunger, an oscillation forever unresolvable, an oscillation which in the end would devour him, and cast him down, and the husk of his flesh be sloughed back to earth. The re-absorbing power whirled the sidereal universe through its shimmering cycle, conceivable but inaccessible, perceivable but unattainable, absolutely amoral because absolutely beyond concern. There was intensity, unspeakable intensity, an intensity so fierce as to break the very structure of matter, but there could not be love.

And what was love? I had used the word; but when I did not mean desire, appetite, refined emotional hunger, I believe I gave it no higher definition than basic human solidarity. Love was the conceptual synthesis within which man unifies his highest ideas. But in the Christian sense, in any metaphysical sense at all, love was a fiction, no more than a mis-labeled insight into the soft abstraction clothing the essential identity of all things; a nothingness, sheen of the gravitational flow, an elusive high-light evaporating out of the compulsive necessity, caught up and objectified by men into a prevailing presumption, one of those pleasant evasions by which we endeavor to ameliorate a bit our loneliness before the unfaceable night into which we go. Below it lay the compulsion, inexorable. That was its one determinant, its inflexible source, the terrible necessity of all the outflung components to achieve adherence.

Pleasure, Pain and Destiny, and the great fate-god *Wyrd* who was the universe, swept all components through their sightless dance. What was its meaning and where was its end? Who could say?

What could change it? Not I, blind with the blindness of the darkness-drenched soul. But all that time, behind the universe yet not of it, distinct yet not withdrawn from it, within Whom it finds its total synthesis, the great, gentle and serene God regarded my absurdities, knowing Himself in His own mystery as no man ever could, contemplating Himself in His own completeness as He can never be contemplated: pure Act, the single Flash of knowledge, the abyss of Love, the infinite comprehension of uncreated Cause.

But I, being man, and fallen, preferred my absurdities to the living truth. For in man fallen from Grace, his absurdities spring from his own disorder, a disorder he seeks desperately to maintain: some deep interior disposal, so rooted in his consciousness as to lodge there, the very fundamental of his thought. He cannot relinquish it until the dissolving light of Divine Grace rectifies his heart. His need becomes his blindness and his blindness all his death. So did I serve out my time, shaping the majestic universe to fit my own disordered soul, falsifying its noble proportions to gratify the turgid misconstructions of my mind. All the cruciality of truth could only glance off the knot in my heart, until the veritable grace of God was given me, for no worth of my own. That grace began in this: there was one thing left in me, a hunger, an immense irresolution, a basic need for totality, for the consummation of being in the unity of love, for the unreckonable depths of that illusive quality I doubted could even exist—a love which in its instantaneous comprehension both exhausts and fulfills, both creates and quenches; a love that will never falter and will have no end, which consciousness cannot encompass, nor death consume, nor pain deflect, nor pleasure vitiate—primal, beyond even the seeming primacy of life.

It was for this reason that my notion as to the nature of things could not endure that challenge when the final challenge came; it had no grounding in the basis of total need, no *quies*, no depth of resolution in the knowledge of love. I could *live*, yes. I proved that in myself. I had known passion and intensity, the satiation of instinct, the complement of thought in books and in music, made serious friendships, held the trust of men, the delight of women, the well-being of true achievement. These were life and I had lived. But what I had never known, nor knew that I needed, was the finality of knowledge and realization, the fullness of being and true felicity which in Scripture is called *caritas* and in its depth we know as Love. It is for this reason that I remained through all those years a man without a center, questing right and left for one thing and another but never achieving purpose. It took me the whole of my life to learn that finality is met only in love, *caritas*, the act of unification; that love was the thing for which I was made; that without love I was nothing.

And that without love God is nothing. This, in its essence, is the thing that would make me a Catholic. Love, the prime existential fact, is sourced in personality, and the person is analogous to God. Intellection and Will, Knowledge and Love, are the two facets of Person, the final metaphysical absolute. In that rigidity which had characterized my mind, the whole depth and complexity of person, of the human soul as true spiritual entity, had been painfully closed to me. From childhood on, there had been compulsions and tensions, cravings and desires, instincts and drives and impulses. But the soul as an existent thing, a fact of qualitative being, in whose embodiment we recognize the delicacy and distinction of person— no, I had no grasp of it, or only such as was too vague, too amorphous, to stand before the powerful forces which shaped my thought. For though I could sense, dimly, what was meant by these qualities, I could not acknowledge them with conviction because they had so little fulfillment in my own life; I had blocked them out in the desperate intensity of my seizure. And it was precisely this insight, this penetration that she provided. Perceiving the soul as she had revealed it, a realization she must herself have assumed in the profound conditioning of Catholic childhood, only to throw it away in the years of that impersonal sojourn, but recovered now, reintegrated into her life, emerging in an intuitive poise and responsiveness, wonderfully subtle, so pliant and generous in its distinction as to leave me breathless, as we are left breathless, struck to our inmost hearts by the unspoken revealments in the face of a child—knowing the soul thus, could I not perceive that if mankind is such, then God must be more, infinitely more? That God must be its prototype, intensified to its absolute condition, expanded to its infinite comprehension? In the claim of the person could I any longer ignore the claim of love? And in the claim of love could I not at last acknowledge the absolute claim of God?

For it must have been the stark insufficiency of my old nature-God that had been my deep uneasiness there. Not perhaps so long as I prospered, back in my young manhood, on my own land, possessed of my own woman, beaver-like threading about me the wicker-work of my febrile certitude. But in the North, in the bad days, the hell of a fallen marriage, a ruined life, a ruined future, then I cried out for a different fare. For the first time in my life I cried out to God, in that wilderness, there on the hill above the sea, crying out to God for purpose and understanding. I cried out on the hill above the sea to the great unlistening God of all things, who had no more concern for the sigh of my outspent breath than the sound of the stick that falls in the forest. Many and many a time in the night I tossed on my bed, in my mortal anguish, crying in those deeps to God who gave back nothing. In all that anguish there was at no time a knowledge of any giving back, a common concern. Remote, incredibly beautiful, beyond pity, beyond love, the vast non-human abstraction—the leaf falling in the forest or the rockslide raking the mountain—what did all my crying forth to such a God avail me save to make the frustration more frustrate? And this is why, when I came out again into the world, after the War, I shuddered back from that brink, sought to live a life among men, took up a new marriage, fed the bodily needs. I had been like a man beating his head on a rock in a frenzy, and all I ever heard was the ringing in my ears.

This too is why, when I came to a glimpse of the Christian God, more in me was drawing there than purely speculative, or purely cultural concerns. All those years of desperate quest I had been seeking the end for which man is made—realization, the *term* of all impulse, completion of instinct and intelligence in the object of the being's total intent. By the excoriate process of elimination, at first, tentatively, through direct action, later, and more crucially, in the cauldron of the imagination, I had exhausted the possibilities of the human attempt, to arrive in time at the understanding that man's last end can lie only in an absolute; and the only absolute is God.

And gazing now across the multitude between me and the sanctuary I saw the tabernacle, set back upon the altar, contained in its own reservation, as mysterious and impenetrable as some thoughtless stone. "Unknown God," I said to myself, "what can you be that I should come here and wait for your word? If the hills and the sky and the stars have not spoken, what hope from you? O lifeless bread housed in the lifeless bronze! If the vast cosmic god hears not, nor cares, why should any man speak to you?"

We had genuflected, on entering, as I had learned to do, and then I had knelt a moment beside her, not merely to conform, but to see if perhaps in the approximation of the empty act the thing might be evoked; but I soon sank sighing back on the pew, as if even so little an effort as this were too much to expend. She herself had kept kneeling, as was her custom, and now in the sight of her presence there at the margin of my vision, I became conscious again of that special quality she seemed always to possess in such moments: the character of a subdued but vibrant expectancy, as of one waiting, fastened upon an interior alertness; the body tensile with a hushed and quickening excitement; the head bent slightly forward in the listener's attitude; the neck, seen from the side and behind, arched with a poised presentiment; and the heavy hair, coifed, caught up and coiled under the scarlet turban. What mystery, I wondered, what revelation did she wait for, something which in its very expectation sealed me off in my plight? What does she wait for, when she waits like this, kneeling, contained within the ineluctable principle of that femininity, out of the knowledge of its very incompleteness made receptive and serene? What does she see there, sense there, across the infinity of the nothingness that faces man? Is it a mystery the soul of woman is made to meet? A mystery the mind of the male, in its terse abstractness, can never truly grasp? Is it a woman's wisdom, a woman's necessity (I idly toyed the question), unreal for any man?

Any man? I asked it again, like an echo, turning my gaze back toward the crib. Can it be true even of the primitive, in all his subjectivity, in all his celebrated intuition? But the vision of those sheepherders, impassive, crouched there on the cold sheep-flats outside Bethlehem struck through me, before the inconsequential question could find its rebuttal. I saw the ridges flecked with frost, the wind crumbling the ruined darkness, blowing into their eyes the very grit of history, the dust of the Assyrian, and the dust of the Chaldean, blowing the bronze dust of the Ammonite, and the flake of the Babylonian bone. And the vision of the sheepherder became the tragic vision of the race, cut off from finality by the unwitnessing layer of darkness that has no edge. And in the hovering night of that vindictive upreaching void an immense terror dropped over me. I remembered all the wildernesses I had known, the measureless night, and sensed their plight out there, those primitives, those sheepherders, watching their beasts through the jackal-haunted blackness, huddling a blaze.

And it rose now, that void, empty and foreboding through the tall lofts of my imagination. It rose over the cathedral, over the city, over the long ribbon of coast, over the continent, breathing and vast on the web of the waters, over the great dream-sunken hemisphere and the planetary earth itself, up into ultimate heights where no life is, ever, and the nameless galaxies grope their way through deserts of space that will never be probed. And sustained in those altitudes the winter constellations walk their great way, bearing yet the fabulous names the Greeks had given them, back there, so long ago, before the time of the epoch of Christian man: Orion and Taurus, Andromeda and Perseus, Cassiopeia and Draco; and the great Ursa, circling forever that nailhead of the North. The Greeks had given them names indeed, but how pathetic! We in our enlightenment know that the gods are dead, the stars no more than titanic blobs of fire, unthinkably vast, and going nowhere.

And the terrible universal enmity, set against the isolate human heart, came into me, and the loneliness of man, trapped in a universe he cannot subdue. Westward that hostile, man-hating sea throws its storms upon all coasts, chews its islands, smashes its ships, breeds its interminable, indissoluble fog. It will be coming in soon, I reckoned, that low invection, that sundering sea-hugging cloud, blowing through the Gate, running its outrider pennant far up-river to cut off the cliffs. And it will spread sideways, and widen, possess the Bay and all its boats, the wharves and the barges. And the great buoys will mourn in it, sad, soughing their thick and doleful note into the sodden ear of that cloud. And gliding it will possess the houses on the shore, all the peninsular towns. And it will cover the highways, and the fast lanes of traffic will be slowed, and men will die in it. And the long trains will nose through it, crying, those sleek metallic runners, in from Cheyenne, from Omaha and Chicago, footing their way cautiously on the dewed iron, anxiously calling ahead to the crossings, crawling between the flexing lights. And the airports will be sealed, the great planes in from the ends of the earth will circle and go elsewhere. And behind the cities the nude heads of the hills will take it too, and the redwood canyons claim it as theirs, for they love it, fog is their element, they drip it endlessly; it is their embrace, their thing of love; and it is beautiful.

But for the men on the Bay, the men in the machines, the pilots and the drivers, those in the long ships creasing the sea, it is not beautiful. Man sets himself over against sea and earth, and they both fight him. The mountain fights him, raiding winter after winter the troublesome road that binds its base, stabbing down its rockslides, smashing its giant pines across that thread. And the river fights him, the dike-breaker. It drinks rain and breaks out. And the storm fights him, gathering its cyclic strength and hurling itself in on the land.

And fog fights him. Crashing on uncharted reefs the split ship shrieks and starts down; deep in its bowels the boilers burst open, disgorging men and metal on the tangled kelp. The crew abandons, pushing off in rafts, riding out the back-surging roil where the hulk sucks under. They drift, float out in the white smother. They call and call across to each other before they divide, before they are lost each to the other, left each alone, the echo of their shout dies out on the water, in the waste of fog.

And the great burden of human life, of the man-life, the great burden of my own life, end-less, without End, rose like a vision seen in my heart: and my mind was drenched. And I cried out in my heart at the doom of man, the doom beyond the brute denial as the sea deals it, beyond death as the fog delivers it; the more terrible doom of which these elemental dooms are somehow the type; the real doom of cut-off man dissevered from God, adrift on the raft of earth in a universe of night, a universe of fog, of galactic dust, and no port to make. I had come without knowledge to the root of one of the great historic dilemmas—that teleological liability, that absolute block by which the quest of man is shut from its attainment; the curse that he only, of all seeking things, cannot attain to his needful goal; the curse of man that he alone may never achieve the essentiality for which he was made.

For the plants have their green sufficiency. And the beasts, complete in their instincts, touch fulfillment in direct performance of their basic acts, each act consummated in some tangible, concrete end: the eating, the sleeping, the playing, the mating; all governed at last to the species' preservation. Even that droll conceit of the chimpanzee, which to us, in our preoccupation with mere things, seems to teeter on the edge of human perception, never transcends the realm of the concrete. The instinctual impulse, despite variation, is the only one it has, the only one it needs; and all its cleverness, and all its affection, remain but elaborations within the stark instinctual cage, constitute the whole realization of the merely sentient creature.

But man has intellection, self-awareness, can reflect perfectly upon himself. We know that we know, are conscious of being conscious, can say, "I am myself!" It is the power to abstract which is the intellective mode, and possessing it man cannot reduce himself to bare instinctual sufficiency. In the very facts of his nature he can do no other than posit some final abstraction, some hypothetical end: wealth, fame, power, pleasure, seen always under the aspect of the good, and bend his effort to that attainment. But since none of such things embodies the All, since each suffers limitation, his insatiable intellect ranges beyond, groping for the illimitable Good, the totality of all the tangential goodnesses meshed in his comprehension.

This was the matter the Greeks assayed with such confident certitude. Man's end, they perceived, is happiness: it is this which he seeks forever; and the supreme happiness, *beatitude*, is the fulfillment of all desire. But of what, precisely, does such happiness consist? Epicurus saw it in pleasure, defined as repose. The stoics saw it in rectitude. Plato had placed it unhesitatingly in the contemplation of ideas: the idea, particularly, of a subsistent Good, the Beautiful. Aristotle, more "realistic," rejected the very notion, and posited, rather, a hierarchical synthesis: contemplation, virtuous action, and the moderate goods of life.

But do these things constitute a true *quies*, a genuine fulfillment, the quenching of total need in utter realization? And are they actually attainable? Beatitude, in the proud Greek optimism, lay like a happy condition within the grasp of man. But between them and us lies the welter of three thousand destructive years, every year of them crying out with a terrible voice that this is an illusion. Time and again man draws himself up to some trembling peak of attainment, some consummate attempt, but he always collapses. He makes recovery after recovery, but he always collapses, the recalcitrant forces groined in his nature drag him right or left, and the tall effort goes down; the barely-glimpsed vision cannot be sustained; the sublime ideal slips ever away, vanishes in the ruin of effort. The natural synthesis collapses, disintegrating in the demolition of all earthly attempt, and is gone.

Why? The mystery of man. Nor may any analysis ever unravel it. But there is another means of knowing, higher, sourced in the fountainhead of life, and ordained to an extra-terrestrial end. East of the Hellespont, on the desert-edges of Palestine, the University gave way to the Synagogue. If the Greek genius was philosophy, Minerva regarding the cosmos, Hebraic genius was religion, Jacob wrestling with the angel. What the philosopher cannot penetrate by analysis the prophet perceives in the depths of an unspeakable vision. And hence it was to the prophet, the religious man, that the solution of man, a religious problem, and the end of man, a religious end, were in fact vouchsafed. For he lived in the knowledge of the one God, and he had a single mode—worship. And out of his worship poured his understanding. And in the wisdom of worship he perceived the mystery, saw to the essence of primal Sin, cried out in the liability of sin, the anguish of that knowledge, its whole consequence; and knew the loss of divine adhesion. Himself the inheritor of that deep defect, that universal human curse, he yet lived on in faith and in hope, and kept a promise of salvation, and looked to a true resurrection, a real immortality—the factual reality of a life utterly freed of the tyranny of death.

But to me, sunken in that spiritual denseness of the truly lost, which like a falconer's hood darkens the strong hawk of the mind and stills its wings, these issues were closed. They lay, dry academic questions, beyond the lines of my consideration. Neither Greek nor Jew, neither philosopher nor prophet, I, like the sheepherder, crouched in my natural indigence and had no hope. But what I could not think through in my mind, I suffered out in my soul. All unknowing I was Spinoza's heir, who had turned "He Who Is" into "That Which Is." And though like him I could love "That Which Is," also like him, I could not expect it, ultimately a categorical *thing*, to love me in return. Yet this must be said: Lovelessness is a clean abstraction, and the mind can accept it. But the heart, that faculty of volition, has love as its mode, and denied fruition it knows no rest. Faced with that verdict it turns and turns, dodges, seeks to escape, refuses to assimilate, so revolting a thing is this in the being's intuitive depths, so dread a sounding does that knell proclaim through the substratum of the soul.

And so despite my ancient disillusionment, I turned again and again to new endeavors, seeking diversion, seizing this way and that for some temporary engrossment, only to be driven back to that elemental terror subsistent there in the roots of my awareness. I was a man, a thing of heart, a being made for love and for God, and this was my need. But I had written in my flesh and etched upon my soul the anguish of the knowledge that God and man are split from each other. There is a gulf, a hiatus between the hungering soul and its final end. Man is adrift. Alone in the prolixity of evolving nature, a creature of terrific impulsion and no resolution, man swelters in the prison of his shut soul, the thing that all his love, all the packed suppressed impulsion is made to achieve, he can never reach.

Can never reach! Not by any act of his own, not by all his intensity, this much I had learned. But beating my head on that rock in my frenzy, aware only of the ringing in my ears, I had at last begun to detect above it the high pulsation of another note, the clear and dulcet syllable, like the whistle of a lark across the roar of an avalanche, the syllable of a religious word, a word containing in its disposition a preponderantly Christian concept. It was the beautiful word *Salvation*. It was a word, actually, of my own cultural heritage, one I had heard all my life but had never acknowledged. But more and more, in my slow awakening, it had been blending into the stream of my consciousness, evocative as a whisper, speaking to me some haunting communication, adapting its cadence to the gauge of my comprehension, as of someone possessed of eternal patience, waiting for me to hear.

*Salvation*! How many times had it thudded across my consciousness, and how deeply had I resented it! Rather I insisted that the natural world be its own sufficiency, bear its own fulfillment. I was contemptuous of people who, given so much, turned to toy with these absurd phantasies, these sentimental myths. They had only to recover the bond of nature, a bond they had broken with their blind machines and their blind cities, to discover again the ancient wisdom whose term is peace. So did I believe before the edge of man's doom began to cut into me. But as my life sped on, and nature itself proved insufficient, over and over failing to assuage, my hunger deepened, drove down to the older areas, the scars of the primal unrest, hidden but unabatant in the human soul. I saw then indeed that something more was needed, some more transcendent fulfillment than nature yields, the quenching of the whole hunger for completeness. But *Salvation*? This antique word? This repellent Christian concept? What could it offer but a brassy conglomeration of hortative effects?

For when Protestantism lost confidence in theology it more and more fell back upon simple evocation, pounded into eventual incomprehension by a million enthusiastic reiterations. In that process the basic Christian tenets slid inevitably under the common spell. Thus the universal mediation of the Incarnation, the central concept of Christianity, became blurred out of all distinction under the impact of declamatory insistence: "Jesus Saves!" I had seen it everywhere, daubed on bridges and barns, carved on fences and telephone poles, scrawled on sidewalks, defaced among four-letter words in public lavatories. How could anyone, with the best will in the world, fight back to prime meaning behind the monotony of such repetition? I did not try. Up there, in that northern encampment, when some of our more earnest brethren sallied forth to carve those words on a roadside bank and the bank caved in on them, believe me, the delicious irony of such retribution flavored many a day.

And yet, beyond all the abuse of the immortal words, and outside all the irony of the mortal ignorance, the magnificent concept keeps its worth, and now I pondered it. Was the Incarnation, in the Christian view, simply the means by which the race achieves the true ultimate, its own necessitous end, the thing for which it is made? Is that what salvation means? The fulfillment of a need as fundamental to man's nature as any that sends the salmon up its thousand-mile trek, fighting that rock-falling torrent to its head-water home, the place where it began? This was something I could see; here was a concept I could grasp. But if so, where lies the nature of its finality, what was its fulfillment, and what was its mode?

And then, in a long correlative insight, comprehension was given me. And all the instrumentality of that search—the witness of the woman; the perusal of baffling, half-read books; Mass after Mass sat through in ignorance; all those sermons falling on the deafest ears in Christendom; my false misguided hope; the intensity of search cramped most desperately into my soul, compressed and hardened there in the ferocious pressures of that agony—now all were fused in the instant of my enlightenment. That night, that Christmas Eve in the San Francisco Cathedral, with the sheepherder hunched by his dung-fire outside Bethlehem bitter in the wind of a ruined world, all, all leaped into focus.

And the knowledge of the Christ, the power of a stupendous disclosure poured into my heart. I saw [that,] beyond the intellective act of the Greek or the religious one of the Jew, the emergent Christ had spoken, revealing what the combined intelligence of all philosophers, the total aspiration of all worshipers, could never have conceived. In a single act of love and expiation Christ plunged the human soul into the very actuality of God, and quenched it there, and its purified gaze met the gaze of that God, was unified in a single look, made face to face. The mystery is open. Man's thwarted end burns in the glance of an unspeakable love—it is the Beatific Vision.

For into the human context, into the ignorant heart of the human sheepherder, penetrated the transcendent principle, the Word. In the mystery of flesh God walked the world; healed men, taught men, was nailed to the sky and killed there; tomb-sealed; rose up out of death's mechanistic chaos to touch on sacrificial fullness, and in the mystery of the Church maintains the salvific principle which makes men of the divine. It is the great renewal a self-offering God casts ever on earth, the immortal fire which finds its kind in the individual heart, and they burn together, they make one blaze.

Suddenly through the spiritual denseness of a man's grossness that Grace is given, and he sees the Church as the Incarnate One, and he comes. Upon Her altars Christ flashes the realism of unsubduable God. In the sacrifice of the Mass God stoops and proffers, stoops and proffers, descends, rises, is nailed to the sky. Over and over, spending and redeeming, He is never done. Out of His joy He yields Himself immortally in the supreme act, the Redemption. The wave of restoration drives through the chaos of the world, dissolving sin, dispelling darkness, casting out rancor and evil, killing hate in the human heart. A man is touched. His pride-stiff soul crumbles before an ineffable grace and he comprehends. The once sinister Church, seen only as evil, becomes in a trice the resplendent Mother of Men, the Christ as pure beneficence, and he skips in singing.

Can this be him of whom the common jibe is given: "He fears liberty as much as he needs bondage"? O foolish men! You see darkness where there is light, and light where there is darkness! How long will you hunch in your fears, squatting there on your ancient earth-soiled loins, the fear of those venal loins polluting your vision? How long will you crouch in the servitude of that sexual terror? Day after day Christ on the altar dispels all that, repeats His passion, pours out the running wave of His grace, the flux of His perfection. It would drown your wrath in its vastness, would lift you on its swift upreach, but you clench and resist, you fear. Adam-wise, you prefer your wretched fig-leaves to prime spiritual nakedness, the blazing exposure of a soul made new in God, brought face to face, burned pure in the excoriate gaze of Christ.

I too crouched out there on the sheepflats of man's terrestrial ambiguity, with nothing but the rags of pitiful pride between me and that death, but something was spoken into my soul, and hearing I followed. When the fir-smell reached me across the closed interior air of the Cathedral, binding as it did the best of my past and the best of my future, shaping for the first time that synthesis of spirit and sense I had so needed and never found, I was drawn across, and in the smell of the fir saw it for the first time, not merely as an existent thing, but as a *created* thing, witness of the Word, the divine Logos, who made all earth, and me, a soul in His own image, out of very love.

And I saw in the fact of Creation the end of Creation; and in the end of Creation saw indeed the unspeakable Lover who draws the loved one out of the web of affliction, remakes him as His own. It was then that I could rise from the pew, and, following like a hound the trace on the air, go where the little image lay, in the Crib there, so tiny among the simple beasts, watched over by the cleanly woman and the decent man, and these humble ones, my good friends the sheepherders, who in that instant outleaped the philosophers. That was the night I entered into the family and fellows of Christ—made my assent, such as it was—one more poor wretch, who had nothing to bring but his iniquities.

And all this while the Cathedral had been steadily filling, and I was vaguely aware of it, though too absorbed in my own thoughts to be conscious of time. But suddenly there began behind me the sound of the rising of people, a sound coming up out of the hush that held it, and filling the hush, gathering in waves from here and there, as section after section, in the gathering awareness, rose to their feet. Even in the days of my greatest resistance this had been one of the most compelling things I had experienced in the Catholic churches: a kind of inner spontaneous coming-up, as a flock of birds of the fields, out of some inner instinctual thing, rises: the commonness of it, the mutual identity of the need, and this, the response to the need. Just before the Canon you hear it. In the better-mannered parishes they wait discreetly for the bell, but in the poorer parishes they do not wait. When the Preface is on and they know the Sanctus is drawing near, they begin to go forward from their seats to the kneeling; you hear the spread of the sound of them moving ahead to kneel. I received it now as the great hushed and expectant congregation rose to its feet, and looking up I saw that the acolytes were coming in, the subdeacon and the deacon, and behind them, in his great vestments, the Archbishop himself. But now he was no longer the Archbishop. He was any priest before any altar in the whole of Christendom, bending into the Confiteor. And the Mass began.

# Part Three

# THE FORCES OF THE PANG

*For myself, it was not logic then that carried me on; as well might one say that the quicksilver in the barometer changes the weather. It is the concrete being that reasons; pass a number of years, and I find my mind in a new place; how? the whole man moves; paper logic is but the record of it. All the logic in the world would not have made me move faster toward Rome than I did.... Great acts take time.*

John Henry Cardinal Newman

IN THE YEAR 1912 a man is born. It is California, the young country, the land of great promise, the Golden West. It is the new century of unlimited hope, the fabulous century of man's fulfillment. It is the unborn century of hope without Faith.

A century of hope without Faith it may be, but it cannot be said, at its inception, to lack for certitude. The Western World trembles on the lip of all fulfillment. America, unencumbered by the restrictive conventions of Europe, applies the machine to production with unprecedented effectiveness. From her enormous resources and her primitive assembly lines already a plenitude of goods pours forth unstinted. Men are intoxicated with the sense of their own potentialities; they stand before a universal prosperity of which their ancestors could not even have dreamed. Peace contains the nations. To many, the idea of open war among the great powers is a nightmare of remote barbarism, unthinkable. Suddenly the dream shatters like falling brick: in 1914 Europe begins a purging of blood from which she is not to recover.

The child is six when the Pact is signed and the purge ceases. He enters, with his formative years, the era of Prohibition, called in the nostalgic journalism of the time, The Roaring Twenties. He lives in one of those quiet rural American towns supposed to be the best places in the world in which to grow up. Perhaps they are. Yet the man next door is one day discovered to be a bootlegger, smuggling whiskey in automobile tires; in this very neighborhood the homes of his childhood playmates are ruptured by adultery, incest, suicide and divorce. On Sunday afternoons flushed bareheaded young men in open roadsters roar down the dusty streets; beside them girls in short skirts, clutching ukuleles, put their feet up on the dashboards and scream. He and his companions, in the morbid prurience of boyhood, learn to pick through those nooks of the rural lanes where the reckless lovers left in the weeds the sheaths of their unconditioned lust.

He has hardly broached puberty when he enters the belly of The Mechanized Age. All summer long his little town works the mammoth cannery which constitutes its chief employment. For though this is an agricultural community, it is far indeed from the subsistent rural economy that formed the backbone of Christian Europe. This is the capitalist's entrenchment—an area of vast orchards, immense vineyards and gigantic packing plants, all developed to exploit the markets of the clamoring cities which engorge the East. At fourteen years of age he is sent into the cannery's cookroom, an inferno of howling machinery and hanging steam. His shift is eight hours a day, the limit of the law. A year later he lies about his age and works the quota of a man—twelve, fourteen, even sixteen hours a day. In that hell the temperature lives at 110 degrees. He stands at the capping machine and watches the cans whirl under his eyes, a hundred and twenty a minute, crowding out of the retort and into the capper and up the belt to the seething cooker. Hour after hour, a hundred and twenty a minute, with a half-hour break for lunch and a half-hour break for supper, and on into the night.

Where were You then, God of this heart, God of this smothered soul, in those hours, in those dreadful days! Here is a spirit famished for light, for whom the poetry of love lives on as an ignorant dream. Across the aeons in which he moved where was Your Face? In the whole of infinity one thing only can make existence tolerable; one thing alone can give this spirit light, this is Your Face, and he knows it not. His mind is lurid with vision, but never the vision of You.

And even before the termination of his common schooling, when he is expected to emerge into the world as a sufficient citizen, the Jazz Age is shattered, and he graduates into the grip of the enormous Depression. For a year or two after high school he idles hopelessly at home, working only in the harvest season, until finally he is sopped up in one of those cure-alls of the Twentieth Century state: a government work camp, the CCC. He is twenty-two years old, by law and tradition a man, but he has not yet begun to think.

It is here, in his new rootlessness, that he begins to ponder seriously the meaning of life. The available possibilities, presented for consideration to the rawness of his mind, may be reduced to two: Christianity or Atheism, with long odds on the latter. His father has rejected the former as a thing below the dignity of enlightened men. Its explanation of the origin of the physical universe can be dismissed as absurd. Its hopes for a nebulous After-Life in a rhapsodic paradise can be discounted as sentimental wishing. It possesses no true authority, and the fictitious one it claims is being steadily reduced. Even in his own short lifetime the young man can sense the vitiation of the authority of religion in the community of men. The tacit acknowledgment all show the civil law is, in the case of religion, notably lacking. Not that they mock openly, but that they tend more and more to simply ignore. The civil law applies between one man and another, and its force is binding. But what obtains between each man and his conscience is his alone. The need for conventional religious observance is still powerful, but no longer has it any real binding force. Everywhere the preachers thunder against the collapse of the traditional Protestant social conventions, but they are powerless to check the deep underdriving trend, the powerful unrest at the heart of the nation.

And if Christianity possesses only a tacit authority, it possesses no unity whatsoever. In his little town of three thousand people there are almost thirty denominations, none of them, of course, predominant. For a few years as a child he attends the church of his mother, a Christian Scientist. His playmates let him well know the inferiority of that affiliation, and they derisively call him "Christie." At the edge of town the Catholic Church presides over its little flock of Portuguese farmers and Mexican field workers. As a social force in the community it can hardly be said to exist.

So the young man finds himself, at a later age than most, in the period of intellectual awakening, wearing his father's agnosticism, but with increasing discomfiture. It is somehow too negative a thing to fulfill the growing demand for centrality, a demand that he does not recognize nor understand, but which from henceforth is to be the determining motivation behind the progress of his life.

Released from camp he takes a year at the local State College, where for the first time he experiences a lively exchange of ideas. The Communist unrest which has seethed on the campuses of the East and is beginning on those of the West Coast, has not yet penetrated to this intellectual outpost. Here the mental climate, not so much of the professors, but of the students he meets, is still that of the late Twenties: the weary atheism of those New York critics, essayists and playwrights who shaped what was then called "the modern temper." And while this is a stimulating refinement upon his father's gross Nineteenth Century skepticism, it cannot assuage his unrest. He encounters at last the sustained and developed writing of the poet Robinson Jeffers, with its cult of violence and social doom, and suddenly all his father's anti-Christian repudiation, and the snobbery of the sages of New York, are made into a powerful transcendental mystique of pure pantheism.

This is unquestionably his most profound intellectual experience before the actual encounter with the Church, fourteen years later. Here is a poetry that touches at last the violence buried in his heart, ignites the smouldering energy locked in the unconscious, and gives it its catharsis. Here, in a poetry rivaling the eloquence of Scripture itself, is the grandeur of God liberated from the oppressive atmosphere of small-town Protestant churches, and flashed in gigantic symbols across the cosmos. Here is a poetry of blood and fury and phallic sexuality: a poetry of the supremely procreative God set off against his own guilt-festered soul, a God reducing his deeply feared, repressed violence of heart to the acceptable proportions of mere anthropomorphic insignificance. Here is a religion beyond convention and morality, and hence one he can grasp, believe in, and painfully try to live. This becomes his climate, his psychological context, his spiritual habitat. With Jeffers, he has found, in a sense, his father; has touched at last his maturity. A year or so later he discovers the erotic mysticism of D. H. Lawrence, and he fuses the two strains together to create an intellectual weapon capable of fully approximating the emotional chaos which fills him. It is, given that prime disorder, a weapon made for real destruction.

He has become, in fact, a kind of unconscious existentialist, though it will be years before he even encounters the term. He has inherited, confusedly and blindly, Kierkegaard's acute dilemma. For in the writings of Jeffers he has at last found a God in which he can believe, but having found it he cannot attain to it. His very humanity seems to cut him off, and because he is convinced that it is his relationship to man, his humanness, that keeps him cut from God, it is his manhood, his humanness, that he seeks to transcend, if not to annul. In this conviction his separation from the world of men begins in earnest. Before, all his deep-down rebellion, his insecurity and his mortal pain have not been able to break the bonds of social convention because they have had no instrument in the intellect. But now the instrument is provided, and he methodically sets about chopping one by one the attachments that have held him to the stabilizing structure of common social life.

He arrives at artistic maturity, and at last determining upon the career of poet, narrows all his activity, canalizing toward the one end, adopting for himself the ideal of the supremacy of the artist, in the great European tradition, the genius as a being apart, remote from the concerns of common humanity, above political and moral and conventional consideration, living a life of intense withdrawal and profound inner preoccupation. The political unrest of that time leaves him relatively unmoved, cognizant but unbending. He maintains his strict autonomy, looking out on the world through the lens of his art, passionate and intense, but emphatically uninvolved.

He achieves marriage, and breaks thereby the predominant attachment to family, as a source of both material and spiritual support. For it is a marriage based on no true commitment, and perhaps nothing reveals so clearly the extremity of his mind as the desperate surgical act by which the sterility of the union is guaranteed. Leaving their families he and his wife move into the neighboring countryside, take work that will separate them out of the community which had moulded their very lives. In time they acquire their own farm and establish a life isolated as far as possible from every relationship with the people about them.

And all through the late Thirties this drive for isolation is forced by the rising threat of war. Europe groans in apprehension. The terror of doom hangs over the nations. A fear, indeed an hysteria, breathes from every newscast. In the threat of this doom he and the woman cling together; they wait for the worst.

And the worst comes. War cracks the world. The man, a pacifist, being drafted, is sent to another labor camp in the Northwest woods. With only so insufficient, so incomplete a marriage for support, possessing no foundation in the structure of society, the woman falls into disillusionment, takes up with another, gravitates to the great coastal cities, drifts in the chaos of that life. His mother has died; at war's end his father dies. Although he did not know it, his old centrality was fixed on a few basic tangibles, and these have been utterly destroyed.

He emerges back into the world in a state of pure quest, the need in him to achieve totality aggravated to desperation, but terribly thwarted in a universe of flux, a life purely transient. With no anchor, with almost no hope of anchor, he doggedly begins again on the farm of friends in the hinterlands of California. Once more the affection of a woman touches him; once more the hunger for love and certitude sweeps him into an alignment. He forsakes his loved landscapes and migrates to the hateful city, takes work, begins again the hopeful endeavor to build about him the very shells of earthly certitude the war has swept away. But the mystery of life remains unsolved; the thing he has once fastened on has proved terribly treacherous: deep in his soul the old problem at the heart of man gnaws for solution.

And now, through the instrumentality of this other woman, it is once again Christianity, after so many years, that rises for his consideration. His father's powerful repudiation is still rooted within him, yet his father's acceptances and his father's rejections have now utterly no value. In this realization he tries for true detachment, makes his appraisal. And yet, laying aside his raw prejudice, it seems to him that whatever may be said for this creed, whatever its use as conditional norm for the masses of men, such is the substance of its metaphysic that he is quite prevented from rendering assent. To do so, in the present state of his knowledge, would be nothing less than intellectual abdication.

For since all possibility of a personal God has been sealed off from him, detachment and inviolability are necessarily the essence of religion; and all attempts, ritualistic and dogmatic, are failures of what the existentialists call "the courage to be"—a kind of cowering behind the blinds of creed. Dogma is unacceptable because being man-made, man-proposed, it cannot relate to the unformulable godly objectivity, it can relate only to the human subjectivity, and hence but falsifies the relationship. "A security system that no longer sustains." The reliance on liturgical externals, the insistence upon the strictly applicable standards of morality and norms of conduct, become perverse crutches, props which enable men to maintain an illusory certitude at the expense of the actual inviolable experience. Hence the true abstraction of God must be approximated in the spiritual abstraction of the aspiring soul, a resolution to cut unflinchingly across every conventional and subjective attachment, and every authoritarian representation, wherever the blazing insight leads. This is the last gasp of the Protestant spirit, the intellectualization of non-conformity when all its other religious attributes have proved unequal to the demand.

He is remarkably like those inveterate bachelors who regard every marriage as a failure of nerve. To them a man, in some obscure manner, loses the courage of his completeness and collapses into the slavish delimitation of matrimony. They can understand the need for sympathy, sexual expression, companionship, domestic assistance, but all these are possible outside so ruthless a compact. They can understand love; at least they claim to understand it; but what they cannot understand is the institutionalization of love in the compact of matrimony. That is capitulation. In the extremity of their isolation they refuse to inhibit the free flow of sensibility by an objective commitment. They do not see that the commitment is the necessary framework in which sensibility is ordered, ordained to its rightful end, truly *engaged*. Thus these confirmed bachelors, in their pitiable separation, drift from woman to woman, and wag their heads sorrowfully over the men who "succumb." And just so their cousins, the marrying bachelors, bachelors at heart but husbands only for convenience or through a transitory fit of enthusiasm, in either case relying upon the instrumentality of divorce to maintain their autonomy, drift from wife to wife, and leave behind them a woeful string of fatherless children.

So, like them, are these other cousins of theirs, the religious egoists. They dabble in the esoteric literature of mysticism, become adepts in the lore of multifarious cults, Vedantism and Sufism and all the varieties of Buddhism, the lives of the Christian saints, and the more fervid aspects of Christian spirituality, each of these inveigles them, and they turn from each to each, restless, tasting and putting down, like spoiled children in the vast candy shop of the metaphysical.

So too, in the same way, are the tortured religious existentialists, more principled surely, but no less desperate, caught up in a kind of compelling negativism in spite of their passionate affirmation, doomed, in the nature of things, to hurl themselves out of context in a willed paroxysm of revulsion from the essentiality of the real.

For the unifying force, the vast totality which invites them to make the sustaining assent is closed to them, the simplifying grace has not touched their hearts. It has not touched their hearts because they do not really desire it. They sense the nature of the cost, which is, hidden deep in the soul, the luxury of egoism, and they draw away. The self, in the supreme agony of estrangement, sees that estrangement is the terrible cost of autonomy, and like a true Protestant accepts the wage, maintains the divorcement, blistered in the agony of its willed apartness, because it dreads its own good, which is likeness, likeness to the reality of an ineluctable Design.

For egoism and God are mutually exclusive (though they exist at war within us each), and in the luxury of egoism, conditioned to see egoism not as luxury but as Truth itself, the soul arrives at this terrible termination: it is, in some mysterious way, actually unable to desire grace. In its naked depths it sees that to accept grace is to capitulate, surrender, betray the sovereign principle of autonomy. It is for this reason that such a one regards every conversion as intellectual violation, pure treason; or, more pitiable, a straight neurotic manifestation, the succumbing to fear, guilt, the queasy compulsion of Judeo-Christian morality, or the psychic cleavages resultant from the baneful Greco-Roman heritage of categorical formulation; or, indeed, merely that Renaissance activist lust for a God of pure power. Whatever the definition, the genuine conversion can only be reckoned an appalling failure of nerve.

He is, then, like all such men; and he is sufficient a temporizer to have assimilated them each in his own equation. Trapped in the disorder of his individuality, born in a chaotic world, shaped to the doctrinaire myth of egoism (nature's darling, the supremely separate man), schooled in the policy of revolt, he can only seek peace through spiritual secession. But because he is impelled into the social context by the very actuality of his human nature, he yet seeks to maintain it at a level free enough to assuage his egoism, but involved enough to fulfill his humanity, and of course he can only fail; so imperious a balance, outside a basic communal commitment, can never be maintained. True order, the order of true equation, pulls him forever in; but the disorder of his time, his heart, hurls him forever out; and in this terrible imbalance he will surely live out his whole life, as his father did, and die the death of the uncomprehending.

In the density of such incomprehension the claims of the Church are no help to him at all. And indeed, were there no Incarnation, his dilemma, setting aside the heroic philosophical rectitude of an Aristotle, is understandable enough. But given the chaos of the world, to proceed as if there were no Incarnation is as ruinous as to proceed in an epidemic as if there were no vaccines. It is to ignore the saving of your life, to die with health at your hands. How can the poor savage, suffering frightfully from his affliction, ever become convinced that so simple a thing as an injection will cure him? Had he a broader perspective, a truer historical insight, a more sober and mature acuity of appraisal, he would be able to perceive the efficacy of medicine in the breadth of the human pattern; as the spiritual sufferer, were he truly educated, could see the efficacy of this more potent Medicine in the tragic history of the race.

But each is entrapped in the false creeds of his fathers. Baneful medicine men and pseudo-philosophers, real witch doctors of the intellect, lure them astray, and the ruinous myths of their cultures suffice to confine them each in his own varietal ignorance. Can a savage believe that because a white man injects a syringe into his buttock, by that apparently absurd operation he can be healed of a terrible disease? Can a modern man believe that because another Man died two thousand years ago upon a wooden cross that he himself, simply by an act of "faith" in the efficacy of that "sacrifice," may gain—what? Perpetual life? Does he even *want* perpetual life? He has in his time tasted enough of life to fill his belly; life is his sickness; give him death, merciful death: He wants nothing more. "Annihilation, the beautiful word!"

Before either can be helped he must assent, which indeed is the terror of choice; assent is dreadful. For make no mistake. If assent is really to mean anything, there can never again be a turning back. Assent will entail putting off the old endearing life of the past, all the delicious corruptions, the care-free fornications and the succulent cannibalism of the old dispensation. It will mean putting on the new man, the new interior discipline: a more trenchant rectitude, a true civilization of the heart, probing even unto the division between soul and body. The choice is terrible because the consequences mean a total change of life undertaken in pure faith. Can we wonder that this modern man, this wretched savage of the soul, sweats in his mortal anguish, sweats before the consequences of a decision that will mean the transformation of his whole life?

Creature of his age, his age is the age of naturalistic synthesis. There was a time when the Church and its supernatural synthesis shaped the whole fabric of the Western temper, so that men grew up in it as consciously Christian as he has grown up unconsciously naturalistic. But five hundred years of passionate revolt have been devoted to the prime task of eradicating that synthesis, and destroying or denying the evidence through which it was achieved. And though much of it is fortunately ineradicable, what has been done with great effectiveness is to break it up, destroy its cohesion, its continuity of strength and force in the community, and to isolate its parts so as to render them ineffectual against the massed, carefully controlled, resonantly evocative forces of materialism.
Creature of his age, contained in the vast probability of unfolding Nature, he is brought face to face with the manifest improbability of the Christian claim. Improbable? The union of God with man in the physical body of an historical personage? Has language lost its capacity to distinguish that it labels as improbable the patently absurd? All his life the ludicrousness of the thing has been drilled into his head; even the so-called Christians hardly believe it any more. In the camp of Objectors, a body of genuinely religious men, absolute belief in the Incarnation was relatively rare; the liberal Protestants had lost it to a man. Not so, of course, among the Fundamentalists, but these evoked only an occasional indulgent smile—sterling characters, all, but how incredibly naive! And even among them, in the more intelligent and educated, commitment often appeared to be wavering. The modern spirit had bitten deep into the very tenets of their belief.
For to the faithless modern mind the essentiality of the Incarnation, which is a religious truth, is an extremely difficult thing to grasp. It cannot be empirically proved. Pursue any proposition of the Christian religion back through the intricacies of theology and in the end you encounter a mystery—a mystery illuminated, indeed, by speculation, thrown, indeed, into a context of rational elaboration, but a mystery all the same, a proposition requiring a definite act of assent based on no more trustworthy a motivation than the obscure impulsion of faith. And nothing, to the skeptical modern mind, is more suspect than that.

All this the man knows. It is not that he ranks himself among the dry rationalists. He fought, as he matured, an increasingly open revolt against the monstrosity of that emphasis, smothering the creative spirit in its own enveloping myth. It is indeed the intuition which he celebrates. It is indeed in the name of the religious spirit, the religious sensibility and the illumination of religious insight that he acknowledges his revolt. But Christianity demands too much for credence. When he learned that not only a few dwindling sects of Protestant obscurantists but the powerful Church of Rome, with all Her astute priests, Her facile doctors and adroit scribes insists that the Incarnation be taken as *literal fact*, he is scandalized. It stands as the supreme insult to the intelligence, the ultimate slap in the face of reason.

Why is it not? How is it that it is no insult to the intelligence, nor a slap in the face of reason? Because, as a mystery, however improbable it is to the mind, it is not, for all that, unintelligible. It is only that its intelligibility consumes itself in the reaches of the infinite. Joining two fundamentally distinct natures (the hypostatic union) in the definitive body of a single man, the Incarnation literally merged the human and the divine into one existential reality, and established the polarity by which the whole human race is assimilated into the Godhead. Faced with the audacity of the thing the mind can only gasp "Why?" and never really know. But though it never really knows, it still retains the fact, and this is the essence of its intelligibility. I do not even know the "why" of an apple, but I know the *fact* of apples. Apples are intelligible, because they exist, and can be grasped as existent. So too the Incarnation. Like any other mystery it simply *is*. It stands up in the temporal continuum as any other historical fact. It remains only to be verified. God took flesh in order to "save" mankind (that is the simplest "why" of the Incarnation), which means that the baptized man is restored out of the indignity of spiritual depravity to the full dignity of a spiritual being. But great, from our own perspective, as that fact is, it in no wise exhausts the vastness of its implication. The "why" reverberates back through infinity.

What we know absolutely we know only by Revelation, and that is defined. But over and above this the theologians believe that God chose in this way to achieve a central uniqueness, a kind of inclusive objectification of Himself, a realization which incorporates within it the extremes of the universe, embodies the whole range and orchestration of Reality, from pure and limitless Spirit on the one hand to base inert matter on the other, assumed into a single transcendent Focus; and by that objectification achieve the final Masterpiece of creation, the Archetype to which it all relates, the Hub upon which existence turns. This Archetype is the Incarnation.

Man, they know, is the one created being engaging material flesh and intellective spirit in a natural synthesis. He is himself the bridge between the paired halves of creation, and as such he stood, ripe for the masterstroke. All the aeons behind his making the physical universe was shaped in being, the elemental stuff of prime matter, rim of the Wheel, laid down at the dawn of time, and then slowly, spoke by spoke, it found construction: man was made, and fell, and in this very falling, in this Sin, in this abject debasement and collapse (foreseen, utilized now in the overflow of Love, man's offense seen as a kind of bait, the Bait of God, drawing forth the divine action), the great creative Intelligence fitted the Hub, and the whole mighty disk, conceived from its nebulous beginnings around that conceptual Axletree, is done at last. Through the sin of man, God achieves the Masterpiece, completes the Wheel. It is in this that the Christ is called King.

O ineffable drama of love! Unfolding of pure purpose! Lifting the fallen human nature out of its sunken creaturehood, fusing it into Himself in an act of perfect love, out of the love projecting the glory of that masterstroke, the merge of God with man, the Incarnate Word. What unspeakable glory did You have in store for us, God, when You foresaw our sin, and foreseeing all, did not prevent, but rather prepared, rather readied the Logos for His great entry into the feeble human history, to choke the Devil's lordship, and swing man speechless up the rippling hegemonies of being, past all the hierarchies of valuation, to quench his Christ-illuminate mind in the great Love-Gulf of the Head! O speechless beatitude! O blessed sin of man that lured the love of Christ! O fortunate sin that brought the Universal Wheel to its completion! O fond failure of Eve that by her fault was earned our Faith! Sing, Immortal Word, great Figurehead of our fate! Sing in the vast lofts of Heaven where You live, and where the soul of man, gift of the fallen flesh, is swept through all those reaches to Thine own incarnate Heart!

Mind and Mystery, and no scanting of the reason. Utterly beyond it, yes, that is what the Mystery is, but opposition, never. The immense corpus of the *Summa Theologica*, to anyone who cares to crack the covers, is witness enough to that. The great Dominican develops the broad Incarnational synthesis under three aspects: proving first the existence of God and considering His attributes; proving next that the true end of man lies in supreme happiness, Beatitude, reached only in the Beatific Vision; and finally demonstrating the manifest fitness of the Incarnation to achieve this necessity, and in the achievement provide the universal End. The logic is undeviating. But after all the massive elaboration of the *Summa* the Incarnation remains a Mystery of the Church, substantially beyond proof through factual demonstration. No possible accumulation of deductive evidence could of itself evoke the soul's assent.

Rather apologetics can do one thing only: prepare. It can dispose the soul toward the moment of its own assent, but at that point its function ceases. Reason may provide a perfect equation between naked soul and naked Truth, but it cannot bring them together. At the last it has nothing to do with the soul's illumination; neither its deep perception nor the sublime movement by which it glides to its assent. That final activation is the inscrutable privilege of God.

True, the Church teaches that Christ's reality is historically authentic; there is more evidence that Christ lived, claimed divinity and proved it in His miracles and in His resurrection than for virtually any other event in ancient history. Modern archeology has rendered untenable the vain hopes and arrogant suppositions of that destructive Nineteenth Century critical skepticism. But History is not enough. Archeology is not enough. All the techniques of factual recovery, literal reinstitution, can never be enough. Where is the man who is going to change his life—throw over his manifold preoccupations and his compelling concerns, to embrace a strange, improbable and frankly bizarre concept of a God who takes human flesh—merely on the strength of a few mouldering papyri, however well authenticated? Not by these will he be moved, no more than by the perceptive elaborations of medieval theologians. Grace may spur the will, but where is the intellect to find the evidence to satisfy its need? For Faith, despite the popular misconception, is never blind. Clearly something more is desired.

And clearly something more is provided. For beyond the historical attestation exists the living attestation, actual and apparent, a manifestation tangible to the senses and open to the intellect, an attestation everywhere in evidence, upright for all to see, offered to every race and nation, set like a beacon on a promontory streaming its light out to catch the gaze and the wonder of every man. That living attestation is the Church, the Church Herself, in Her own being.

And not only does She attest and celebrate the Incarnation; She does more: She exemplifies it. With the Incarnation She came into existence; by it She lived the long millennia of Her life; of it She exists today; through it She preserves existence to the end of time. Were there no Incarnation She could not be what She manifestly is, just as Christ, if He were not God, could not have been what He manifestly was. The Church verifies the fact of the Incarnation as vapor verifies the fact of water—the same thing under a different form. She is what She is. I AM WHO AM said God. The Church, being God, claims nothing less.

And to those who thirst She quenches thirst, and proves by the quenching. But to those who thirst not, She is merely irrelevant. Why should one who has never desired water concern himself with a mist? It is all so improbable. But the true thirster sees the mist as the sign of the living pool, which he desperately desires, and his pace quickens. Is it merely a mirage? About him swelters the wasteland, arid and bleak and vast. Can there possibly be water here? Then he sees the veil gathering against the horizon, and he breaks into a run: he has now smelled water. And running he plunges through the gathering mist, plunging onward in his quest, plunging onward in an act of pure faith, plunging into the deeps of the Cloud of Unknowing. And his face finds the Living Pool.

But for this man, hemmed in ignorance, it is not so much that the improbability is canceled out or explained away; from the natural point of view the supernatural is by very definition improbable. Rather it is that for him this improbability becomes in fact the warrant, the real pearl of great price. The chaos of the world has ground itself into him, Nature *qua* nature has riddled him. The dichotomy between his material existence and his spiritual existence is too complete to be final; the probable only enslaves and crushes. And when he at last perceives it, the evident improbability provides him with the clue—not to escape the chaos of the world (for only in death will he be released from that), but to understand it, to understand it in the present and to provide the means by which it may eventually be transcended. For in a universe where the probable kills, the improbable itself takes on a new dimension. When he becomes convinced that the improbable has indeed occurred, it instantly eludes its definition. Grounded on the realm of fact it is no longer an improbability. It is as *fact* that it frees.

The fact, indeed, in the order of time is historically remote. But that tremendous Fact has never ceased to reverberate, and now these reverberations begin to pound about him. He feels the throb of them in the living body of the Church, the throb of life, the Incarnational impulse throbbing up time to form the warrant and the witness he so much needs. He sees it in the testimony of the Christian saints. He sees it in the Christian miracles, a continuous stream of divine fire pouring up time through all ages until like a great conflagration its light fills the world. Or like those motes of the air which take the rays of the sun and amplify them innumerably so that the whole of earth is illuminated through their radiance wherever the light of the far sun falls, so these miracles of all time, ancient or modern, and these testaments of the saints, yesterday and today, take their light only from the single Sun two thousand years away, of which they are but the extension, and like the dancing motes of air one sees through them to the Source.

So it is indeed by the Fact, the fact transcending the improbability, that the man is at last compelled, as the old chaos of the world had for so long compelled. As that tore from his hands the things he craved, so this will slip from his fingers the very things he craves again. One by one these needs, these engrossments, these sensualities will be eased from his fingers. Their worth, in the light of a greater Worth, diminishes, and he lets them fall, so that he stands at last on the edge of the final renunciation. This is the first time in his life that he has ever really made an assent. And now, strangely, he has to make the final, the terrible assent. When he does he will once more be stripped in a trice and thrown naked of all his human attachments, just as the brute world had stripped him and cast him down. That was by violence, against his will; he was hurt and he howled. This too will be by a kind of violence, and this too surmounting the stiff intractability of his will; and this time, too, he will be hurt, hurt deeply. But this time he will not howl.

I began to write *The Uncouth* soon in the new year. After the midnight Mass, that Christmas morning, we left the Cathedral and took the last train over the great bridges home, across the Bay, down to that long but narrow shelf of earth that tables, between the water and the hills, the cramped cities of our life. Days went by, but whatever I did in them that I now no longer remember; I know there walked with me the image of the sheepherder as I had rediscovered him, the thing I once had been; but more than that the thing I still was—a heart swaddled in darkness. As far as the things of God were concerned I was an utter barbarian. I knew for the first time how callow was my mind, how shadowed my heart, how stunted my soul. But like the sheepherder I was the material of transformation, that much I sensed. And in the great smothering city, with its sweat, its bawl, its omnivorous gut, I felt the touch of that grace. This was hope. It would be in hope, a hope born of knowledge, a knowledge born of grace, that I would take up that grappling, and in such areas of the human heart as I had never believed to exist.

### i. The Uncouth

A mild autumn, rain, and the high pastures
Greened again with good verdure; but at solstice
Wind northed for cold, and they brought out the sheep,
Nights crippling, frost in the hollows at dawn,
The wind blowing as out of the depth of a void,
Blowing as out of the nethermost places of earth;
And on the third day, near dusk,
Being come at last to the wilderness edge,
Drew in their flocks, made nightfall there, the sheepherders;
Built weedfire, would go next day
Down to the valley, warm,
To the sheltered fields,
The snug sequestered folds,
A more tolerant winter.

For the sheep only. As for them, the herdsmen,
They'd rather hug out the year on a juniper ridge
Than enter now, where the hard-bitten settlers
Fenced their acres; where the merchants
Wheedled the meager gain of summer;
Where the brindled mastiffs
Mauled the wethers. For the sheep were hated;
Themselves were hated. Their ways were of sheep;
They wore rough skins of sheep;
And the stink of the sheep
Hung everywhere about them.

And they made their weedfire,
Gravely.  This for them was the last night.
Tomorrow was the world's,
And the world disdained them.
They had no knowledge of the world

Nor had they knowledge as yet of the Angel.

For these faces were fated.
The fire, in its fletch and dapple,
Fretted the countenance of a humanity
That had demonstrated only the crude
Capacity to survive; the brows
Hardly clefted by thought,
Where hope, as on the face of the ram,
Never had recourse.  Something there was about to happen,
As if a soul were to be bestowed,
Where the naked intelligence,
That prime, animal aptitude for life
Retained its purity.

And the world, of whom these the uncouth were most despised,
Mocked off the streets to keep the cold nightwatches there
Over the wilderness-hearted earth,
Dreamed blindly on of the transforming grace
These were now to receive.

I wrote in hope. And in hope the sheepherder moved into history, out of his isolation, his high sheepwolds and his narrow thoughts, out of his great indigence of soul, into the making forces of God's way among men. Everything he was he brought with him, his innocence and his guilt, and the great wounds of his divided heart. He too, like humanity itself on the eve of the Incarnation, was a thing of deep divisions. For the divinization of the natural order means that each of its attributes takes on the urgence of a godly dictum. The machine of the universe becomes the unimpeachable absolute from which there is no redress. In the hegemony of nature the instincts loom supreme, the good beasts inhabit it with the clean conformity of a matchless accord; and although they too are torn between the exigencies of instinctual demand, for them, even though they perish, there is no inherent culpability because there can be no choice. Choice and culpability constitute the unique domain of man.

For though we too, like the beasts, may be torn between instinctual demands, there, with us, the matter only begins. In man, endowed with both an immortal soul and a discursive intellect, not only does the factor of choice set him irrevocably apart, but the consequences of it extend drastically beyond physical survival, so that at every turn the unprincipled man is swept from anguish to anguish in the terrible extremity of his decision. And the man who is principled indeed, but whose principles end in nature, is only a little less vulnerable: his body, as St. Paul writes, becomes his god, he has made his impulse holy. And because the impulses, in fallen man, are not thoroughly coordinate, but exist in an overlappage and tear at each other, warring one with another, the final extent of progression is limited only by the simple capacity to endure the strain.

Hence we see among primitive peoples, as well as in the age of classical paganism, how men deify one aspect or another of nature, and, seeking a principle of selection through which the energies can be canalized, worship that aspect in the personification of a god. In modern man, of course, this process of deification is largely symbolic, but its mastery of the mind is virtually as complete. A modern man compelled by circumstance to choose between two conflicting demands of nature has all the anxieties of an ancient pagan appeasing two conflicting gods. It is nothing strange to observe men pouring the whole of their lives into one aspect or another of the natural order. As these emphases continue and deepen, the cleavages between man and man also deepen, just as they deepened through Rome, until chaos is their end.

I was one of those men who divinized nature, and I worshiped its attributes in my attitudes and my acts. In the terms of nature these things became holy simply because they *were*; their very existence was the certificate of their sacredness. Through habit and training I might conduct myself in the conventions of men, but in my heart the gods I served were instinctual; and because I had no concept of such a thing as *fallen* nature, I had no defense against the weaknesses of nature, nor the influences of evil, nor the ancient and ingrown habits, the ancient, ingrown sins that held me in possession since the days of my infancy. These attachments, these habits and compulsions, these old inveterate affinities were rooted in the authority of nature, and they had to be torn up and cast out before I could become a Christian.

What were these affinities, these compulsions, that had so entangled my heart? They are each exhibited in *The Residual Years*, where all unknowing I set them down as they struggled for mastery in the structure of my thought. In the depths of his imagery the poet does not lie; and the poet's truth is often a terrible thing. The poet's truth, insofar as it springs from a twisted nature, is freighted with annihilation. His congealed hatreds and his disabling fears will here, in the heart of his poem, be hushed no more. They eat their way out, and leave the testament of that torture, the past, in the depositories of his words.

I was never prepared to recognize the principle of active evil in the world, but certainly, very early in my childhood, I witnessed its most evident manifestation. I could not have been more than six or seven years old when there moved into our neighborhood a family whose children, all of whom were girls, had through some indeterminate circumstance become thoroughly corrupt. Everything they did they managed to endow with an engrossing nastiness. For the first time (and I was never henceforth to cast it off), I learned the secretiveness of evil. And I learned the lurking craftily-done violation of the body, and the filth of the bodily functions. In the tall weeds, in the deserted sheds, in the vacant lots and unpeopled corners of the summer schoolyard I learned, in the impressionable depths of newly awakened conscience, the magic ritual of depravity; and in that earliest, most consequential of choices, I, with the choice to be made, did not choose to reject.

It was a choice which, in one form or another, I was to repeat many times in the years of my youth and my manhood; a choice, in its long sequence of error, not fit to delineate here, and not necessary. For sin has this character: in the repetition of detail its chronicle of deviation becomes merely mechanical, the frigidity of soulless action straining to achieve what is already lost. Sin can do one thing only: violate. That is its single shock, and in a trice that goes, leaving the impotent after-action straining pitiably on an empty gratification.

And yet, to temper the impression that I lived a life more dramatic than it was in fact, it must be said that I was not a vicious nor even an adventurous boy, but only a weak one, though I cannot over-rate the powerful impact of sin on my whole psychology. I had entered with my earliest thoughts the frightful domain of guilt, and I was nevermore to leave it. From thenceforth it could only accumulate, for I had neither Confession nor Absolution to assuage me. My father was an agnostic and my mother a Christian Scientist; perhaps no combination of spiritual obtuseness is less likely to foresee, prepare for, or recognize what surely must have been the open manifestation of evil. Though my parents were by any standards admirable people, the marriage was nevertheless flawed by terrible psychological divisions, and this is a factor to which no child can ever adjust.

In a truly stable home a child of strong character might well have thrown off the early seductions and followed his father forward into a life of rectitude and equanimity; but given that twisted polarity at the heart of the family, where no certitude may develop, and where the father, repudiating the child, annihilates before his eyes the image of the man the child is to make, no such recovery is possible. The male child moves in the esteem of the father and in the familial accord. The image of the father is the male child's great criterion, his god. The whole function of the father is to lead that child from strength to developing strength, and in the end, through his own consummate worship, effect for him the transference to the true God, to Whom all the fatherly function has been conformable. But when the child is brusquely rejected, or when the tension between the father and mother quenches that love, the child, in his rootlessness, wavers and is lost; he falls back on the clamour of his senses; in his misery he gravitates into the orbit of his purely appetitive needs, and caught there he begins to lie a little, cheat a little, sin a little; and although manhood may well straighten him into some acceptable norm of conformity, at heart he remains essentially insecure, essentially untrustworthy.

The defection of the father takes many forms, many modes. Brusque repudiation merges into painful weakness, weakness merges into mere boredom. You see them everywhere, unhappy frustrated men with the faces of discontented children, or the impervious masks of willed insensibility, or the horrible grim death-faces of those who have given themselves utterly to plain work. Night after night they go home from casual trades to apartments where possessive wives invert the role of woman: play mother to the husband and lover to the child. And the sons grow up over-sensitive and far too wise, learning to play out the mother's game with a calculated disdain because it "pays off"; or with that brittle brightness of the overly eager; or with that terrible passive muteness of the truly thwarted soul.

This is the seedbed of homosexuality, choked with malignant growths, its poisonous soil the very death-bed of souls. For in that cleavage between the father and the mother, where somehow the full flow of loyalty and trust has gone frustrate, the son, by his father unclaimed, drifts in that vacuum. Then let the mother so much as waver and that boy is lost. For when out of her own need she turns instead to her son, and all unknowing seeks to find her full love there, loses her mate-love in her mother-love, then will she only stifle that son, and he will grow twisted, hungering for the fatherly trust he never had, but hating the excess of female affection he is made to bear. He is not her mate; he is not meant to be her lover; he cannot bear the burden of it. He smothers, chokes, rebels, grows up malformed, and in the full power of his young appetites, his oppressive past gravitates him into the company of men, and he finds delight there, and solace, but mostly understanding, for that is what he never had, and these men know it; they too lived it through; and so he succumbs. He will mingle with women, fascinated; he will even marry one, but he will trust them never.

Unless, of course, he gains the gift of Faith, in which all twisted souls are healed, all hurts cleansed, all deeps made light, though it will take years. For we are made for the order of nature, and in her balance are blent; and her balance, once broken, is only slowly mended.

Behind it all is the really ruinous failure of manhood, which is the failure of authority, a failure through abuse on the one hand, through capitulation on the other; a failure to grasp the role of husband and father, because there is no grasp of the role of God; the abdication of the clear demand of duty, because the idea of complete parental dedication is gone. The father repudiates the child because in some way his relation with the woman is awry, or neglects it because he is dangerously bored with his life, or because he sentimentally projects upon it his own lost youth, having in the relativity of modern life no true principle upon which to act, and becoming the ultimate anarchist: why should he interfere with this little person, this individuality, this uniqueness, just because it happens to be his child?

As for me, in some way, certainly, I came to stand in my father's mind as the thing that kept him from happiness. He would have been shocked and hurt to have been told that he hated me. I dare say he did not. But he made me hate him, with the worst kind of hate: buried hate, hate crushed under fear, fear twisted into the very texture of the natural affection. That hate and that fear consumed me.

And I too must have stood at the threshold of homosexuality. But my mother, in her sanity, in her great heart, never poured out upon me the thwarted love she lacked. Rather, she took it resolutely into her own room to weep alone, and to beg, in my father's return, the full gift of trust that he, in his own thwarted heart, never could give. So the mother, if she is wise, will turn away from her Favorite.

Yet this very turning away is itself a wounding. It is, given the father's defection, necessary, but in the hungering heart of the child it is truly a wounding, so that he grows into the full status of his ambivalence with the father-hunger and the father-fear, the mother-hunger and the mother-fear at war within him. He knows neither what he is nor what he ought to be. In women, he seeks the mother, the comforting breast, the protective embrace; in men, he seeks the fatherly certitude, the beneficent guidance. And he wades through confusion, driven by the internal dilemma he cannot resolve because he does not understand, seeking he knows not what, a blind quest, a baffled, fruitless odyssey. He is ripe for sin, and he will fall where his senses take him, provided they are stronger than his fears.

O terrible paradox! It is in sin that he will learn! Most terrible of teachings, most frightening mystery of life! How could it be that it took sin to teach me? I would rather have died in the womb, dear Christ, I swear it, than learn as I learned the real errors of life! Great God! In Your all-seeing gaze You know the temper of my clouded heart! Look and lay bare the thick complexity of circumstance and equivocation that made me what I am! You have placed in the human family the true formation of Your souls, and it may never be rescinded. Not by the schools, not by the governments, not even by the churches. Send us then parents of great prayer, men and women who every day, enriched in Your sacraments, lay down their lives before You, in whom all vacillation is consumed in Your mighty purpose, in whose God-centered homes children grow toward Your light undeviate as the tall corn grows toward the sun! Here the righteousness or the ruination of man is dunged and nurtured! From here is Your harvest!

And so I arrived, in my maturity, with the full list of those subterranean motivations I had no way of appraising; and when I gradually broke the safe restrictions of small-town conventionality, I became aware that in the broader intellectual climate of the day there is indeed a technique of resolution, there is indeed a new sacrament of penance, and a contemporary absolution. These are to cure not by sacramental grace but by ritualistic exorcism, and the ritual is this: banish sin by denying it; eradicate guilt by rejecting its provenance; what one did once in secrecy and stealth do henceforth deliberately and with assurance. Be no more ashamed. Guilt is the great crippling bugaboo of the heart, avoid it like poison. The high places of learning are full of sane young men and women who smile to hear the sins of the past called sins indeed; who saunter into their sins with the relaxed insouciance with which they wade into water.

In this emphasis the whole relationship between the sexes incurs a profound shift of emphasis. Under the Christian ethos a young woman regarded the fact of chastity as the first line of defense against the liability of recalcitrant human nature. An ethical safeguard, it was nonetheless real, sourced in the supernatural mandate, and the highest warrant by which she fortified her man against his fractured nature, and her own. She bore no illusions as to the status of the human race. Any violation of that chastity was understood to be the debasement, not simply of a convention, but of use, a function; if calculated and deliberate, then the perverse mutilation of something made for a most noble enterprise; if impulsive and hysterical, then an unfortunate bungling, a ruinous collapse. Beyond it lay the act in marriage, lofty in the sublimity of a sacrament, understood and revered because its end was understood, and all its impulse heightened in the knowledge of its ultimate worth.

In my time all that had gone, or was going; and now the standard of the new paganism flaunts from every billboard. Although a young woman still seeks indeed to sustain the man she regards as singularly her own, such is her conditioning that the impulse is not to withhold but proffer. Once more the act assumes, as so often in the long course of history, the aspect of an ancient pagan mystique, its true sacramental character reduced to a kind of unpremeditated plunge. Where once she thought of herself, thought of man, as a being created whole, disastrously fallen from perfection, but reinstated in a perilous recovery, a rescue purchased at ferocious cost through the sacrifice of the Christ, with all the consequent responsibility to maintain the recovered integrity intact, now, through the insidious conditioning of a thousand pervasive influences, she has come to regard herself as something essentially other: a biological end-product, a mutation realized across aeons of evolutionary elaboration, species to species, breed to breed, to arrive at last at this *homo sapiens*, this curiously unstable blend of instinctual drives and psychological compulsions, malformed by years of ignorant parental misguidance and perverse social taboos. Where once she stood beside her man, proud to strengthen him with the singleness of feminine purity, now she prostrates herself before him, not in a blindly procreative urge, the raw surge of biological reproduction (as one might suppose, were that celebrated instinct the true determining factor) but rather, in an act of appalling romanticism, throwing her body down as a vessel wherein he may disemburden his being of the uncontainable tensions which rack him. Her role is to assuage, to absorb the excessive activism which motivates him, and in her loins she seeks to restore his psychic peace and her own completeness, quench his need in hers. And though she feels it meaningless to give herself to someone she does not love (save perhaps out of pity, *noblesse oblige*, the last gesture of human fidelity), she has no convincing reason at all for refusing someone she does love. That would be a rancid self-involvement, a narcissistic toying with her own immaculate exclusiveness, when what is needed is the sharing, the release; a proud defiance of nature, when she ought to comply; a rigid erectness, when her whole conditioning is to relapse.

This neo-paganism, which has great persuasive force because it appeals to the immature romantic imagination, and hence finds its staunchest adherents among such astutely evocative forces as the *literati*, gains intensity not only by its counteraction against the residual Christian ethic, which it hates as a perverse and diseased inhibition, ranked as a dying thing which need only now be ignored, but more desperately against its dominant rival, the materialistic school of clinical sexual experimentation, which, as the age becomes more and more objectively "scientific," bites deeper and deeper into the social consciousness.

Here the approach is made from the opposite side of the biological hemisphere. While holding that some more objective training program than presently afforded by the natural family will find itself in the collectivity of the future, involving the separation of sexual activity from the whole child-rearing process, it is nevertheless recognized that at the present level of social development the family is irreplaceable, so that if the race is to survive, marriage must be sufficiently perfected to perform the interim task of carrying the species forward. And since the chief source of marital discord is held to be sexual incompatibility, it is in this area that it hopes to achieve its solution.

Marriage, in its definition, is a relationship based on (1.) the instinct of sexual attraction, a powerful excitation achieving spontaneous resolution in (2.) periodic physical copulation, which, if successful, results in (3.) that psychosomatic harmony essential to the proper rearing of children. Now marital disturbances may be expected to arise from defects localized in all three of these phases: defects of attraction, defects of copulation, and defects of harmony. Actually, it is insisted, the key to any of them lies in the central one: copulation. If copulation is defective, both preliminary sexual attraction and subsequent emotional harmony will vanish. On the other hand, if copulation is effective, attraction itself will certainly increase and domestic tranquillity will assuredly prevail. The key to happy marriage, therefore, lies in one crucial area: the perfection of the copulative act.

Now since the act is basically physical, it demands primarily an adequate matching of two juxtaposed sexual mechanisms. It is the failure to provide for this matching which occasions the disastrous inadequacy of traditional marital procedure. Heretofore, because of liabilities arising from the arrival of children, society has insisted that copulation be postponed until after the marital compact, a requirement that throws the choosing of sexual partners back on subjective factors alone, while the all-important problem of matching the physical mechanisms is postponed until both emotional and legal involvement have proceeded too far to be rectified, with ruinous consequences to both parents and offspring when common physical incompatibilities inherent in so blind a procedure inevitably develop. Contraception has, however, now made it possible to permit sufficient physical experimentation *before* emotional and legal involvement dominate the relationship, with no danger of undesired offspring to complicate what should at this stage be only a very tentative alignment.

But it must be stressed that mere sexual freedom is not enough. Romantic love, a purely subjective factor, is as deluding an element in pre-marital copulation as in pre-marital abstinence. Under its spell sexual deficiencies are often overlooked or ignored, merging after the birth of children, when the subjective factor vanishes, to reveal insuperable obstacles. It is essential to be absolutely certain that basic physical conformation of the sexual mechanism has been achieved, and that definite physical attraction based on sustained instinctual reaction is in operation, rather than illusive romantic-subjective factors. This can only be ascertained under conditions of ruthlessly objective analysis, and may require prolonged experimentation.

Hence pre-marital sexual activity must operate purely as a calculated prudential measure, an experimental test-run on a basic biological function. In a field where performance is an unknown factor due to a total lack of statistics and where physical specifications are usually concealed and can only be estimated, the whole project is necessarily reduced to the hazards of all trial-and-error procedure. Objectively speaking, the primary aim should be first to isolate the factor of basic physical conformability, the actual engagement of part to part; and, second, the further isolation of solid instinctual sexual attraction, completely dissociated from confusing sub-marginal sentimental accretions, proceeding, thirdly, only thereafter to the cultivation of accompanying subjective overtones, which are so highly important in the end product, but which cannot be permitted to bias the fundamentals. For as no one is happy with an automobile unless it has a beautiful finish, and this is correct, how foolish to sign a bill of sale before it is even ascertained whether the gears will engage.

In practice, however, ideal as the above hypothesis might be, the experiment does not admit of such logical step by step procedure, for it can only be conducted under conditions of initial sexual stimulation, which renders the isolation of phenomenal aspects difficult. But even so, every care must be taken that within the field of genuine, fully instinctual sexual attraction, actual physical conformity is insisted upon, otherwise sentimental factors may intrude prematurely into the program, objectivity will be lost, and only too late will basic physical incompatibilities become apparent. In no case should the relationship be permitted to develop into more refined areas until basic physical parity and sustained instinctual attraction have been demonstrated. Only thereafter should subjectivity be permitted, and then, preferably, only following a period of thorough training in basic sexual techniques. But it should be obvious that unless some such experimental procedure utilizing objective standards is adopted, the present situation of marital chaos will continue, with disastrous results to the offspring of the race.

Thus the bleak world of laboratory realism. And though we may not yet see it in such unrelieved crudity, that its values point logically in some such direction is apparent; that its influence is growing is evident; and that its attitude already exists as a powerful conditioning element is undeniable. Just as the housewife may not be an expert on vitamin research, but is canny enough to take their existence into account when she purchases, so the coed may be only nominally curious about clinical sexual documentation, but as a woman of an empirical age she can hardly have escaped the temptation to know at least what kind of performance she can expect, and is herself capable of, before she makes her commitment. At any rate, neo-paganism, whether of the Romantic-Oblative or the Scientific-Objective variety is hinged directly upon the lurid myth of materialistic evolutionism—an hypothesis so universally accredited as to merit the appellation "the greatest confidence game in history." It has enslaved souls by the millions, and in that delusion they fall like flies.

I myself do not wish to indict here the theory that man is a biologic mutation, though apparently Thomistic philosophy finds the theory untenable. What any Christian, evolutionist or not, objects to, is the widespread assumption that man is *nothing but* an evolutionary mutation. It is this attitude that stands at the heart of the ruin of modern man.

In that delusion, like summer's bumptious fly, snapped by cold in the brittle frost of autumn, I listened and I fell. As man, as male, I sought of woman the vessel in which I could expend myself, and fulfill myself, and find quietude from the forces that riddled me. And from such rash premises, elementary logic could only indicate that in the absence of woman, onanism was the simple unquestionable alternative. Do not even the better youth directors candidly assure the stripling that a little discreet masturbation relieves tension, quietens the nerves, and establishes poise? I needed no such assurance. I had learned, in my "liberation," to laugh at the follies of my elders, but my laugh was bitter. At heart I was furious that the stupidities of society, the stupidities of religion, should have imposed upon me their unreal and barbarous malformations. Henceforth I would be free. In the new shamelessness glares the sun of mental health and bodily fulfillment. A savant of the times, whose sexual documentation is shaped to fit the biologic myth, when asked by what criteria he evaluates his findings, replied, "Man is a mammal. I use the criteria of the mammal." So I. By the criteria of the mammal I would conduct myself; I would lose myself, like it, in the inclusive mutability of evolving nature, and there find peace.

And there find peace? It is not so much the genus which governs individual behavior, but more particularly the species. The weasel and the whale are both mammals, but who in his senses would be so rash as to appraise the needs of the one by the habits of the other? And yet *Homo sapiens* is separated from the rest of his genus by a distinction more vast than all the inequalities of bulk and instinct that divide *Mustola vulgaria* from *Cetacea mysticeti*. It is in terms of its intellectual nature that human behavior attains its radical demarcation, throws its conduct forward to the spiritual being, not backward to the brute. But the time's dry rationalism, preoccupied with physical considerations, has lost faith in the most elementary spiritual distinctions. Lulled by a blind empiricism, the disordered soul most rashly hungers for an ever broader equation, finds the species too confining, turns hopefully to the genus, and frustrated even there (for it too has its laws), launches out into the welter of multifarious creation, to seek, from the amoeba to the ape, the guerdon of its hope.

In nature, therefore, I sought my peace, and nowhere else. Nature was the context, and in its inexorable dimension surcease ran in a direct line from the mother's breast to the loins of the mate. Is it not in the repetitive mechanism of the universe that man's whole destiny is contained?—the journey of the sun, the pursuit of the moon, the paths of the planets, the courses of the stars, the pounding of the rain, the reaching of the tide, the rhythm of the dawn, the springing of the blade, the falling of the grain, the swelling of the sap, the migration of the birds, the passage of the salmon, the pulsing of the blood, the menses of the woman, the circling of the year—these are the context, the all-sufficient fact. Sink here, thou man. Find here thy peace and come to thy rest. Thou hast worn thyself out with too much constraint. Sink down and be still.

And I sank there. And in *The Residual Years*, the residue of those years, contained like former lives in the siltbeds under the earth, my old attempts are stratified, but not the peace. The peace is not there. In the Autumns, perhaps, sunken in the knowledge of mortality, the nostalgic reminder of a once real, once near joy, a surcease touches the heart of the poet, and he is content. But it is the inexorable Springs that he has not reckoned with. In the never-ending Springs the great fertility of the earth sweeps about him, the million seeds of the spendthrift grasses germinate in the warm rain and come thrusting on. All nature, mad with procreation, will not abide. Litter after litter pours into life from the flesh of the beast, and the beast drops, is ground under and gone; the processes of life consume it and spew forth their own carnivorous young, and of all its vitality not a trace remains.

Was this perhaps the Great Lie he sensed in woman, that underlay all his poems of her, a doubt and a distrust?  Earth-Goddess, the omnivorous Female, the consuming Womb, where he lost his identity and found annihilation?  Was this the compulsion, and this the revulsion his aggressive masculinity could never hide? Yes.  The dictates of the mammal, once they are deified, prove stringent indeed.  He shudders back alarmed, to where the cast-off claims of the forsaken intelligence languish in disrepute.

Such, indeed, was the thing I had come through, but on the eve of my conversion I had fought forward to a more trenchant resolve.  I had fought forward because she with whom I had pitted my life refused at any time to play out the game of the mammal that I brought to her.  And in her outrage strove to reclaim in me the human personality I sought to renounce.  And because in that war she was successful, I moved forward out of the biological and into the personal.  And I stood at last in the new knowledge, which was indeed a still new bewilderment, and sought for the secret that could make it clear.  The claims of personality, as I had seen it, could have no function in the wheel of pure nature.  That was something of a different order.  But where and how that order impinged I had yet to understand.

But as the sheepherder, in his beautiful credulity, had come forward to attend a thing no shepherd had ever seen, a virgin birth, so I too, in the awkward diffidence of an unbelief that had worn too thin to last, I too came forward.  A Virgin Birth—a thing clearly beyond belief because utterly unnecessary:  did not procreation suffice?  Until gradually I sensed in it something of the secret I had sought, something beyond the blood of the beast, some finer, more favored marriage than body and spirit had yet known, but might aspire to—not sexless, not soulless, but a mastery  of the two, a fulfillment at a rarer level, which loosed them from their urgency, and made them govern toward a more stable norm.  In the ambience of this exquisite event, the supernatural revealed its most gracious touch.  And suddenly all the consequences of that first willed act of the self, that primordial Sin, the trap that caught the world, lay broken; and through it poured the knowledge, the certitude, the mystery and the faith. The whole planned, powerful misconstruction collapsed into the dust and ash of all fleshly emphasis, and in my awe I understood.

    ii. The Coming

Blood, and the black
Bull-trodden earth, where the cow
Had bled of the womb-blind calf,
Where the shuddering ewe
Had bled, in the beast's
Fortuity, the beast's
Groan.

It too, it also: birth,
Like death, ravenous—
An unspeakable rank fertility of earth
Splitting its pod—
But this time a difference.
That lull in the air, that lapse!
As if the great device of the flesh,
The need of the flesh
Made flesh, the flesh
Founded forever upon the flesh,
Blood on the blood—
As if, on the instant, the stroke were checked,
And the flame sprang through,
Purely, between the forces of the pang,
Hued with the flush of Godhead,
Set round with the tongues of angels,
Burning and flashing
In the strewn litter
On the somber floor.

Nor would that night contain it.
There was an age, insurgent,
Scrawled on the stonework of the temple wall.
There was the massive aftermath,
Flanked with the doom of kings,
And the secret seed
Spored in the bowels of Empire.

> There was the powerful regrouping of the mind,
> Where the sotted puppets
> Snored on their grosser thrones.
> That. And the bare power,
> Which is love, forged now, in the frighted human soul,
> As the force of a love, larger than it,
> Swells the wizened heart
> To the stature of a faith.
>
> Birth, like death,
> Transcended. The blood
> Burned out of the stable floor.
> Outside, the oxen and the ass
> Crunch their corn. But the man!
> The man! seized in that vortex
> Breaks on his knees
> And prays!

In awe, out of the remote sheepwolds of my imagination, and into the making forces of God's way among men, I came, and I understood. It was an understanding that had once shaken the core of history. No more the old hegemonies, no more the rotten affiliations, the hoary kings and bloated emperors of the mind. Mankind was touched. Henceforth each age, in its servile attachments and its weak resolve, would too be touched. So crumbled ancient Rome, the masthead of the world, the pitiful hope even of Christians, pitiful because founded upon a thing unfit to survive; so too our own great technological age, it also the pitiful hope of Christians, and the more pitiful because the less fit, it too will go down before the mustard seed of that Grace, before the secret germ in the bowels of this Empire, to make, out of the blistered earth of another night, a new Age of Faith. And I, who grieve out my own time, rejoice in the far resurgence, rejoice in the bare power, forged again in the human soul, and the stature of the Faith.

For why should I not rejoice in the liberation of my age as I rejoiced in the liberation of my life? In a single poem, whose short and labored line was like, indeed, the throes of a birth, I had laid the ghosts of a score of nightmares in the poetry behind me; I had broken the tyranny of nature, and at last arrived at that detachment from which the sequential errors of my past could be surveyed. The uses of the intelligence, which I had so long discounted, could now be gathered into perspective, a perspective attained not by a kind of calculated adjustment, but through liberating faith—the transcending of the limits of the natural vision, and the willed and accepted exposure to the inflow of God's activating grace.

Nor is this merely a fanciful substitution, the mystique of Christianity for the mystique of Nature. It is, rather, a spontaneous cognitive act, the perception of the essence of reality, in terms of source and fulfillment: true recognition. Obviously, I do not mean that with Baptism I would suddenly emerge into the assured status of an intellectual master. I mean that Baptism would remove barriers that had kept the mind from its whole fulfillment, great or little, in God's comprehensive plan; and that its native powers would indeed be augmented by infused knowledge, providing, insofar as it was needful to know, a dissolving insight into the denseness of that most august of mysteries, the mystery of God and His means among men. Grace is not mere influence, an effect, as one would conceive of remote control from an omniscient Heaven. For God is immanent. The universe is God-thrusted, God-mingled. Not an atom of it but is kept in being by His conserving force. Moreover, sanctifying grace is His own true bestowal, a participated likeness of the Divine Essence. At Baptism we become not merely reconciled to God, but through that speechless incorporation into Christ Himself, *of* God, grafts, in St. Paul's vigorous terminology, into the magnificent tree of the Divinity. And though the mind, at most a part, never can grasp the whole, it can be fulfilled in the function of the whole, and this is its greatness. In the conformity of its place, the mind achieves its maximum utility, a utility occasioned by the ease of its acceptance. Outside that, all its wrestlings and strivings are but the juggling with effects. It perceives, but does not fitly comprehend; it seizes, but does not justly assimilate; it collects, but does not truly synthesize.

And where there is no true synthesis, no cleanly harmony, there is no invincible knowledge, no final, compelling truth. Could it be for this reason that the intellectual, the man of mind, was not at the Incarnation? Where were they all, the philosophers and the poets, great men of letters, astute scholars? Off there in the thick cities, Athens, Alexandria, Antioch, Rome, they would, as a class, never admit to having shirked their responsibilities. The intellectual had, in history, brought the art of thinking to a final ordering. Painfully, through generation on generation of slow speculative application, of cancellation and rebeginning, he had constructed the tall superstructure of human thought, the final end of the purely natural reason, and it was an achievement that would be the wonder of all time. But it had not brought him here. For him there could be no reason why the inherited myths of a dispossessed race should be conceded any premium on the truth.

But what of the Jews, who, in the Incarnation, were supremely proved the Chosen People? Were there none among them capable of such comprehension, no class or profession trained to ponder the Event, comprehend its significance, and translate into usable terms, for the enlightenment, the joy and edification of their own people, the meaning and the might?

For no society is really whole without the intellectual, though nothing so demonstrates the collapse of thought in our time as the ambiguity and derogation with which this term is used. In the intellectual the direct vitality of the peasant and the adaptive genius of the merchant find a kind of illuminate synthesis. He is, culturally speaking, their equipoise. He understands the strong things of the one and the fine thing of the other in a way that is itself a synthesis, so that his acuity and detachment may permeate the social fabric and give it a final balance. The Jews, indeed, had such a profession, but its fate is a ruinous story, and not one for these pages. And however it may be described or what forces adduced to explain it, the salient fact emerging from the remote historical context is the utter failure of a class.

We know from the words of Christ how terrible is the judgment upon those who govern and who abuse; but will the failure of the thinker be less? The failure of the governor tears the flesh of a people, but the failure of the intellectual tears its very soul. In that failure governors too go down. The weakness of the thinking man is intellectual pride. Pride strikes at the very center of his gift, and transforms it from a delicate gauge to a thing like a cold chisel, no longer sensitive to the intricacy of Being, but stiffened into a weapon for the hewing of the will. In this atrophy nations fall, kings go down, cultures vanish, races disintegrate and pollute the land, and the miserable squalor of the unenlightened man makes an infestation of the earth.

When Pope Leo XIII declared that the tragedy of the Nineteenth Century was the loss of the proletariat to the Church, he might have added that the tragedy of the Eighteenth was the loss of the intellectual. When the intellectual deserts, sooner or later the proletariat falls away, to leave in possession only the *bourgeoisie*, the merely institutional man, who transforms Her exterior into his own conventional image, and smothers beneath his inveterate conformism the divine life hidden in Her heart. But if the Eighteenth Century saw the desertion of the intellectual, the Twentieth is witnessing his return, and the Twenty-first will record the recovery of the proletariat. We see, then, that the intellectual holds the key not only to his own destiny. Voltaire, when he said of the Church, "Destroy the infamous thing!" was condemning more than himself. His curse fell on millions.

This failure is always, in some obscure way, a failure of faith. It was among the Jews doubly deep because although the intellectual elite was not precisely the priesthood, nevertheless it was the instrument of canonical interpretation, promulgation of Sacred Law, and hence served as the agency of divine authority. And though the manner of the failure was complex, the totality of its results permits of no doubt. Christ documented it to the full, and in His flesh.

It is a well known fact in the psychology of conversion that the complicated person is rarely won, and, if won, remains curiously unstable in the framework of his choice. To the simple soul, conversion comes with relative equanimity, and the equanimity gains, the soul stabilizes, broadens, becomes indeed more and more simple in the gradual concentration of its whole purpose on the finality of God. The complicated soul, however, is so riven with cross-grained inversions, so wracked with a futile thwartedness, that it is with great difficulty, and only out of a most painful suffering, that it is able to make the great interior grasp of faith. Conversion is the free, fulfilled and consummate act of assent to the transcendent motive, the sudden stripping away of the self, the forthright all-clasping embrace of an utter trust, and it is a thing which must occur in the life of every man if he is to see finality. That it did not come to these men who were destined to play out the role of the unregenerate in the life of Our Lord, these intellectuals, this elite, who should have been by natural and supernatural fitness the spiritual flower of their people, is a lesson the intellectual must never cease to ponder. It remains in the naked account of the Gospels, and it began in pride and blindness and ended in the lynching of God. And it is not over. The men with the cold-chisel minds are everywhere and in all things splitting the wrists of Christ.

But still, it is a gracious and comforting thing to know that the intellectual was not, in fact, denied his place at the Incarnation. He came, though belatedly, as he was belatedly to arrive at many a similar significant manifestation in times to come. Somehow, at this kind of event, the sheepherder would always be there before him. And indeed here the sheepherder had his moment, with the angels singing plain-chant, row upon row of them banked above the underbrush, out there on the sheep-flats, treading the buoyant air in their dance of jubilation, breaking forth in the vast ethereal liturgy, a rising and swelling sublimity of modulation beyond all the Gregorian modes!

Yet it is not of him, not of the sheepherder, that we were speaking, but rather of the intellectual, and how he found his place at the Incarnation. For there were, in fact, three of them, coming twelve days late behind a flying star, bearing odorous gifts and broaching the news all over Jerusalem. We do not know a great deal about them, these extraordinary migrants, save that they were said to be wise, but that fact is sufficient. We know also that they came out of the East, and this too is of note. For at even so early a date the mind of the West had been given up to arrogant rationalistic squabblings, disputes over terms, and resignation to the refinement of sensuality. But in the East the contemplative faculty there was of ancient endowment (though unfecundated, it is true, by the active ingredients of speculative truth, without which it was to rest to this day relatively inert). This was why it remained, and the adjective is crucial, essentially *receptive*. In these men, these contemplatives, the uses of the mind had not crystallized into an edged iron. And this being so, when the revelation was given, there was not the resistance in the will, there was not the attachment in the world, there was not the inertia in the flesh, to keep them from coming.

As for me, scribe and Pharisee I had been, though without their distinctions, and in my own crude way had also cold-chiseled the mind to shape the nails of Golgotha. If I could not claim the full status of the intellectual, it was because I had never submitted to the disciplines of that exacting category. As a thinking man I had taken the line of least resistance, fumbling my way alone and in darkness, and hopelessly wasted the gifts which God had planted within me. But in spite of this I was brought. I was brought out of attachments so poignant in their impingement as to count almost for the whole worth of my life. I was brought in the face of a thousand resistances and distractions. A host of old inurements begged me not to stir, seduced my strength, made flaccid my will. *Brought.* Torn out of context and swept like those desert storms that whirl westward from Arabia, to that consummate Event in the world's need where the contemplative East and the speculative West were fused in the flesh of a Babe, hid back from the coldness of the year in a drover's cave, a cave for the breeding of beasts, hewn out of a hill in Bethlehem.

### iii. The Wise

Miles across the turbulent kingdoms
They came for it, but that was nothing;
That was the least. Drunk with vision,
Rain stringing the ragged beards,
When a beast lamed they caught up another
And goaded west.

For the time was on them.
Once, as it may, in the life of a man;
Once, as it was, in the life of mankind,
All is corrected. And their years of pursuit,
Raw-eyed reading the wrong texts,
Charting the doubtful calculations;
Those nights knotted with thought,
When dawn held off, and the rooster
Rattled the leaves with his blind assertion—
All that, they regarded, under the Sign,
No longer as search but as preparation.
For when the mark was made *they* saw it.
Nor stopped to reckon the fallible years,
But rejoiced and followed,
And are called wise, who learned that Truth,
When sought and at last seen,
Is never found. It is given.

And they brought their camels
Breakneck into that village,
And flung themselves down in the dung and dirt of that place,
And kissed that ground, and the tears
Ran on the face where the rain had.

In a stockbreeder's cave cut in a hill, then, the sheepherder and the intellectual were at last joined, after many prolonged separations, there among the hoof-prints of the beasts, on the damp placental earth, at the crossroads of the world. The lectern of the schools and the high sheepwolds of the steppes were merged together in the Infant Christ, that miracle. For it is only in the miracle that the instance was achieved. Nothing else could have done it. Only here lay the purpose to resolve such evident cacophonies. Only here lay the insight to seal such wounds, close such abrasions. The abstract dubiety of the one and the earthly skepticism of the other were both confounded. For though the intelligence, whether complex or simple, failed at the fact, the Fact remained. It was the fact that verified the *event*, in its precise historical certitude, to be proved in full thirty-three years later, on another hill called Golgotha outside a greater town called Jerusalem, when He Who entered life through a slit in nature would leave it by another that had become a rent, and rise up from it, and in proof of His rising give verity to many ancient prophecies, and birth to many new ones.

# Part Four

# THE FALLING
# OF THE GRAIN

> *But to whom am I telling this? Not to Thee, O my God, but in Thy presence I am telling it to my own kind, to the race of man, or rather to that small part of the human race that may come upon these writings. And to what purpose do I tell it? Simply that I and any other who may read may realize out of what depths we must come to Thee.*
>
> St. Augustine

> *But he that is with wife is solicitous for the things of the world, how he may please his wife: and he is divided.*
>
> I Corinthians 7: 33

ADAM WALKED IN THE COOL of the evening, under the fragrant eucalyptuses, among the redolent ferns, and communed with God. He moved in an inexpressible equipoise, simple and sublime. His roving eye regarded the reality in which he was engaged and perceived with a cool detachment each intricate detail, all closely occasioned, as earth, plants, air, water, beasts, birds, and insects moved in their just ordainment. Not only were his natural faculties unclouded by any trace of imperfection, but he enjoyed as well a profusion of supernatural graces. He was, for one thing, endowed with an awareness remarkably clairvoyant. No overhead branch could fall unseen and strike him to the ground. No hidden beast could, unsuspected, spring upon his back. He moved not merely as if God had thrown about him a zone of suspended animation, keeping him in a languid lack of real connection with the brunt of things. It was nothing quite so tame as that.

Rather he knew the exhilaration of true dominance over nature. His powers of discernment were such that he could launch into the onslaught of transient event with perfect timing and emerge unscathed, as some great ball-runner, almost by a sixth sense, eludes the lunges of his adversaries. Nor was this but an instinctive reaction, as the night-time bat follows his beam through the thick forest unhindered. Adam achieved it by a true instantaneity of discernment and judgment, by an exactitude of mind and body flowing with flawless decision into a complexity of forces, each gauged and overcome. If he tired, he could withdraw to some known eddy in the flux, as a swimmer pulls out of the breasting flood to rest. The marvelous consciousness, the undeviating intellectual perception, the unbelievable sensitivity and preciseness of his choice kept him clean of any error. With all the fullness of the flesh he yet possessed, if not the spectacular intelligence of an angelic being, something nearly of that kind.

And yet, for all his specialized distinctions, he need not ever lose the whole immediacy of the Godly presence in and about him. It was as if he were forever cast in some sublime orchestration, some absolute harmony that never closes, but reveals in its unfolding dimension the pulse and lapse of limitless variation, brought forth to the view and sustained there, but always contained in the larger music, of which it too was ingrediential, in which it also was suspended. In the depths of his soul God spoke to him, and the voice was of unending love, and he knew love, it was his full life, his larger existence. The directness of that flow kept his soul eternally sustained in the measure of tranquillity.

When the Woman was given him, as of himself, out of his very side, sharing his powers and proclivities, his life took on an even deeper dimension. Between the three of them, God, the Woman, and he, the flow of love moved triangular and full, a new modulation introduced into the unfailing harmony. In that ambience time flowed by like love itself, so total as to be without diminution, and certainly without end.

One day the Woman came to him and told him what she had done. Adam stood there in the cold instant of his comprehension, and saw with utter clarity the consequences of that act. In an existence where every instant was engrossing, where desire merged into its just fulfillment in a smooth sequential bliss which nothing could impair, what motive impelled?

There came, she said, a resplendent Stranger, and he was very wise, telling me God had hidden the secret of infinite wisdom in that very Tree, of which we are forbidden, cursing us with ignorance that we, of all the creatures of intelligence, might never know, as even the Angels know, the meaning of good and the meaning of evil, be therefore as gods. He swore, moreover, and his testament to me seemed true, that no such thing as death ever could ensue, was but God's scarecrow, set up to frighten us from knowledge; and listening I did eat.

And Adam shook his head, grief-wrung, and wept at the willfulness of her, the cupidity and the wantonness that could so have done.

Then Eve touched him on the arm, saying: Look. I have sinned before God. This has made me alone. He gave us to each other, each for the other, each of the other, inseparable. Take then this fruit, and do thou likewise eat, so that at least we may be together. Having each other we can bring forth children from out of ourselves and find sufficiency in our sons, and in our daughters, and they in themselves, and thence fill the earth, and subdue it; but alone we are nothing. Do not forget, she added, the distinction that from this moment divides us. I have of my act the hidden knowledge that is not yet yours. I would always be wiser than you, who were and must be master. Is this not intolerable? Do you not perceive how impossible it is? Already there obtains a vast area of understanding we can never discuss; an area of which you simply have no comprehension, something other than all the pristine limitation of your innocence. And oh, Adam, if only you knew how terrible and awesome a thing this knowledge is! And what the use of it entails!

And Adam shook his head, and groaned, and wept at the pride of her, the cupidity and the perverse self-will.

Come, she said, take up and eat. Would you let me be cast forth from beside you? No more to walk in the pleasant groves? Is your love so little you could still call paradise *Paradise*, and I not near?

And Adam groaned, and weeping hid his face.

Then Eve trembled, saying: I am afraid. What will become of me? I will be sent far away, never again to be near you. Take pity upon me, Adam, for I have done what I have done!

And Adam groaned in his heart at the pride and the will, the wantonness. And with his eyes blinded by tears he caught up that fruit. And he ground it between his loathing lips, and flung it aside.

And in his terrible nudity he cowered on the ground.

Paradise dried up. After the Banishment brambles broke the grotto wall and took the garden. Spikeweed struck root in the sandy earth, and the poisonous vine encroached. Then the dry desert winds entered in, and it was no more. Back there, before, they had watched the natural world with all its apparent chaos grind through its metamorphosis and had no fear. It was perfectly comprehensible then. They saw it somewhat as God might, in its final ordering, and in that order the mild clashing of its parts was but a variation of the music, and equally beautiful. Now the chaos, apparent and real, closed in upon them. Before, the lords of nature and its friends, they now became its victims, stumbling through their days in a fatal restriction of vision, the consciousness drastically reduced to the pitiful limitation of their senses. Suddenly they had become like the night-loving owl, driven forth in the sun-split day, to flounder down the sky, half-helpless, the air's most aimless fowl.

Nor seemed they any longer to be glad. They sinned often: pride, anger, hate, deceit, lust. Even their comings-together were painful, painfully wrought on the mean grass beds, or along the rough sands where the stale water seeped. The sublime passion they might have used so well now used them at its will. Children came crying out of their loins. Age bit deep in them. Their coarse food hardly sufficed to keep their stingy lives. In the winters they sickened often, recovering only slowly in the weak malarial light. Many a time they despaired.

When Cain was born, they had good hope in him, but that proved false. After the Expulsion Adam might have believed that since only the supernatural splendors had been stripped away, he could at least have gone about his life in the same rigorous sufficiency of the beasts. God had reduced him to the level of the beast; ought not that to mean at least the wholeness of a beast? But man, an animal indeed, has intellect, the very property of the angelic beings. Part beast, part angel, this is the astonishing complexity that makes him what he is. And Adam began to realize that while indeed God, out of sheer generosity, had in the beginning heaped on him graces, there had been an eminent practicality in that generosity as well.

For it is precisely because of man's uniqueness, the unstable juxtaposition of an intellective and a sensory nature, a union of such delicate precariousness, made by the very fact of their conjoining more viable than either nature alone, that God had strengthened him stoutly with such great supports. As in mechanics, where use requires the composition of two radically different metals into a given part, the resultant "weak join" requires careful reinforcement, a need so urgent that, if not provided, the device is left so friable that a simple tool becomes in fact more useful. Thus man, stripped of those sheer supports, actually stands more vulnerable within himself than any insect. This is why Adam who, in his repudiating sin had declared *I will not serve*, was given, in God's grave reply, *Then be on your own*, precisely what he had bargained for: the sweeping away of those all-important strengths, leaving him in a position which, while "natural" indeed to humanity, that beast-and-angel complex, was in fact a thing of such positive liability as to be virtually a disorder, and to earn in Christian thought the very concept of a "wounded" nature consequent upon the Fall.

And this is the terrible thing that Adam began to see in Cain. He watched him, often, going about his work. He looked a perfect man, Cain did, well-fashioned, the son of sound parents, but deep in his nature that baleful weakness lay, the hidden flaw, and Adam knew it: he had put it there. Cain stood in his full maturity, the beautiful geometry of an adult man, but hidden in his heart he had not the stability of a snake. Adam could see it in himself, for he was the head, and it is the head, the spring, the fountain, that stains the whole long stream. Before Cain came he used to wonder if it would actually transmit, and now of course it had. In this beautifully proportioned man there lurked a viability that nothing on earth, no endeavor, no aspiration, no surgeon's knife nor chemist's drug nor the salubrity of athletics nor the fine discipline of the mind could ever remove. There a weakness had been exposed like the vitiation of an incurable disease, which precisely when one stoops to use his expected strength the treacherous limitation spoils the perfection of the act, and he crumbles in his attempt.

And what is this? Concupiscence, the reduction of intricate human nature to a ruinous liability. Eve, like Adam, created in the superabundance of grace, could never have been tempted through the senses: all the blandishment and enticing of sensual provocation fell unheeded about her, simply lacking any power to enflame when reason demurred. Her sin was something other, something more considered than this: you shall know good and evil, and in the knowledge become a superior being. And though the sin in both Eve and Adam was certainly pride, self-love, one suspects that in either case the underlying motivation was somehow complicated, as in a world of multiplicity, choice is always complicated.

Perhaps it can be said that Eve's temptation was gauged on otherness. Her feminine receptivity and self-containedness must have been susceptible to what are essentially distinct and rival states of being, seeking not merely some additional segment of self, but perhaps an utterly different self, a new, more immanent ego, the elevation to a new status, the status of a "superior being." Eve was the first social-climbing woman. But for the male, more dominant and forceful, temptation verges between rival fields of activity. And perhaps Adam, in the pitch, when he chose not God but Woman, chose that in which he could absorb himself, chose that which he could dominate, activate, fecundate. It is in this sense that the Fall of Man may be brought into focus as a sexual offense: the woman like an adulteress exposing herself to unwonted potentiality, craving to be re-possessed, made other than she is; the man fawning before what he can sexually exploit, perverting his plunder to the poverty of self denial. His sin was the more outrageous and debased became he had the intelligence and the sensitivity to gauge the full nature of the cost and accept it. And the result was this terrible reduction, this fearful exposure which means, practically, the hopeless inability to accommodate the sharp stir of appetite to its reasonable end, with utterly suicidal consequences for the race. Before, there was no rousing of the senses without the prior assent of the mind, harmoniously governed to the being's greatest good. But now each appetite lives unto itself. Stimulated, it can wrench free from the proper synthesis, demand assuagement. Hunger, sex, fear, anger, jealousy: all strive together for mastery in the body's shut domain.

Over and over Adam proved it in himself. Each morning on his knees before the crude stone altar he had fashioned for his worship he would pray. Where it once flowed in him like consciousness itself, the very play of his thought, prayer now came hard. And he painfully prayed, remembering how God and he had communed together among the stately eucalyptuses and the odorous ferns. And he would pray God that for just that day he might do no wrong, for just that day, somehow, he might make every act a perfect act, every thought a pure one. But no matter how he prayed, nor how he tried, it never happened. Between appetite and will the bond was too frail. And though on some days of gracious accord it almost seemed to be granted, always enough defection would come through to let him know that he was not the true sufficient self he once had been. He came to see then that he was in fact a cripple, and Cain and Abel, and all the host of children he had got through Eve. Whatever henceforth came into life through the gate of the flesh of Adam would so be crippled, save two only, the Christ and the Woman who bore Him. But for all the others, their race was like a weak-winged bird, that could take to the air, indeed, but it would only be a matter of time before it failed and fell.

There would later be men who scoffed at the whole development, crying that God would never so punish for the mere eating of a fruit. For these Adam could have had nothing but scorn. Man's life with God is a love affair, and the code of love prevails. If a man gives the pledge of a great love to a common strumpet, his offense is not measured in merely monetary values. It may be but a kerchief or a rose, but when he sheepishly returns, the door is barred. He seeks to press on in with his old assurance, but the footman throws him into the street and sends him packing. There is always an Expulsion. No, Adam understood thoroughly the nature of his offense. Before, in the superabundance of God's love, he had wanted some way to show his gratitude, some tangible means, purely of his own, by which he might demonstrate the greatness of his debt. Then God had told him of the Tree, and Adam knew that this would be his pledge, his token. In a way that made him love it, though he was warned away from it. He always passed it with reverence and profound respect. It was the one thing he could really do for God, respect His covenant, and he knew perfectly its worth. No, when Adam ate, he was being the man who took the pledge of a great Love to braid in the coif of a strumpet.

For of course his heart had become divided, that was his great downfall. After the creation of Eve he somehow lost his singleness, and once the slightest flaw was made in his allegiance, from then on he was vulnerable. He never coveted what was not meant for man until Eve did. He never wanted to be greater than he was until Eve told him that he might. And always she was so soft and dependent, she made him seem so necessary, that when the time of the test came on, and she stood there, in that great and solemn moment, with the light breeze in her hair, and all the consequences so meaningful about her mouth, then bawl as later he might, and rant his tragic abjurations, at the bottom of his heart it was his own evasiveness that brought him down. He took God's pledge, the pearl of greatest price, and sniveling, thrust it to a strumpet.

This is the crucial thing he had hid from himself under the guise of Eve's defection, but now he knew the appalling corruption, the towering self-love, and the ferocious pride that in his heart of hearts he had permitted to usurp his trust. And somehow, in his abject contrition, he was able to see what, in all his spectacular intelligence, he had only blinded from himself before. Self-pity, which is the sickness of pride, is the pride's greatest weapon. There are prides which we may confront and face down because they are recognizable, are indeed unmistakable. But the pride that comes under the guise of an injury or a loss is the deadliest pride of all. For then, legitimized by an injustice, how the ego seizes it up, and feeds on it, and sickens and grows bad! And how the rot spreads, and with what rapidity! As when some morbid infection, rooting near the vitals, will sweep into the body's bloodstream, and blow through the reaches of that fevered realm, from organ to organ, from limb to limb, until in that pestilential conquest the whole being is utterly brought down.

Adam died. Eve died and the children of Eve. The tribe of man fanned out from the native basin and faced the night. That was a million years ago, back at the beginning of the long Bone Age. On the changing earth the last of the glacial series was slowly retreating North. It was an age of giants, the mastodon and the sabre-toothed tiger, and for three or four hundred thousand years man survived by food-gathering, hunched over faggot-fires, shaping his tools from wood and bone. He learned in time that rock could be worked, that flint could make a weapon, and for five or six hundred thousand years more that fact sufficed him. Slowly the Old Stone Age gave way to the New. And then, suddenly, the astonishing emergent proliferation: from the Age of Stone to the Age of the Atom only twenty thousand years.

And emerging out of that enormous primitivism men became tillers of earth, grew crops, built permanent encampments, ditched water, learned to fashion the softer metals. Families merged into tribes and tribes into nations. The nations, enlarging, subdued the earth, raised true civilizations, achieved a common collective security. Out of taboos and customs they formulated Law, the slowly wrought disciplines of control, the long gradual gaining, force put to the lofty purposes of order. By diligent training the raw surge of appetite was steadily reduced, and out of his accumulated generational span the progress of man was forged.

And with civilization came leisure, and with leisure, confidence, and with confidence the growth and particularization of the secular spirit. The horsemen cantered before the kings, shouting their oaths of fidelity, shaking their lances against the sky. The warriors exulted in the power of the sword; the lovers, hot from each other's arms, rose to the knowledge of their great desire, trembling with the certainty of all earthly hope. The warriors and the lovers, in the intensity of the possible, rose up out of their passionate engagement, and flung into the future. The prophet might howl from his sandy wastes, the temple priest might warn and rebuke, but the warriors and the lovers, in the flush, in the peak of desire, rushed headlong into each other's arms, kissing and killing, and shaped the future. And the poets, crazy with vision, chanting the great theme of war and the noble theme of physical love, chanting the celebration of all earthly hope, sang the vision of the earthly dream, and deified the future.

Look, they cried, the world wakens! The guilts of our fathers were foolish guilts, and their fears were foolish! We have everything here in ourselves! Break off the bane of that sterile past and emerge from its shadow! Stand forth in the light of the new time, taste its savor! We must win for ourselves abundance and freedom and men will find peace! None will murder for none will have need! Sin is a myth! Lust is but the outburst of repressed desire! It is all because of the conditioning past, but the future is open! Man alone is the measure! Man alone is the means! Man alone will forge the future! Man alone will share the reward!

And there were many great cities. And in the gathering secularism there rose up many great thinkers, and many great philosophers. They studied the fact and the meaning of man. They pondered the mystery of who he is, where he came from, how he is made, what he can do. The religious man, the prophet and the priest remembered his origin; but that was a story the poets had swaddled with many myths, and the secular man was scornful. In his great effort toward objectivity he took man as he found him, man in the immediacy of his exigent reality, and studied him there. He studied him ever so carefully, but in all his astuteness he never discerned any such positive manifestation as might lead him to acknowledge the existence of a Flaw. For to a man engrossed in the natural emphasis the Flaw was a thing he might not posit, could not afford to posit. The Flaw was myth, and myth was the realm of his rival, the priest. The Flaw, in fact, was the very thing he set out to disprove.

For the Flaw is concealed. It cannot be seen as a positive wound, some interior gash or inherited scar that divides in itself. Call it rather a spiritual deficiency in the psychosomatic synthesis, a lack of true proportion between the intellectual and the physical natures. It does not emerge save in terms of the greater thing man was made to be, that he once was, is now no longer. In a universe that is, obviously, ordered, the spiritual nature must consistently govern the physical one, and in man it does not. That is the slit in his troubled being, and is not so veiled but it glares to the sight when one really wants to see. But so oblique is its narrow concealment, and so complex is the web of human nature; the correlation between body and spirit so shrouded and vague, and so various the forces that impinge upon them, that any apparent discrepancy may always be seen as springing out of some physical factor. The very shortness of human life, the very lateness of human maturation, never permit the exhaustion of all the possibilities. Man dies before he has explored himself, discovered himself, and his fierce thought leaves but its shadow residue, a film in his books. Under all his attempts, all his cumulative progression, the Flaw remains, outlasting the advancing wave of his thought, the mighty upthrust of his intelligence, and in the darkness he eats his doom. This is the tragic view of human life, but it is the fact. Man, in the natural order, is doomed, and the thing that dooms him, deep in himself, has no accounting in the order of nature. It is only explained as the positive result of some immense and significant violation, some latent, primordial sin.

And the knowledge of this sin, with its effect, Concupiscence, is the possession of the Church, a knowledge given at the Primitive Revelation, set down in Genesis, preserved in the Hebraic tradition, and verified by Christ. This knowledge is Hers, that She may tell man what he is, how he is to guard against his potential defections; that he may have no hope in himself alone, but that his whole hope is with God. It was for this that the Church was created, so men might know their nature, their end; in that knowledge be healed, achieve that end. For this the sacraments were given, the channels by which the forfeited grace is restored again. For this Christ came: not merely to teach; show men how to live good lives as the world would have it; not merely to witness to a superior truth—many prophets had done that. But to change, to set aright, to rectify, to heal; to heal, indeed, the individual man, the leper and the man born blind; but the race as well, the whole of men; strike off the leprosy and blindness that have lain since Adam on the heart of the world. He came as an individual, as the single man Christ Jesus, God assuming human form, incarnating, to rectify the race; but He perpetuates Himself in the institution of the Church. For the Church is Christ. When the Church acts, Christ acts. When the Church heals, it is Christ who heals. As that was the mode of His life, the efficacy of His death, so this is the mode and the efficacy of His Church, for She is His. They possess each other.

And the Church holds the knowledge of the Flaw up like a mirror in the face of all generations, crying out to them to see what they are and beware. But they do not beware. Like somnambulists they strike down the mirror of knowledge from before their eyes and trample it, and stride forward to seize with their own hands the future, to wrest from it what they desire.

The craftsman at the forge is confident in the strength of his arm, the skill of his fingers. Look, he says, see, I can make. He turns the tongs, and the iron, red, is deftly withdrawn. The iron is struck and twisted; the form emerges out of the forge. Look, scoffs the craftsman, it is my own hand, my own eye, and none other. The woman at the stove warms the broth for her child and hands it down and the child eats. The broth had come from the grain and the grain from the earth; the woman cooks the grain to make broth and the child is fed. She does not scoff but she does not believe: the grain is always there. It is gathered up and makes broth and the child is fed. This is enough.

And the Church cries out: It is false! You cannot go on as if you exist in the sufficiency of simple nature! As if no disabling weakness crippled the soul! As if all instinct and all appetite are wholly conformed to reason and to will!

But the craftsman strikes his iron and scoffs, turning it cherry-red in the forge, hammering out of its resistance whatsoever shape he pleases. And the woman turns back to her stove, and pouring out grain makes broth for the child, and shrugs and forgets. There is always more grain.

Day by day the sun rises, the clouds fly out of the adjacent sea and flow rain on the hills. Night comes on and the continents lie somnolent under its shroud. The sequence of the equinoxes walks the sky through the recurrent years. And the civilizations fall, fall. They have risen up out of the shells and fragments of those that have gone before, and each seizes on some new relevance of life, some new salience, and working it out pours into it its generative strength, and prospers, and extends itself into the imbalance of that dominant attempt, and then tips down, falls. And the craftsman drops by the forge and the woman sinks. The great civilizations spin out like galaxies breaking and abandoning in the web of space, in the limitless night.

And in their falling the races of man rush on each other with a savagery unequaled in the ferocity of beasts. The cities smash up under storm after storm of rapacious men. Whatever is helpless and weak, whatever is innocent and pure, whatever is steadfast and true, is hunted down with a pitiless hate, smashed with stones and clubs, trampled under the boots, thrown in the latrines, obliterated. Fiercer than the fierceness of hawks and eagles is the split heart of man, swollen with cravings and fears, black with a thousand ranklings, blind.

And the Church cries out with an imperishable voice in the days and nights and will not be heard. She holds up for all the world to see this tremendous fact, this Flaw, the clue to the mystery of man, the mystery of his confusion, calling out to all men that they might know themselves, take stock, and seeing, avail themselves of those sacramental remedies that She alone affords. She cries out with an imperishable voice the terrible realism of the truth of man.

And all who will listen She gathers about Her, for this is Her life, Her love. This is Her great passion, the passion of Christ Whose Body She is, crying out yet from His cross through Her voice, crying out to all men. The very wounds of Christ cry out through Her voice to the hearts of men that they might come.

And indeed they come. One by one, from here and there, they listen and they come. These are Her few. They come out of their old ignorance, their spiritual torpor, the clogged sloth of their lives. They awake and come. She welcomes them, cleansing them as they enter; and She heals them, and gives them the gifts by which the flawed nature may be secured, until the ultimate day when all error is past, and the flawed nature is wholly transformed in the vast perfection of God.

And it was that imperishable voice that rang in our ears all through the spring of the year 1949, as the rapid pace of our hearts drew us on to our own tall hour of decision. *Triptych for the Living* contains the whole impact of its opening assault. But even as I wrote I would not have believed that the summer solstice would see the attack accomplished, the citadel taken, and the victory complete. Nor even now does it seem real to me that a mere six months' interval could have achieved so total a reversal. It was a thing the actual transaction of which took no longer than the time required to pack a few boxes and summon a van. *But the cost!* One thought it would have taken years to steel the will for such an act. One still thinks it, in retrospect, and in truth to the poignancy of human nature. But lo! the swiftness of God is like a thief in the night, and none may predict His coming.

And because the thing has such an apparent brutality about it I have delayed its telling, seeking to probe back into the substance around it, so that it might be seen in its wholeness, as one seeks to penetrate into the involved moral complicity behind some great crime of passion, or else the atrocity stands forth in so great a glare as to blind the understanding. Here also where no crime is at all, but rather the rectification of a crime. But in the eyes of the world it is the violence that is the crime, for it sees the thing only in the wrench of its sympathies, and it counts it insane of those who so abuse themselves, and criminal of those who require it. The penitent and the Church alike stand condemned. Abraham, knife in hand, stooping to slit the throat of his only son, is a picture that fills with revulsion. The world hates the God who would so command, and the fanatic who would so comply. But the Church and the penitent do not see it in the crudity of such unrelieved detail, but rather they look through to the relationship, for that obtains and persists after every atom of the detail will have vanished in the pervious transience of all tangible things: the relationship of direction and response, one to one, and crowned with forbearance, transcended in the crowning, which was not capitulation, but mercy.

For the warrant of all assent is sacrifice. It is this which gives gratuity what worth it has. Sacrifice cuts through all the convolutions of the either-or, all the involvement of a dear self-gain—what one has and what one may expect. It is in the act of sacrifice or in its declination that we come to know our most elemental hearts.

So the spring of the year 1949 ran through its rapid pace, and all before we knew it the hour was shaking the door and the door swung inward. She had gone more than once to the parish rectory, in the glimmering hope that some way, some loop-hole, some little crevice might manifest itself through which two weak ones, who nowhere in their hearts could find a grain of the fortitude of saints, might slip on through; but no crevice showed. She went then again, a final time, and laid the matter before them, formally; and they took it, and turned it over to the diocesan marriage board, but the board saw no hope. And the great need for finality, for resolution, that now gnawed like a hunger was with us always, and the flesh like a thorn. So we put down the flesh forever then, and she took our plea back to the fathers, that we might perhaps be granted the dispensation of those of deep friendship who wish to share the married state, as brother and sister, not touching in the marriage act. A long time we waited. We made our own pledge before God as a seal of our earnestness, that we would not touch again in the marriage act, in order that at least a life in common might be spared us. And we never touched again in that act.

But this is a thing I never told any friends of that time. It could not have been understood. Only a Christian, no, only a Catholic would have understood, and I knew no Catholics. In the secular world, in the religions of the day, even in the heterodox Christianities of the day, the primacy of the flesh is undisputed, but in the Church a more ancient wisdom abides. This much I had come to: marriage is meant for that touch, certainly, but this was no marriage. That is the crux of the matter. And since it was no marriage, the act was not to be indulged. But if it was no marriage, what was its term? I her brother? She my sister? Could two who had lived as we had, in the pagan recklessness, count ourselves so now? We were willing to count it. Where once it had been the bodies that joined, it must now be the souls; and a truer join than ever the body owns, touching in the oneness of the spirit who had never achieved the sacramental oneness of the flesh. It was our last try. Call it a compromise, if you wish, and a pitiable one at that; we did not think it so. But sought rather to give to God and each other the utmost of what we owed.

Then one night among many too remote from me now to remember, it came about that we sat late after dinner, sipping the good wine and the good coffee, in the afterglow of a spring dusk, that we might hush the heart of each other in the presence only. And in that twilight the telephone rang in the room, and getting up she went to it, and hearing what was said she came back to her place, and spoke nothing, and I thought no more of it. And then she said: "It was one of the fathers. To do the thing we ask, to be as brother and sister in the house, is not deemed prudent in any but those with children, or those who are old." She looked out of the window to where the last of the light lay yet on the street. "But we have no children," and she made another pause then, which I remember now for the note of exquisite delicacy that lingered in it, endowing it with a hushed significance too final to be disclosed, "...and we are not old."

I made no reply to her, but sat in the suspension of the deep fatefulness that was shaping about me. When I looked at her again the great tears sprang from her eyes and she lifted her face and cried out: "Who will take care of you now! Who will cook for you and make for you and see that you go properly clad! Who will wait now that I will be away, and comfort you when you are sad!"

It was not a protestation. She knew, as did I, that the time had come; that to go on as we had, knowing God so near and yet denying Him ever, living the life of a lie—to go on could only in time tear us to pieces, drive both insane, and in us each destroy the soul. She did not protest. But in the stunnedness of that moment it was out of her very womanhood that she cried, knowing in truth that it was her hand, her guidance that had brought the two of us where we were; and it was in the shape of this deep functional necessity, now to be relinquished, that she lifted her voice and wept. But she stood in the deprivation of her deepest usefulness, and thought not of herself but of me. I got up and went quickly round to her and made her be still. I knew that we dare not falter now or we would be truly lost. I knew that if it was indeed her feminine strength that had drawn us so far, it must now be my masculine strength that broke on through. She never wept again, at least not in my sight. In a few days we settled our affairs and separated. She went immediately to Confession and Communion, and the wounds of her long estrangement from the Church were all instantly healed.

And so was brought to a close another phase of a relationship which, in retrospect, reveals through its mounting ascent the elementary journey of the soul. It had begun in the passion of blind self-fulfillment: two lost ones, hurt in their hearts, flinging themselves upon each other in a devouring rapacity, seeking to assuage the fire that ate their souls. That passion stabilized into the tacit conventionality of the Common Law, and this union of the Common Law became in time legalized before the civil courts. These phases may be taken as a growing objectivity, a deepening social concern. Furthermore, that old fear-dictated cancellation of the loins, that surgical stroke by which the man secured his sterility, was itself undone, the severed interior channel rejoined, so that the gift of seed might once more run its true course, an act which marked the high reach of the natural ascendancy, for though the link was joined no issue graced its term.

But the forces of ascent would not be stopped there. The forces of ascent in man never remain contained at the level of the purely natural. Beyond, the supernatural proffers its greater claim, and in that claim the great heights of physical relationship are shown to be, in this instance, actually a misalignment. Thus it was that the very line of ascent, built phase by phase, level by level, between them, led inexorably to their own renunciation. But not, mark well, to their loss.

For in that renunciation of the natural alignment they gained each other in a richer way. This is the thing which, in the purely natural emphasis, is never accredited, or if plainly shown, is never truly trusted: that God, once gained, flows back graces in a sweeping flood to drench and invigorate the shuddering souls who in His name find the means to make that quittance. And if any reading these words do find themselves in doubt upon that pitch, fearful of the cost, let them be assured in us. Not easy, no, but once decisively done two souls soar up. Two souls ascending find in their upflight the great fulfillment of all promises: God tells no lies. For it is not love that is renounced; the very heights of love are gained. These two will find a love as yet not known, coming to regard each other so delicately in the blessed Christ as no hot intimacy of the unrelinquished bed could ever teach them. Believe this. Its truth cries from the souls of two who had the grace to dare, and the further grace to activate the dare, putting all fast-clasped passion down. Believe this. The crowning resolution follows fast, and Heaven is its end.

But yet, arises the persistent rejoinder, if what you have said in regard to your dispositions, the niceness of your affections, this platonic brother-and-sister impulse of which you speak—if this be true, why did you offer so little resistance? These things are technicalities. The mere advice of a local board, relayed by a parish priest over the telephone, is by no means an absolute decision. If, at that time, you meant as much to each other as you assert, and in the particular way you assert, why is it that you took the first response, rather than the final ultimatum, as your cue to separation?

There are, on the surface of the matter, many things that could be said, not the least of which was our complete ignorance of the technicalities involved; but searching down in my heart I believe the truer answer lies another place: the rapid state of our spiritual transition. When we made our initial petition we were still in the clinging necessity of each other's presence, but by the time the answer was given we were, unknown to ourselves, on the verge of spiritual independence. As long as we lived but for each other, each other was our tangible end, and we gave ourselves to each other. But when the knowledge of God flowed into our lives, this each-otherness of our absorption was transcended.

For remember, and it must be again noted, this had not, in fact, ever been a valid marriage, even though duly legalized in the civil courts. It is the Church, not the State, which holds in keeping the warrant of the marital bond. Remember too, we had no children, and when the knowledge of God was given into our lives, the very insufficiency of our relationship became apparent. There was no crucial, no truly final reason why we any longer had to live together. I mean no reason founded in the intellect as well as in the affections. And I suspect that we began to realize, in the development of the God-life within us, that outside sacramental marriage the life of God is really lived alone. It must have been this deep unspoken understanding, this mute knowledge beneath all the passionate protest of our natural fondness that made us, in the casting of the die, take it at its given value. In this deeply realized rightness necessity becomes a kind of suffering joy. It was in such suffering and such joy that our separation was achieved.

Yet how well I am aware, knowing my mind of old and the way it worked, that there are those who, reading these truths, will never give them credit, picking behind my sentences for some hidden flaw in the relationship itself, some deficiency to prove to their dubious minds that any so confused as to accept total separation at the dictate of the Church must somehow do so really to escape that union. They discern a hidden liability, a fatal erotic defection to show that such a deviation from the line of physical fulfillment is actually an inversion into narcissistic subjectivity, a specious mysticism.

But that is a charge no friends of the time, appalled as they were by that separation, and searching their minds for some clue to comprehension of what might motivate so drastic a device, could point to. We stood too evidently in a rich compatibility to warrant that claim, had gained too much beyond the woeful, nervous and pathetic wanderers they knew at our first meeting, for them to believe that a subversive maladjustment was our hidden cause. For our hearts had grown blithe in one another's presence, and this was their own joy, who had watched all the intoxication of initial discovery fill out into the natural sympathy of truly fruitful lives.

And what do I care now for these insidious doubts? I trouble to raise them and reject them only to justify the Faith that transcends passion, a justification the squalling world engrossed in its gratifications always brooks ill; and to sustain in the living hope those who, involved in such a fault themselves, may overcome the doubt that surely haunts their hearts, as the warped emphasis of the time leads us to forever doubt the very warrant of our souls.

And so we made the separation out of an insight given, a strength given, and I have told the truth of it insofar as I have seen it, but I have told nothing, or very little, because the mystery remains. What actually occurred was something other than anything I have said, and this must never be forgotten. I, more than any, must never forget it. Circling and circling in my ever-expanding area about the center of that consequence, sometimes in my passion for communication I assume that if only I could sufficiently explain the vast contingency projecting from the center, the center itself would achieve illumination, would emerge into focus; that if only I could say enough *about* it, I would eventually be able to lay bare the thing itself—the mysterious interior event by which a man in the positive knowledge of his unbelief wakes up one day to the full knowledge of his certitude. It can never be. All my positing of the need of "bridges" to span the gulf between two cultural emphases comes to nothing before the awful fact of a basic lack of faith. This is why every conversion story is a disappointment. The crucial thing always goes untold. Down in the soul's subliminal depths a transfer indeed will be made, but it will not be occasioned by any elaboration of cultural bridges. It will be occasioned only by a force outside itself, a force which, far below the level of its consciousness, will permeate it, and will transform it, and make it into another thing. It will be transformed only by a bestowal, a supernatural gift. And this bestowal is the ineluctable Gift of Faith.

Faith! How can a Twentieth Century man accede to so obsolete a doctrine! Is this not the formula of primitive peoples, subjugated by natural forces till physical survival compels them to fabricate a religious compensation? The modern skeptical mind is too suspicious even of itself; it thinks it knows too much about its own subjective convolutions to be taken in. It is too aware of its concealed liabilities; psychology has so thoroughly exposed its instinctual drives, its capacity for self-deception and aesthetic sublimation; anthropology parades before it the whole range of ritualistic mystification behind which the unsophisticated primitive mind masquerades its motives, for credence to be placed on any such transparently evasive phenomena as might be tricked out under the guise of "faith." When the heretical Modernist theologians define faith as "a sentiment erupting from the subconscious," they are stating the formula of skepticism, the only formula the Rationalist can grasp. What he demands is no kind of subjectivity but fact, empirical and objective: proof positive. All he can make of faith, the key concept of Western Civilization, is a pious word for self-deception.

But for the Catholic, who is the true inheritor of that civilization, and will preserve it after the depredations of all the rival Isms have left upon it their deathly gash, faith is something else, involving not merely his own subjectivity, but a motive far more trustworthy than any of its bewildering vacillations. Faith is the adhesion of the intellect, under the stimulus of grace, to a God-revealed truth; an adhesion not made on the basis of any intrinsic evidence, but solely by virtue of that authority itself.

And the skeptic, trapped as he is in his secular perspective, is scandalized. He sees categorically rejected the only criteria the intellect can trust. How can it assent to a proposition that is, by definition, unintelligible?

—Not unintelligible, rather super-intelligible; not absurd, on the contrary unspeakably above rational comprehension. Faith is indeed in the intellect, with all its consequent need for evidence; but the will intervenes, the movement of the will spurs the intellect to its adhesion, dissipating the intellect's dilemma, and enabling it to rise to that luminous strike of assent despite the absence of intrinsic evidence.

—Fah! Sheer subjectivity! A palpable case of self-induced deception! When the evidence evaporates and the intellect bogs down, then whistle up the will, and force yourself to believe!

—No, the intellect gets its evidence, truly, but not in the way you skeptics expect, and not the kind you insist on having. The intellect needs evidence, certainly, but the Divine Truths often do not provide it. Their very loftiness constitutes the difficulty, for they surpass the whole rational capacity of the mind. You have to understand that the intellect is confronted by truths which are totally outside its domain. Like an eye that is blinded with light, it cannot achieve focus. But because the eye cannot see shall we say the light does not exist? Left with the insufficiency of his truth-blinded mind man could never arrive at finality. And this is the very reason why faith, the influx of grace, is provided. *Provided!* Can't you grasp the conceptual implication here? Only stop thinking for a moment of dynamics and think for a while of persons, of God as giver. The will, intervening through sheer homage to its Maker, moves the light-blinded intellect, agonized in its own hopeless impasse, to acknowledge the truth, incomprehensible as that truth is.

—Deception upon deception! What is so simon-pure about the will that *its* stimulus should be uncritically accepted? Ascribing an impulse to homage to God rather than to subconscious motivation may have a noble ring, but the truth lies deeper down; lies in fact, as Freud so tellingly indicated, in a most unedifying locality, which is precisely what the sentimentalist cannot bring himself to admit, and precisely why he concocts these high-sounding phrases like "homage to God" to account for something a little straight biological correlation would put in its place. The question is *what* moves the will?

—Efficacious Grace. A personal God makes a personal gesture, the gesture of divine compassion. Though faith is certainly a free submission of the reason to supernatural Truth, it is really that Truth itself, God, who makes Himself known to the soul, quickening the will to move the intellect to make that adhesion, that free submission. This quickening, this stimulus, this sublime interior in-movement is the hidden work of grace, the veiled gesture of God. We may speak of it as a divine influence by which the will, freely but infallibly, is determined to act.

—Fantastic! Your whole proposition comes down to no more than a simple two-way equation between one impulse labeled "grace" and another impulse labeled "faith," fancy names, poetry, perhaps, but hardly science. The grace-impulse somehow creates the faith-impulse, and the faith-impulse reacts to the grace-impulse; and all going on conveniently out of sight below the level of consciousness. No, until it can be shown how the intellect acts on the basis of authentic evidence, *facts*, enlightened men will hold to the subconscious-motivation theory.

—In the act of faith the enkindled intellect certainly does make its adhesion on the basis of evidence, but it is not the *intrinsic evidence* of science or mathematics—that kind of self-evident equation fulfillable in itself which we get in such propositions as [that] *the whole is greater than the* [sum of its] *parts* and which the intellect seizes up and accedes to instantly, unshaken by doubts. But in most of the choices of man's life the intellect does not have that kind of certitude. It makes its choice on the basis of the extrinsic evidence of practical affairs.

For instance, a merchant opens a store in order to do business. He receives a cheque drawn on the account of a man who he knows is a safe risk. Now although he did not actually see the money earned, or the cheque written, and certainly the money is not there before his eyes, nevertheless, the signature, the extrinsic evidence, stands. The merchant's need to do business moves his will, quickens his intellect to acknowledge the sufficient probability, and honor the cheque. If a merchant waited for intrinsic evidence before he acted, he would starve to death.

So too with faith. There is in every man a need to achieve his end, union with God. This need is existent; call it a fact. Furthermore, reason confirms that God exists, is essentially good, cannot deceive. On no more evidence than this, man knows he must worship. But how? Then comes the authoritative pronouncement: the mode of worship desired by God is given to the whole human race, given once and for all, with irrefutable finality. Can the man really believe that? Certainly, because the pronouncement was verified, confirmed by events analogous to the signature on the cheque, marks that stand in place of the guarantor Himself. These marks are actual supercessations of the natural order: miracles. For the thoughtful man, like the prudent merchant, the case is rapidly approaching probability.

Certainly sentiment, subconscious motivation, could precipitate the will, induce it to opt for intellectual assent, but that would not be the act of faith, and it would fade with the fading of the sentimental impulse. We see this happening constantly: a person experiences conversion, pursues a period of intense enthusiasm which after a time fades away, and the convert relapses into his old life. It might have been genuine grace, repudiated before striking deep root; but it might well have been merely a complex of psychological factors that had no ground in genuine faith at all. Who can say?

But in the true act of faith the soul has been transformed in its naked depths, so mysterious a process we do not even know whether or not we have it. Certainly religious sentiment accompanies the infusion of Faith; one may experience intense feeling, profound feeling, but that is not Faith, and must never be confused with it. True faith can be judged only by the long pattern of a religiously dedicated life: persistent undeviating adherence, according to one's state, to the dictates of divine truth, despite all the diversions and counter-temptations of earthly existence.

The skeptic is amused. So you don't even know you have it, save by the token of fanaticism! And yet, if that kind of motivation is not held to be self-engendered, simply doled out from Heaven by divine whim, so to speak, why bother with all these formulas? Either it's given you or it isn't. There's nothing, apparently, you can do!

—It is not conceded there is nothing one can do. In this equation a man can do a very important and terrible thing: refuse. We know by revelation that every man is given sufficient grace for his adhesion to as much of the truth as falls to his lot. What we do not know is whether or not we, in our willfulness, have abused the confidence, whether or not it has been withdrawn from us. And never think this bare capacity to refuse, which seems to restrict the role of man to so negative a function, is a trifling thing. What? The ability to spurn the force that every instant keeps the galaxies in being? O weak-minded men, who hold in their hands such enormous power, and find it so trifling!

But the skeptic is unmoved. It is maintained that natural reason proves the existence of God, but what is more convincing to him is that a multitude of naturally reasonable men remain unpersuaded. It is maintained further that in the act of faith the intellect assents on the basis of evidence attested by miracle, supervention of the natural laws. But when this guarantee is challenged, what it is, where it came from, how one knows it, all most elementary precautions, the prime evidential object turns out to be merely Scripture, which, despite the asserted array of archeological support, remains a bundle of man-written documents claiming any number of unlikely prodigies, compiled sometime after the event and composed in a primitive period when the criteria of objective documentation were hopelessly inadequate. And even conceding some small surviving trace of residual veracity, it is admitted even before examination that any analysis, no matter how well-disposed and patient, can only lead to one more mystery. And that, to him, is unacceptable. Faith or no faith, grace or no grace, religion at this level is not to be thought of.

At bottom the skeptic is a man who has never learned to distinguish between the kinds of criteria, a man to whom the word *truth* has a fatally narrow definition. As an historical document Scripture has proved itself to be undemolishable, but the faith of the Church is not founded on historical documentation. It is no use insisting that the criteria of spiritual reality conform to the standards of empirical demonstration. Until a man is prepared to acknowledge this radical and obvious demarcation, he will never comprehend, his soul will remain blind. At the end of all his enquiries he still arrives, as he says, at a mystery, a whole complex of mysteries, which are the revealed truths composing the core of the Christian religion. And the mysteries are a scandal to him. This is a pity, because as things stand he has no real grasp of what is going on. He does know something of what is going on in the one sphere of reality, the natural order, but it is in no wise the most important, and he really knows very little about that. Name a physical phenomenon that does not itself, upon analysis, end up in a mystery. How far back will he carry his research before he admits he is against the wall? Clear back to the mystery of cosmic energy?

He is, in fact, only partially awake. And until he becomes fully awake he will never learn the end of man, and not knowing the end of man he will never really discover how to resolve the manifold problems which surround his life. He purports to be making out well enough just as he is, on the basis of things as they presently proceed. To the Catholic, however, he seems really very insecure and not too happy, and collectively he lives in a kind of chaos, but this is no argument. For what presently proceeds, be it good or bad, is not the end of the process, and it is only there, at the end, the Afterlife, that the adhesion of faith will be verified. But the end of the process, the Afterlife, is to him only the cessation of cognizance—the point where apprehension ceases. This is because he accepts things only by halves, the physical half. For him death is a terminal point, indeed, the end of a process, but what else it is, is simply the Unknown. For though he dislikes the smack of the word mystery, he does not hesitate to acknowledge the Unknown. The Unknown must eventually yield before the penetration of human knowledge, and as such he can salute it. It is simply what remains to be conquered. But he refuses to glorify it with the status of a mystery.

But nevertheless he ought to know that there is an unimpeachable link between reason and mystery, and that it is, at the level of religion, intense and profound, and the religious man finds it extremely absorbing, most consequentially central to his quest for truth. We have got a glimpse, all too brief, all too insufficient, into the action of one mystery, Faith, or, more properly, into the impingement of the mystery of Faith upon the understanding of man. The same tentative outline could be provided for all the other mysteries and articles of the Catholic religion, with greater or lesser elaboration, depending on one's time and ability. But so long as he clings to his hopelessly inadequate view of the limited function of reason, and of the nature of evidence, these would remain quite as unacceptable to him as the operation of faith. At the end he will arrive, as he has said, at one more mystery, a mystery of the supernatural order, which is the kind in which he is definitely uninterested. But he must never be permitted to forget that the prime fact here is not the deficiency of reality, but his own disinterest, his own lack of spiritual acuity, blind to grace. For in this perspective, no matter where one turns, it is the fact of grace with which one is everywhere confronted.

Such, more or less, is the position of the Catholic. Or perhaps I should say, in the more prudent qualification, one presentation of the Catholic position. For I have not the right to saddle the Church with my own definitions. St. Thomas soberly cautions us that our intent should never be to convince by argument, but rather that argumentation should only be made to answer objection, and in contradistinction he takes the positive approach. For he says flatly: "The sole way to overcome an adversary of divine truth is from the authority of Scripture—an authority divinely confirmed by miracles." Contemporary Catholics do not quote this remark of St. Thomas with noticeable frequency. To the modern ear it sounds very Fundamentalist, even obscurantist, and hardly the pronouncement of the man whom a recent Pope has called "the special bulwark and glory of the Catholic faith." St. Thomas does indeed go on to say that certain "likely arguments" may appropriately be used for "the training and consolation of the faithful," but he insists that these aids to belief must never be used against "confirmed adversaries": "For the very inadequacy of the arguments would rather strengthen them in their error, since they would imagine that our acceptance of the truth of faith was based on such weak arguments" (*Summa Contra Gentiles*, I, 9).

It is, alas, advice which I have too often ignored, and I can only hope this book may never, in its peregrinations, fall into the hands of any "confirmed adversary," lest he too be deluded into the supposition that such "likely arguments" as freckle these pages constitute the very bonework of the Faith. No, it becomes apparent that my book must make its witness in another way. Such figures as the merchant and the cheque doubtless owe their ineffectuality to the fact that I have no genuine relationship with such things. They possess no vital reality in my own awareness, for I have no real interest in them, and in fact they bore me. Our Lord employed the commercial metaphor with great vividness, and perhaps I hoped to touch something of the broad reaction of the people He addressed. But here it is mere imitation.

I say "mere imitation." And are we not invoked to the imitation of Christ? Let this be understood: no kind of imitation is Christian. Christ, in the existential engagement, confronts through us the counter-reality of a sin-smutched world. It is the Christ in us, not our pallid imitation of the Christ, which must be brought to bear. Christ did not incorporate us into Himself to make of us a sort of superior substitute, but rather so that we might become utterly of Himself. And we become Christ by being in the most exigent manner the wholeness of our individuation, which is all our perfection is. Christ takes us precisely in the measure that we become conformed to our true selves, because we are each a likeness, a projected facet of His uncreated Godhood. "To thine own self be true" strikes to the substratum of the Christian Faith.

Actually, the positive evidence in a man's life, the true line by which the intellect is led to its assent, is something extraordinarily subtle and complex, and the very fabric of this book is meant to summon up the way the soul engages it in the context of the real. For me there was the earth, the Church, and the woman. The earth spoke to me of God, the Church spoke to me of worship, and the woman spoke to me of love. She lived in my life the long act of love, and its vicissitudes, and it was the evidence of love that moved me. To the secret and mysterious love of God bestowed into the soul and experienced there in an act of direct intuition, she added the evidence of her own love of God and of me, gauged in a Catholic context, endowed with a Catholic wholeness that was like the taste of nothing I had known. Love springs from the person, and in the denseness of the personalism of her love, my soul touched a new breadth of existence. There was everywhere about her, in her presence, on her clothes and among her effects, hovering about her person, the ingrained culture of the Latin. It was basically an attitude, a perspective, and it remained forever aggrieved and amused at my blunt Scandinavian crudeness. She never succeeded in making a complete lover of me, though it was something she set herself most earnestly to do, out of that pity with which one friend endeavors to extricate another from some delimiting myopia that has no reason for existence, and must be made to go.

Latin Catholic culture is possessed of a wholeness sprung out of that balance a true metaphysic deeply endows in a people, the union of the intellectual and mystical elements, the fusion of Semitic spirituality and Greek rationalism. Any system of values other than Catholicism is bound to be deficient regardless how much worth it might have in specific areas, and that deficiency will leave a corresponding imbalance in the very soul of a people. American Protestant commercial ethics are probably superior to those of any Catholic country in the world, but they do not inform and permeate the personal morality of the American intellectual because he intuitively perceives that they spring from a deficient causality. As a boy I have seen my father walk back a block or more to a restaurant in order to make restitution for the slight error of a cashier, but powerful as this example was, it did not later deter me from writing college theses for money, or later still, appropriating the goods of my employers, because this morality was not sourced in any truly vital sense of natural law, and still less of the supernatural mandate. It remained a commercial ethic, the "rules of the game," contained somehow only at the level of one's pride of place in the community, and one's self-respect as to how one ought to behave. As a developing artist I perceived that this was no more than it stood for, a kind of game, and that it was emphatically not my game. Insofar as I was an artist, the Protestant commercial world was against me, it had no place for me or my values, and in order to survive I had to repudiate everything it stood for. Once I had done this, there remained no reason why I should be true to its pristine ethic, an ethic which for all the rectitude of its adherents is established invincibly in favor of the mercantile classes. I proposed to be true, indeed, but only to what I could believe in, my conscience and my art. I was true to my impulse and my art, for these were holy, but I was true to very little else.

The great baroque Catholic culture of Italy and Southern France and Spain, which is still present there, though undergoing corruption beneath the onslaught of the technological age, contains the heritage of the total Catholic impress that sourced the full worth of Western Civilization, and with a kind of atavism she inherited it all. Her father was of the peasantry, a man of the Italian earth, dark and rich as the wine he made, hands blunt and sensitive from the planting of many grapevines, and a soul given, in his later life, to the engagement of God in a kind of rocklike integration. Her mother, however, was of the artisan class, and proud of her heritage, and her sensibility was the sensibility of the artist. Out of that commingling of peasant and artisan traditions, the daughter bloomed in the new world expansion, and I knew her, and perceived the superiority of the forces that shaped her, in the fullness of humanity, in the broad Latin humanism that was her heritage and her possession.

And so it was that her every gesture, as I say, spoke to me of the superiority, in terms of human breadth, human sympathy, human sensitivity and reaction, even human passion, to everything I had known. In the evenings, at the dinner hour, smiling among guests, warmed with the fragrance of wine and the wonderment of music, she was all poise, all graciousness. And I saw that basic cultural assimilation break the dominance of the brutal biological force, tame it, make it pliant and adaptable, give it delicacy, reserve, movement and liberation. The music of her femininity was point and counterpoint, melody, theme and variation. She was a Catholic. And out of her Catholicity she gave me the comprehension of wholeness in its totality of engagement. This, indeed, we abused, and in this too I was fascinated: the terror of temptation. For below my fascination I feared her like Luther feared Italy, like Adam feared Eve smiling across the apple. Her very comprehension disturbed me, her very knowledge, the subtle artifice of civilization. In such artisanship she lived the whole delicacy and modulation of her mother's people.

But in the deeps all this was stripped away, and she became her father's daughter, the gravity and earnestness of the peasant. I do not speak merely of an elemental abandon; rather her love had a kind of tragic starkness about it; the rouge rinsed from her face, the expertly coifed hair, graying already in her early thirties, loosed like a cowl around her shoulders; and from her plain nightgown emerging only her peasant's feet, her exquisite artist's hands, and the masked and tragic nobility of her face. In her passion all the lamplight voluptuousness was swept from her; even her body took on a kind of beautiful glyphic angularity, like the hill-line of the Abruzzi, as if the mounting intensity were reducing her to the fundamental bonework of her being; and her great eyes, fastened on mine like an eagle's, or half-closed in the drench of a commitment too total to be endured, gazed into the deeps of a sorrow my soul had yet to drink.

And yet, subsumed in the bed's paradisal latitude, she was, to tell the truth, all artist. Or rather it was as if, elemental as the Italian earth, she bloomed, under the solar masculine invigoration, into a rippling field, became a cultivated garden. Transforming like a growing thing before me, I saw she was a grove, a spark, a stately town. I saw she was a rich magnificent city, with its avenues and lanes, its hidden places, its sunfilled walls, its deep inviting arches—all those singular richnesses to be explored, all that exotic wealth reposing there for one man's possession: him to whom she yielded up the key. Mistress of such a hoard, hers to fashion and refashion, truly she was all artist.

And so between us, artists transported, we moulded the pliable bronze of our mortality, seeking to fashion in the cast of the embrace that masterpiece—the absolute delineation of the erotic act. I had of her the unbearable need to unify myself, to clarify upon the impress of her body, in the mature loveliness of her configuration, my fractured self. And as I clasped her naked in my arms, to take her wholly into myself, to make her me, I found that rather it was I who was transformed. It was as if she had thrust those sensitive hands of hers into the very clay of my inchoation to draw me forth, evoke me, shape me to her vision of a man; and such was the paragon she could call forth, I hastened to believe it. In her magnificent creativity she had reshaped me to the proportions of a myth, a prototypal hero. In the deep embrasure of her body, the unifying sheath of her potentiality, I had indeed become one; and taking of her art, worked with her.

Swept up in the ecstasy of that art we toiled and strove, shaping and reshaping the nebulous vision, to make between us the vision come complete, be somehow true. The strong bodies, which the long experience of conjugal love had brought to a kind of habituated understanding of the act, a deeply pondered consideration of its uses, rose now to their work. Neither the hectic frantic youths we once had been, nor the faded memory-haunted wraiths we feared to soon become, we seemed to find at last the mode of our true genius.

Proficients in the beatitude of carnal joy, we brought to this great joinure the impetus of those who seek to forge an unexcellable work, to strike the perilous and terrible equipoise, gained at such prodigious cost, that in a moment will slip and vanish into a nothingness, our phantom dread. Fused, sustained there, we achieved between us, out of our hollow selves, a veritable god, a being almost fit for worship—one of those copulating idols the heathen make, figment of the pathos that man in sin hurls against the infinite to cancel out his death. Flesh oned with flesh, mouth clutched on groping mouth, our eyes, enormous arcs of quest and appropriation, merging together in a concentrated vision of unity, the god we had become towered within us, momently immortal. Then it collapsed, and fallen in the ruin of our art, we stared in terror at the prodigy we had achieved, that instantly was gone.

Gone! I shall not forget her; she will haunt my memory forever, as one evokes the subsumed emotive impress of some great tragedienne wrung in the storms of passion. But how can I speak of actresses! She is existent yet within me! Level upon level she abides there, lover and demon and saint! Almost, in the memory now, a kind of spiritual ancestor, from out of whose fictive brain my own existence springs. Almost, now, a kind of racial memory, as one bears in his heart the recognition of an immemorial people, expiating in bondage some inflexible ancient pride, serving the captor with a kind of magnificent totality, throwing down ransom after ransom, to stand at last in an invincible nudity, and nothing more to give. I, in the terrible paradox, was that captor. And looking across the ransom I saw to the sheer religious heart of her grief, which was my own destruction; her grief in the toils of that sovereign sin, my ruination; the grief-shaken face in its terrible contrition, caught in the engagement of a force she had used to enslave rather than sanctify; the great luminous moments of her culpability, the assent of her utter remorse. Such is the evidence that proves the soul. All that inherited Protestant rectitude, like a Pharisee convinced of the virtue of his willfulness, proud to stand neck-deep in vice and swear to the world I did no wrong, swear to the world that my conscience was my God and my conscience was clean—neck-deep in sin and too proud to know it—for me to see this Catholic woman, in the throes of physical passion or convulsed with guilt, plead of the immanent God, acknowledge and acknowledge and acknowledge her own corruptness, and break in twain in the corrupted knowledge; this is the evidence. It is in these extremes that the soul comes to its proof.

The soul comes to its proof. I, proved at last, stood to the bare edge of it; and the mystery of faith was alive in me, and working there; and my intellect, illumined now by the action of that grace, seized in the sublime gesture of God, responded to its summons; and I saw in a new way the old truths I thought were dead; and the wonder of reality woke to my gaze; and my soul drank of those springs which were henceforth to fill it full.

But to return, to revert now to the moment of the going, and the decisive act that broke the established bond. There was a poem that I had written, before the time of separation, though in the awareness of its approach, and it is a cropped poem, a poem pruned back like the bare shape of the vine, in the winter vineyard, where the pruners walk in the rows, and their shears make a far clopping in the frosty air. Though it is a summer poem, I think of it as a poem of the pruning, nonetheless. Or maybe, since it is of summer, that sound of the shears is only the plucking off of the fruit, who knows?

i. Toward Solstice

Wrapped to the branch the runner
Rings its yearly span.
Man is made for the woman,
And woman for the man.

Stalk of the weed is stiffened,
And stands, and will be dried.
But the word of God is prior;
It may not be denied.

The summer burns and blazes,
The year begins its drouth.
I watch the one I nevermore
May kiss upon the mouth.

Who knows, indeed? In the burgeoning of all seed-bearing things the fruit was ripe. The bite of the shears in this poem is the bite of a thing I could no longer reckon. Shaken by a presence I could not possess I felt only the grace of God between me and the portals of Hell.

For it is in the knowledge of Hell, at last, the permanent cancellation, that one is able to push on through. All I had touched of Heaven was fast going out of my grasp. Many a time I had recalled the old scoff of my father: The Churches! They tempt you with Heaven and they scare you with Hell! How I lived out your retorts in my life, old scoffer! Tempted indeed by Heaven, scared now by Hell! How I etched them in my flesh, sealed them in my blood! But all in a way you could not have intended. I had reached the place where I felt the imperious trembling of the earth beneath my feet, as one who walks but on a crust, and the heat tells him.

Strange words, I confess, to come out of a modern mouth. "Poor man," clucks the knowing world, "his guilts have got him indeed. See how old Oedipus draws in his ancient net! See how, in the old man's frown, the boy still trembles, the youngster gulps! His own hell, the bogeyman of his harsh youth, he hugs about him still!"

If there is a twist of the subconscious possibility that I have failed, in my circumspection, to draw forth and scrutinize, I do not know where to seek it. Guilty I was, and I confess it; guilt-ridden, if you prefer the more damaging reading, but this I know: mere guilt would never have made me give up what I did. If guilt is healed in natural, bodily-fulfilled sexual compatibility, and this is the modern thesis, then why should guilt have made me give up the very thing that healed it? Social pressure against an unorthodox alignment? But with the legalization all the social was brought to bear the other way. No, guilt there was, but by this time that guilt was holy. *There is a shame that bringeth sin, and there is a shame that bringeth glory and grace.* Hell was not the creation of my past; I was never taught that doctrine. Not by my father, certainly. One scoff from him sent all devils packing. Not even from the Christian Scientists, who airily waved it away. Hell came to me as a concomitant of two things: free will and immortality, and, in my mind, more or less rested on those claims. But at this time it was the *permanence* of that awesome possibility that shook me out of my trance. Faced with an irrevocable after-life, a man may not intelligently dawdle his time away. Hell is Liability Unlimited. Had it never been heard of, one could go about his affairs in the serenity, at least, of ignorance. Even with a man like my father, who took his stand on these matters with a simplifying directness, your difficulties are comfortably reduced. You dismiss the whole possibility as so much hocus-pocus to goggle the simple-minded; shake it off; shut it absolutely aside; refuse in any way to trifle with it. There is no such thing, has been no such thing, can be no such thing. You die like a mule. You are, after death, precisely what you were before life: Nothing—a memory in the mind of the living, to vanish utterly with them. Ensconced in your impenetrable detachment you screw the iron lid of skepticism tight on your mind and push on through.

But once you begin to make allowances, it becomes a different matter; for as the possibilities emerge so do the consequences. As soon as you so much as suspect that eternity is actual, your speculations cross from the theoretical to the practical with terrifying alacrity. For the consequences are so ferocious, the chances gauged at such staggering odds, that no gambler ever known would even so much as look at them, not if he had any idea of the nature of the stakes. Eternal Damnation. The phrase is so hackneyed we have to stop and take it apart to let the mind get at the reality of it, and even then we cannot keep it. It disappears back into the sub-stratum of our consciousness where all consequence blurs out and is lost in the pervading torpor of our sensual complacency.

Once you stop the scoffing and attempt to understand, seeing the abiding dignity of the soul in the Christian ethos, its marvelous capacity for choice and the grandeur of its immortality, its fundamental uniqueness that survives all phases of the body, from cradle to grave, whether it be a pound or two of flesh at birth, through a towering stature in middle life, to a wasted form on a sheet at death, remaining always the essential Ego, looking into the beyond with the obscure but persistent realization of its unquenchability, then the cost of the scoff becomes too prohibitive to entertain. Immortality is a truth of faith, but it is also a truth of reason. Long before Christ the philosophers had proved it. Even Kant acceded to its claim. And if the contemporary ones discount these proofs, may it not be because they discount all rational veracity itself? They know, and they seek to prove they know, and failing in their proof they doubt the very certitude of knowledge itself; yet the simplest of men knows full well he lives, full well that he is, full well that he knows.

Would I not then be a miserable Oedipal cripple indeed if I let the mere scoff of my father force rejection from me?

Hell is the necessary creation of those supercilious souls who decline to face God. It is made in the image of their own disdain, nothing else, the condition of the character of their repudiation. Hell flows from repudiation as death flows from suicide, and the Damned accept it with the same terrible seizure, the same compulsive embrace that the suicide accepts self destruction. The hatred of life that leads them each to the repudiating act enables them to pay the totality of that price, to *desire* the price, to *will* the price, bring it into being. At the moment of death they fix themselves in the totality of their life hatred, and in their act achieve the rigidity of a frozen concentration that staggers the imagination, so dreadful is it in its density of repudiation.

There are many ways of hating God. I hated Him in His Church. If it all could have been stopped, I thought, before ever it was started, how much misery the world would have been spared! Spared centuries of superstition, spared popes and bishops and priests, all the blind and presumptuous men who dare to thrust themselves between God and the people; spared centuries of guilts, psychic fears, obscure terrors, sexual repression, masochism, the accumulated anguish of hearts made abject by an entrenched authority feeding on their fears. The value of Christ was not worth the corruption of His principles. I hated God most coldly in His Church. But being not yet out of this life, my will was not fixed in my hate, and the grace of God reached to me, and thawed my set heart, and in this thaw I escaped the imminence of that repudiation.

It was a little book by a Fifteenth Century mystic, St. Catherine of Genoa, which first brought home to me what may be called the Economy of the Afterlife. In the impact of that book, *A Treatise on Purgatory*, the next poem was written. I needed to look into the heart of Hell in order to do what I had to do, and this poem is the look. I saw my sins, those that I had long cast off and those in which I as yet lay entangled, but unabsolved because I had not been baptized. And here again I must say, at the risk of leaving the impression that sheer terror harried me into the Church, that when you begin to see, in the reality of the spiritual life, the real dangers of such a condition, once again your alarm deepens. Established in the knowledge of baptism, that *impending* quality begins to invade your thoughts.  A friend once entered a darkened cellar and struck a match in order to see, only to discover a pool of gasoline from a leaking drum.  The instant between the striking of the match and the desperate breath that blew it out is the long instant of the unbaptized who feels that that sacrament is the one surety between himself and the eternal fires; and that he is without it.

I speak, of course, of psychological attitudes, not theological realities.  Nobody knows which souls suck down, which souls soar up.  The Church is not empowered to say.  Many a solemnly baptized Catholic, replete with all the formal assistance of Her rites, may never ascend.  Many a miserable unshriven pagan, living his life in utter ignorance but doggedly clinging to the truth he sees, will find himself aloft.  For all we know, there are more souls saved through the Baptism of Desire than through the formal Sacrament itself.  But that is no consolation to one who, struggling out of the web of his sins, perceives his utter spiritual nakedness, unweaponed in a world of ferocious conflict.  He feels only that he is not baptized, and that he might die.  I said I was walking on a crust, a crust only as thick as the little space that separated me from death.  It was this character of taut untenable urgency, of impending consequence, that colored all the action of this time and made the generation of the poem.  It has been brushed aside as no poem at all, but I cannot agree.  In it I deliberately dropped back to the level oratorical style of the Early Fathers, who knew what paganism was because it stunk in the very air about them, as it stinks in ours; and for whom the sense of smell was not so dulled as to make them leave off speaking truths.  Could that be why there is so little lyricism in it?  Still, I did not write it as a preachment to my generation, though I am afraid that on occasion I have read it as such.  Rather, I sought to drive back to the cruciality of the *choice* of the thing, the act of will that is the hidden, often overlooked condition, and it is this aspect that is apparently so misunderstood.  I should more properly have emphasized the Divine action of Christ, who draws all to Himself, outside whose imponderable mercy no salvation can be.  A theologian once objected to it on that ground, and on the ground that I did not sufficiently distinguish between original and actual sin, but I have never been able to rewrite it.  At the time, I was steeling myself for the great effort, and I knew it would take my whole strength.   I had to smash my father's scoffing caricature of God as a kind of egomaniacal Judge, arbitrarily relegating trembling wretches to their particularly outrageous anguishments. I wrote it so that the reality would be forever stabilized in my consciousness, so that I would not fail to do what I had to do.

    ii. At the Edge

*Let not the tempest of water drown me, nor the deep swallow me up.*
                      Psalm 68:16

There is a mark
Made on the soul in its first wrongdoing
And that is a taint.
And the mark of that taint,
It must either widen or wane—
As the soul decrees in its inclination
So will it be.
For this world is the place in which the freeborn soul
Creates its destiny.
It becomes, at body's death,
All it has tended to make of itself,
That which it wishes to be.

So will it be seen,
That there is no necessity of this life,
No hurt nor harshness,
That may, in the consideration of the soul, assume precedence
Over the decisiveness of that final end.
For its hurts and harshnesses are not permanent things.
They are as tests.
Their use is a way of working on that soul
So that it may truly determine its preferment—
What it intends to do.
Whereas the ending is an absolute—
An absolute as dense as the immutable past,
As irrevocable as the moment just gone,
And now forever assumed
Into the majestic finality of the past of time,
For the ending act is the soul's last choice,

In which it declares itself,
Which is, for the most, the totality of its choices
In the determination of its end.
Save this: that even upon finality,
If it has done ill in the choices of its life,
It is not yet too late.
Not until death drives it over the edge
Is it ever too late.
But still it may,
By a great thrust of the will,
A wrench so fraught with contrition,
The split pain of a guilt self-owned,
Acknowledged and deplored,
And in the blaze of that knowledge
Sees to itself,
A thing so frightful to its sudden sight,
Fungoid, so spongy with sloth and the foulnesses of its use,
That in dread it recoils,
And from the grasp of fiends,
Screeching, hurls itself out—
Only, at that hour, into such a stabbing of the heart,
May the Word
Move and redeem.

Rare! Rare at the final!
Rare at the last!
Too soft, too easy and too slack
Is the self-willed soul,
That never in its time made move to right itself.
It goes into its death
Bearing the debilitate burden of its ease,
Which is the ease only of the pleasure of the world;
And like a coffin at sea,
Weighted,
And the weights are its sins,
It swings outward,
Tips down,
Drops,
And sinks fast down into the body of the Sea of Death,
Which is the Hell;
And the weights of the coffin

Take it rapidly down to that scrupulous mark
Where the drag of the sin
And the buoyant life of the mercy of God
Hang in exquisite balance—
There does it sustain,
Suspended,
And it will never float.

Nor will it ever seek to.
For whoever in life has rejected God
Will never in death desire Him.
For over the Ocean of Death
Shines the great ambient light of the Lord,
Which is pure;
Which is the totality of all the impelling pureness
The soul had rejected in life.
And as that soul in life
Preferred the darkness of sin to the purity of light,
So in the depths of the Sea of Death
Will that soul prefer the darkness of death.
For to be drawn to the surface of the Sea of Death,
And in the open light,
Which everywhere on the islands of the Sea of Death,
Glitters and gleams;
And to have that coffin
Opened up to the Eye of Day;
And to have the thing therein which it is,
Which it has made of itself,
Which it has *created* of itself:
That thing, rotten with slime and the slimy bone,
To have that thing of the self
Revealed to the very Eye of Day—
No, that it would never do.
But rather would hang down there in the grim balance,
Crushed under the tons of the weight of the Waters of Death,
Where those sea-monsters,
Who are its masters now, attend it.
There does it suffer and suffice,
And has its way,

> Which is the way of death,
> And constitutes the sufficiency of death;
> Which is the terrible
> Contentment of the damned.

Contented, that is, only in that the will is gratified, but not the desire. Their torture is to be never filled, but their gratification is in the exercise of the will, which is all impulsion and no fulfillment, and this is the conflict which consumes them. At death the will goes either toward God or against God, but regardless of which, it goes totally. The Damned have willed, therefore they have. The will is their pride and their pride is to fulfill the will in utter self-assuagement, which is hopeless. Their will is to have taken what is not theirs by right, their existence, and made it theirs by usurpation, to possess solely for themselves what they have no right to possess at all, which is to retain the impetus, but be denied the fruition.

We too through pride have usurped what is not ours, and gathered it into ourselves, and lost it, and exulted over it, as it passed out of our possession, never really our own. We know of rebellious boys who have left home and endured the severest privations of the road rather than return and be reconciled, seeking a fiercer gratification in perversity than they ever had in compliance. Nor must it be thought that this perverse intensity, since it is self-preoccupation, a kind of self-fulfillment, nullifies the punishment. The punishment of Hell is in that unfulfillment of violent rapacity; but the more intense the rapacity, the more intense the preoccupation of the will consumed in its own endeavor, however hopeless. For each soul in Hell, as each soul in Heaven, experiences the full realization of the will; the complete *demand* of the whole faculty of volition. And because they have chosen, the very heart of their perversity is the knowledge that their hopelessness is actually self-inflicted. As in our own suicidal impulses we hunger to bring every possible tangent of intensity back upon the ego in a passionate self-impelled desire to cancel disparity within us, to achieve in cancellation the quintessence of experience, and so annul it. It is the ultimate lust.

So the souls in Hell painfully exult in their self-preoccupation, and the souls in Heaven exult in God, but they all exult. Nor can the perverse exultation of those in Hell be denied an ultimate exultation in God, and this is why they blaspheme, because being His creatures their whole intensity redounds to Him, and joins the exultation of the whole of the universe in the Divine Presence.

St. Thomas says that God is merciful in the sense that He proceeds to remove the unhappiness of creatures as though it were His own unhappiness, but not in the sense that He feels sorrow Himself. For some this is troublous, for since God knows His creatures, and the knower "becomes" what he knows, he is modified in a sense by the object, and united to it, so that it is difficult to see how God can know the soul in Hell which will be forever evil, and Himself remain without any experience of pain; for if there is no experience of pain, how can there be knowledge of evil? How can God *know* evil if He is infinitely perfect and can suffer no pain?

Evil consists only of privation, and all privation is consumed in wholeness. The evil of Hell, transcended as are all contrarieties in the wholeness of Being, has become a good in that wholeness, as all contrarieties, privations, become goods in wholeness. Hell and evil are as ingredients in the wholeness of good, and cannot detract from it, but indeed complete it. This is a mystery which we sense intuitively in the tragic. For sorrow, even joy and delight, are transcended in the sublime. In tragedy we experience the fulfillment of comprehension transcending the imperfection of experience.

We suffer revulsion, that is to say incomprehension, when we see a thing mutilated, for we do not grasp it in the totality of its relationship; but in the tragic synthesis we see around the mutilation to the more consummate perfection that is achieved through it. We rejoice, not in the mutilation, but in what the mutilation proves: the overmastering preponderance of the wholeness of reality. Sadness indeed is necessary to the tragic, and God cannot know sadness, but we experience sadness because we are of the self, we are apart, but God is not apart, nor do the Blessed so experience it, for there is no longer self in them.

It is in this sense, in the sublimity of the tragic synthesis, that are resolved such difficulties as how a mother in Heaven can rejoice while her son is in Hell. She rejoices in God alone; but the rejoicing is in fact deepened, because it is complicated, enriched, by the disparity transcended. Even on earth this is recognized as one of the supreme Christian virtues: the capacity to rejoice in personal tragedy of every kind, not only to oneself but to one's dear ones. For though the Christian knows anguish and sadness to the depths of his convulsed soul, he knows as well the great gladness of God beyond.

It is quite comprehensible that the Blessed rejoice even in the suffering of the Damned. We may say in a sense that they glory in it.

For they face God, who is pure simplicity, pure Act, but behind them the vast multiplicity of creation amplifies and projects the Godly will, with all its disparities realized in His wholeness. And it is the great shout of Creation, that exults in that consummate Fact, so that the chanting of the Blessed and the groans of the Damned are only as one tremendous voice of assent.

Here then is its necessity, a necessity not of rigid compulsion, but of fitness, the appropriate disposition of the constituents of possibility, whether guilty or innocent, by seeing it as wholly ordained to the consummate majesty of Being. In the awfulness of this majesty we understand how even the existence of Eternal Hell does not outrage the perfection of the universe, but truly ennobles it.

But these meditations I had hardly begun before I was alone, and I seized up the loneliness of this life that I might not suffer the loneliness of that death. She, as I have said, went immediately to Confession, and the wounds of her estrangement from the Church were healed. But as for me, I could not proceed with such gratifying swiftness. My own wounds, wounds of a different kind from hers, must wait a time for their healing. I had begun instruction in an Inquiry Class at the parish church, and this I must suffer through before I could write my name upon Her list. In my importunity and my very great need, I must be content with these two nights of the week when we catechumens gathered together, and the structure of the Faith we were soon to embrace was drawn before us. It was an instruction gauged more to the mind of those recognizing at least a rudimentary Christianity than mine had been, for it is from such a background that the bulk of American conversions are drawn. Unconditioned as it is to the defections of my particular generation, ignorant of the depth of our bias, uncomprehending the unique chaos that reigns in our neo-savage hearts; too conventional, if I may say so, too unimaginative and too pat, the prevailing Catholic perspective would never of itself have occasioned my assent. But even so, it was good for me to go there on those nights, content to sit among these neighbors of mine with whom I had so little in common, and hear from the lips of a priest what Catholics believe about their Faith. And when an issue arose the expression of which might seem, from the point of view of my special liability, unconvincing, I could well listen in my mind to the way she would have phrased it, with that acute feminine instinct not so much for the objective rational core of the matter, but rather for the particular psychic complexity, the pre-conditioned rigidity of assumption which forever keeps the problem suspended and aloof from true reflection; and with a singular movement of warmth and comprehension she would contain it in her gaze, and there dispel it. For it was because she had lived out its contradiction with such anguish that the truth for her had achieved so compelling an absorption. Not, indeed, that it had always been so, but it had come to be; and I learned to gauge to it, alert to it, understanding it; and to draw from it many acute disclosures.

One day I had brought home a liberal magazine, engaged at that time upon a diatribe against "Catholic Power." Its political views I would not have countenanced for a moment, because as a radical anarcho-pacifist I had long considered its socialistic machinations nothing less than blood-letting, slave-making folly, but whose anti-clerical bias I had not yet the penetration to despise; and reading it, there had been revived again in me all the old latent apprehension. She herself would not so much as touch it. "Never," she said to me, "go to the enemy for your information. The Church can answer these charges, and they will be answered; though you can be sure that the people who delight in the indictment will never read the defense. As for these men, you and I lived out the sum of their errors before we ever set eyes on one another, and it would be a sorry thing if, after so much, we listened to them now. If it is facts you want, you can come to the Church with confidence. Those who fatten on untruth will always be found in such extremities as these."

Now that is no argument to allay the misgivings of even the seriously dubious, much less the congenitally skeptical. The Communist will claim as much for the Party, if not with the same confidence in the convolutions of the Party Line, at least with the same intensity, the same subjective conviction, and the same amatory zeal. It is singularly unfortunate that sincerity and truth form no absolute equation. But I have yet to forget what she told me, or to find it false, call it "woman's reasons" if you wish. *Never go to the enemy for information.* That is basic. What you will get is complete misinformation, plain lies, and very little else. The Church is the most lied about, vilified and denigrated institution in human history, a distinction it shares with its founder, the man Christ Jesus. Let the neophyte, therefore, be cautious, for whether the charges are true or false, he is certainly not able to distinguish between them, and ends up with nothing at all, save the ill-smelling weeds of his doubt. As for *You can come to the Church with confidence*, to one who has learned to know the Church as the epitome of Truth, the vehicle of God's incontaminate Truth, to come to Her with anything less than confidence is an act of real irreverence. Why? Because She is of God, who can neither deceive nor be deceived—though in the working-out it must be allowed that the quest for truth will often take one high and low before he finds that person who is able to lay a finger on the quick of his concern. For it is almost certainly not so much a matter of objective truth, truth *per se* (even the Catechism gives us that, with a stark take-it-or-leave-it finality), but rather a matter of meeting one's mind, misshaped by many conditioning years of obverse thought. It is our own minds, not the Truth, which is always the relative here.

It was to this same magazine, I remember, upon the occasion of one of those alarmed pronouncements on population and its cure which periodically afflict the liberal press, that she sat down in exasperation and addressed a letter opening with the trenchant salutation: "You Contraceptive Curs..."! It was, I am afraid, an epithet peculiarly offensive to the good men and women who preside over the stream-of-consciousness of liberal journalism. They themselves would never be guilty of such indelicacy—except, of course, in their references to the Pope! Stunned by so "anti-scientific" an attitude, they conjure up a picture of the Church as a kind of swarming rabbit warren, its irresponsible cohorts, of unabashedly carnal dispositions, procreating away at an appalling rate, breeding a host of equally gross-loined and sub-intelligent progeny who will shortly devour the world's shriveling resources, and by sheer numerical inundation capitulate the socialistic future to the baleful forces of Catholic Fascism! What happens to such fears as these in the course of a conversion? They are certainly dispelled, first, before the fact of Catholics as they actually exist, sane men and women, mature and responsible, deeply integrated in a cosmic perspective which takes care the things of God are not parceled out wholesale to Caesar; and, second, before the sublimity of the Catholic concept of the family, and of the individual soul.

For the full process of human life, which is holy because it participates in the God-life, and is inviolable, begins not with the act of birth, but far earlier, going back to the initial recognition between a man and woman that they were meant for each other (for the *end of* this recognition is parenthood), and proceeds thence through the solemn engagement, and the great sacrament of matrimony, and achieves the physical act of sexual congress, and impregnation, and gestation, and at last the birth of the child, and the all-important sacrament of Baptism, and thus through infancy and puberty and adolescence and maturation and senility, and into death, and out of the twin facts of conception and Baptism terminates beyond death in the highest union, the ineffable union with God, which is not a stasis, but an ever-unfolding eternally recreative relationship; and to obtrude in violence on this process, directing the limited human perspective to wrench it in twain, is to interfere—there is no other word for it—with a growth that is sacred.

Those who, in their abysmal incomprehension, can be heard to glower: "The facts of modern life will *compel* the Church to reverse her stand on contraception" simply have no grasp of Her supernatural position. She can no more sanction contraception than she can sanction murder. For though contraception is not murder in the sense that abortion is, its chaotic nature is the same. Abortion splits birth from impregnation by an act of willed violence. Contraception splits impregnation from coition no less arbitrarily and no less violently. They each represent the intrusion of chaos into the cyclic order for some lesser end, which is always the mark of lust. Lust is the act by which some singled part is seized up in an attempted gratification grasped at the expense of the fineness of the whole.

This is not to say that God has left man helpless, capitulating willy-nilly to the blind procreative urge. It is indeed the instinct of the Church that coition is truly exercised only in complete awareness of the consequent fact of birth, and in profound humility before the sanctity of the procreative cycle; that the act of coition is undertaken in the holiness of creation, seen as creation, never as isolated gratification. It is the attitude of the married saints, and in it the coitive act becomes a thing of humbleness, of delicacy and force, purpose and consummate wholeness, because it is governed to the universal life of God. Nor is this merely an abstractly calculated program of controlled abstinence, the family reduced to the status of an intelligently run hatchery; but rather a whole responsiveness to spiritual motivation, the movement of husband to wife after the fullness of contemplation in that basic spiritual force which constitutes the marriage state; and out of this movement, this contemplative fullness, the fact of childbirth is seen as consummation, enacting through these forces the consequent creation of a new being.

But in the context of human nature as it exists, nature after the Fall, with that mortal cleavage between intention and actuality, such intense spiritual consummation is very rare indeed. In the fact of marital existence the sexual force dictates, so to speak, its own terms. It is there, potent, evocative and compelling. The man and the woman in each other's presence move into that communion, and the release of the sexual force, the sexual realism in the substratum of bodily being, establishes an equipoise that resolves, as nothing else can, the thousand daily tensions of family life. As soldiers feed heavily that they may keep their stability in the liabilities of their state, so in the common matrimonial condition the man and the wife, in their need for love, possession and resolution turn to one another, and find that solace in the body's bed. That is human life, and the Church knows it.

For in Her wisdom She never endeavors to *enforce* sanctity. She enforces only preventively, guarding Her charges against deliberate sin by Her sternest mandates. And recognizing the fact of human biology She acknowledges that the reproductive process may be governed by the biologic norm; for it is evident that the woman is fertile only at intervals, that in the menstrual cycle there is only a relatively brief period when the woman may conceive at all, and there is no moral offense in sexual congress in the long infertile periods, and no moral offense in abstinence in the brief fertile periods, provided always the supernatural mandate to reproduce has been faithfully fulfilled, in so far as the conditions of one's time and circumstances permit a responsible fulfillment of this precept. And now since the discovery of the relation of basal temperature to the menstrual cycle, it is possible to control without contraception the frequency of impregnation. And though such regulation is perhaps distasteful to many deeply sensitive souls, felt to be, to a certain extent, destructive of any higher relationship, yet it does not in fact violate the natural completion of the sexual act. It is not a sin. It does provide a legitimate alternative.

For in that three-way conjoining between man, woman and God, the part of God is not blocked out. Nothing has been done to artificially inhibit the possibility of impregnation, which must never be closed. For while the man and the woman fashion in the flesh, God indeed fashions in the spirit, crowning their achievement in His own measure and in His own good time, with life. But if they are capable of neither the sanctity of contemplative creation, nor the prudence of natural regulation, then let them relinquish themselves to the Providence of God, and know that what He brings into the world He will never abandon. But to absolutely block Him out by the contraceptive device, excluding Him from the natural participation, is sin, the repudiation of God. It makes the act a kind of theft, a surreptitious deed of spiritual treachery.

The advocates of contraception are wrong precisely because they do not view the processes of human life, individually and collectively, from the supernatural point of view. Here we have the exasperated rejoinder that most non-Catholic theologians now sanction contraception, and how can the Church have the effrontery to accuse these highly principled religious men of lacking "the supernatural point of view"? Well, it is true that they acknowledge affiliation to the cultural continuum that has its root in the Incarnation; but lacking the wholeness of the deposit of faith they do wrong in appearing to assume the prerogatives of Christian morality, endeavoring to legitimize their bias by the approval of their congregations, officializing it, so to speak, and falsely endowing their errors with the psychology of dogmatic certitude. The fact stands that they have truly cut themselves off from the springs of Christian wisdom, and this proves it. No more than fifty years ago their own theologians condemned with harshness the errors their very sons today so blandly propagate. Is this not sufficient testimony that the farther away in time they go from the initial Revolt the more complicated and confused the position of these sects becomes, so that they have truly, in St. Paul's prediction, turned to fables? The more blurred their vision of the end of life becomes, the more false becomes their understanding of its processes, and in their ignorance they abuse the ancient Christian trust which they have preempted, and inhibit and corrupt its essential sacredness. Their secular compatriots, the materialistic socialists, are generally wrong in this matter all down the line, from moral principles to statistics. Their criteria, based upon a hypothetical standard of living, are often excessive. For behind the whole psychology stands fear, lack of faith, no comprehension of the providence of God, and hence no comprehension of the providence of life, a basic self-preoccupation masquerading as humanitarianism. This I know because I lived it out myself, its whole perspective, and was more extreme than most. It was by surgery itself that I insured no generation of mine would intrude upon the free play of my sensibility, nor rob other mouths of the limited sustenance of the earth.

But yet, though I speak bluntly here, how well I remember the difficulty of grasping, or, once grasped, of accepting, the traditional Catholic point of view on the matter. In me, I confess, it was one of the last resistances to go. For in the psychology of the non-Catholic (and, alas, of many Catholics) such is the pre-eminence of the sexual emphasis that contraception is hinged in direct equation to the deepest sense of social responsibility. In the prevalent Freudian emphasis anything more subtle has become unthinkable. Sexual inhibition haunts the roots of ailments, all neurosis, even all involuntary error. From the proletarian folklore of the pub to the dogmas of the medical intelligentsia, nothing will do more good than the orgasm, and it doesn't particularly matter how it is come by.

These concepts, so prevalent and so deeply entrenched in the mentality of our age, make it evident that no mere remonstrations about the liabilities of our "lower nature," no tight-lipped admonitions to suppress the "baser passions" can divert the impress of the mind from its deepest preoccupations. Grounded on such hungers and such fears, stimulated endlessly by the incessant barrage of erotic propaganda, usurping all the prestige of a pagan mystique as well as the agonized search for true psychosomatic integration, sex is reduced to the status of a universal hysteria. And since what is now demanded of it, it can never naturally provide, contraception has, in such a juncture, become an indispensability. By no other means may be preserved the autonomy of the sexual function as supreme act of release. Procreation, its true end, becomes a subordinate, almost an accidental. Its implemental aspects of assuagement and gratification, or, perhaps, of ecstatic mysticism, are elevated into the most dramatic pre-eminence. And thus it becomes inevitable that the minor aspect, forced to the status of a major one, results in no less a debasement than the reduction of its true nobility to the most ignoble of uses. In either event the result is a catastrophic distortion.

All this I knew, having lived it out, and now in the Inquiry Class I pondered it again, assimilating it into a radically altering perspective, sustaining it in the depths of the regard that is the comprehension of the Church and Her proclivities. I had come a long way since I lived through that ubiquitous compulsion, but there was much for me to learn. It was the time of learning; it was the time for me to wait.

I had time. The previous fall I had applied for a Guggenheim Fellowship, in the hope that the year ahead would be one of freedom and release, a year in which she and I might work together, each at his art. I had applied for it more at her instance than my own, for in the hyper-principled extremity of mind in which I moved after the War I ranked all such endowments as tainted money, though in my heart I secretly envied their beneficiaries. She would hear of no such intransigence, and I confess I was easily enough persuaded. Under my principles I deeply craved the prestige that such endowments carry, for I had given myself to many years of poetic endeavor, with little recognition, alienated by region and temperament and intellectual commitment from the various forces which govern literary politics, gaining artistic maturity as yet shut off from the audience I deserved, and in my vanity nursing a wounded pride, morose and sullen at heart that I had not been acclaimed. There was, moreover, the actual crying need for sufficient leisure from the drudgery of livelihood to do the work I was born to do, for I was earning my living as a janitor, out of the belief that only in menial tasks could I keep my aesthetic integrity, the creative freedom for those deep purposes the soul is made to serve. Her logic here was irrefutable. Nor should I neglect to acknowledge the general civilizing process which began in my life when it entered her own, making me more amenable to all prevailing accommodations, a process in which my old rock-rooted reserves were mellowing and tempering. Then in one of those unbelievable strokes of fortune which every poet covets and rarely receives, the Fellowship was granted. Time, at last, was mine, but the days alone now, and the nights a new singleness, the house vacant of its soul, all the rooms redolent yet of her presence, but her voice unheard. In the new age of her absence I flung myself on God, and into work.

And I wanted to make some kind of testament to her, some final acknowledgment, in the glory of the thing which had befallen us. I wanted to render to her some more than purely private asseveration in the fullness of what she had bestowed; to somehow acknowledge, if only in a general way, the whole impress of her life on mine, as incident after incident, seen as we had lived them through, steadily transformed me. For it was these very incidents that stood as focal points in my memory, to come back over me, and bring me once again the power of a meaning made, a new awakening, that clarifying impact of knowledge and light thrown into some area of obscuration dark in the soul, and waiting on grace.

I recalled for instance how, just before the separation, a casual acquaintance of mine, an older man of considerable experience and penetration, had heard of my interest in Catholicism, and in conversation referred to it, curiously; and asked me, probing me with his eyes, how it came about. I drew down into myself then, steeling myself, and said squarely: "It is through my wife," and the thing I expected indeed occurred. For he looked at me a moment and repeated softly, "Your *wife*," accenting the word with that particular emphasis, as if in its syllable I had disclosed to him a world of suggestion; and his look of rather curious, though transient contempt, as the words fell from his lips, revealed the fullness of the thing he had surmised: I was a man succumbed to mere female religiosity, nagged into a pew by a pious woman. What could be more abject?

I answered him nothing, in a new freedom of heart, letting the faint suggestibility of his scorn settle about me. He was, I reflected, everything I once sought to be: mature, experienced, successful, urbane and accomplished. Now I understood him perfectly, and why should I regret? I could have answered his question a dozen ways less offensive to his sensibilities, for I knew what they were and how to mollify them, but I had not. I who had hedged so often wanted to prove my fidelity to her in some consequential way, prove it to myself, in a manner that was of cost to me, and this was one way I proved it. For the truth is inescapable. I was to enter the Church, as I had entered the world, through the medium of a woman, and I cannot deny it.

It was in this same period, the last of our life together, that I was introduced at a party to an old lover of hers. There had been a time, not too far distant, when I would almost have welcomed such an encounter. For as a pantheist in an impersonal universe my relation to such a one would have been that of a special kind of brotherhood, a mutuality of experience which linked us together, gave us a pronounced significance for one another, a uniqueness and an intimacy centered in one salient fact: we had shared the same woman. We would have savored this, and in that savoring touched an area in ourselves deeply dangerous, and curiously unhealthy.

For there is in every man that element which reacts, one way or another, to such a grouping: males thrown together by some social circumstance into a juxtapositioning exposing the latent factor there, and which takes all the certitude of an ordered mind and a profound system of values to discount and ignore. There is danger there, deep danger, a danger mounted upon an affinity that can lead, if cultivated, to an inner softness, a kind of psychic spoiling. For it is here, in these very areas, that a man all unsuspecting stands on the verge of homosexuality. And yet it is precisely here that such caution exasperates the confirmed homosexual. "Why discount it!" he cries, "Why ignore it! It's a fact of nature! How can you honestly discount the obvious truth!"

It is truth in its wholeness, not a partial truth extracted out of the synthesis, that the Catholic acknowledges. The fact of the homosexual element in man does not justify or condone the overt homosexual act. The feminine exists in him, like the masculine in woman, as a concomitant of basic biological unity. The feminine in man is one of the most valuable factors of his nature, tempering his masculinity, giving him balance and perspective, sympathy and comprehension. Certainly the thing exists. But because in fallen human nature all elements strive to break out of synthesis and achieve mastery, the impulse must be curbed. The valuable conditioning element, gone out of control, ruins life, collapses it into sin and destruction. The homosexual, unfortunate as he might seem to be, nevertheless has remarkable insight, sensitivity and intuition, great gifts indeed to offer the well-being of the social whole. But when he seeks to be "liberated," as he calls it, to activate the liability, releasing the imbalance to cut into the fabric of human conduct, the social fabric in which the human act is contained, he destroys himself and the society he could fruitfully serve. It is one of the terrible results of the over-civilized mind, bred in an epoch of appalling confusion of value, that men seek release from basic human nature on the plea that they seek release from a mere convention. The relativity of hypercivilized thought abhors an absolute, and the mind murders itself in its flight.

As for this man and me, there was of course nothing so overt as such a recognition between us. I speak rather of a basic situation, inherent in the relationship between the sexes, which opens, and all unexpectedly exposes the liability inherent in the basis of being, and forces one to regroup intuitively around that core of values he has previously cultivated, for good or for bad. Earlier, as I say, such were my values I would have looked to this man with special interest, for although we would not have referred to the fact of our distinction (not, at least, on so casual a thing as a mere encounter), nevertheless we would by a kind of unspoken understanding have felt the identity as a certain authentic touchstone between us, if only out of curiosity as to what the woman had meant to us each, and we would have savored it.

You will find many men of a militantly erotic cast of mind, professedly anti-homosexual in their attitudes, who yet do not understand that their need to share a particular type of masculine relationship is in fact obscurely homosexual. Not that male friendship is such in itself; that is absurd. But when two men use the heterosexual situation as a point of establishment between themselves, narrating their adventures and analyzing their affairs, comparing notes, reliving in each other's absorption the evocative subjectivity of the erotic thrill, evolving and refining in a kind of worshipful ritualism their elaborate conquest of women, what is quite evident is that here the absorption is nothing else than their own relationship, tangential but intense; that it is this very obscurity, diffuse, radiating the prevailing sympathy of enveloping sin, which makes the meaning. It is in the gesture of the sinful deed, in the suture of their deep anarchic shame, that their souls kiss.

You see it plainly enough at the crude proletarian level, where violence strips away and reveals in its hideousness the corrupt inveiglement only glimpsed above. Soldiers and lumberjacks will take their buddies to the same brothel, share the same prostitute, each exploiting the inert female element with his own breed of rapacity, in the same woman's flesh each merging his being, seeking his buddy or leading him on, desperately attacking in the corrosive act the unfaceable void that is his separateness, straining to attain by brute seizure, by a savage appropriation, what he could never touch in understanding. Or else, more ruinous, take prostitutes side by side on the selfsame bed, and match themselves in defiance one against the other, brandishing the sexual weapon and the febrile mechanistic potency as elements of power by which each seeks to dominate, calling across the insane darkness that divides them, a pathetic comradeship of union and separation, their challenge and their curse, in all their terrible triumphant masculine subjugation nursing the hidden homosexuality that flings them together and forces them apart. They are its brutal victim; they bleed between its tongs.

But your declared homosexual is both more overt and more subtle, for while he does understand himself better, yet he accepts himself in the comprehension of his perversity, and that is his culpability. The root of his malady teeters on the lip of a double flaw—a perversity both of love and of fear. Love of one's self, one's own, one's kind, one's sex, of one's sexual organ; and fear of the other, the mystery of otherness, of woman, of the other sex, of the woman's sexual organ, the trap that devours the very male identity, cuts him off at the groin. Intercourse with a woman becomes for such a one a terrible deed, an act of stealth and great daring, the foray into hostile territory, the audacious penetration to deliver the death-stroke at the enemy heart and then escape, flee back to the safety of one's own familiar self, and there exult, secretly swagger in the hectic flush of the accomplished deed. Oh, he's been a fox, all right! Wormed his way into her good graces. When she dropped her guard he sneaked on in and hit dead center. She went all to pieces. The whole terrifying female edifice blew up under him like a dynamited bridge. But he rode out the storm, pulled free, got out and away and never a scratch! What a rare raider he turned out to be! He never thought he could do it!

He sweats and trembles, listening breathlessly in the dark for the first sign of the counter-attack, listening most fearfully there in the dark for the awful moment when she starts to recover, when she rouses to the knowledge of her terrible betrayal, grabs up her weapons, and comes raging in her revenge.

Is he doomed then to this? No. In the freedom of the human will, in the decisive liberation of human choice, no man is trapped. Let him seek God, and he will learn truth. Let him learn truth, and he will touch love. He is, actually, more capable of responding to woman than many another. He senses, as few men do, her delicacy of response, her hushed quiescence of soul, her tremulous sensitive comprehension. These are the areas of intuition he deeply perceives. But because he does not know God he does not know ultimate value, and in his separating blockage he cannot trust the best he perceives. Life holds him in its terror because his divided heart holds him in its confusion. As a child, too acute, thrusted too fast into the blunt world of the adult, in life's earliest encounter he fell obliquely wounded, and in his isolating sensitivity the wound immobilizes. Out of such suppressed anguish, all distinction, the crude flanges of reality, and the very nature of categorical definition become wincingly painful—the brute mechanism of a lacerating machine. He would perhaps like nothing so much as to fade away, lapse in the amorphous flux of undifferentiated existence, but he cannot. Rather he lurks behind the shell of his ambiguity, and only comes out, most tentatively, most cautiously and painfully, to his own wounded kind.

There is, of course, a straight biological homosexuality, a discernible imbalance of the hormones, but this is a special problem, and is not our concern. It does not constitute the broad homosexual problem. Homosexuality as it infects civilization is commonly a neurosis, a confusion of identity resulting in a corresponding inversion, the thwarting of love and fear, haunting the disintegration of all social value.

As the culture proliferates, and the natural lines of demarcation become blurred and indistinct, everywhere the untrammeled ego hungers across the basic categories, and this is a real decadence. Decadence might be defined as a state of mind, an intellectual climate, in which the true categorical distinctions inherent in reality are lost sight of, or repudiated willfully, and men seek gratification outside true definition. In fallen human nature our need for love and possession is omnivorous, and when we eliminate the true God, the value of the Ultimate, this need flows sideways through the whole of being, and we long to possess and take into ourselves all its shimmering aspects. We become decadent. And when we are deeply decadent, then we actually come to hate what is distinct, whatever holds itself aloof. The Jews are the most distinct people on earth, a divine demarcation, and therefore the most hated. Their persecutors long to reduce them to their own indiscriminateness, their own baseness, to soil them with their own filth, like a Nazi raping a Jewess. He has to soil her utterly with his own soiled self before he destroys her, carries his degradation to her very vitals, smears to the screaming heart.

And the Church, like a raped Jewess, like the ravaged Christ bleeding on the bed of the Cross, manhandled and defiled by ruffians and sadists, fingered and defiled to slake the lust of perverts, the Church on the brutal bed of history takes the attacks of the arrogant men, the manhandlers, who seek to reduce Her to their own corruptness because She insists on the purity of distinction, because She avers and defends the holy categories of divine being, refusing to give Herself to the overtures of their recklessness who out of that terrible disorder seek to annihilate all value, to wipe it out. The indiscriminate Oriental mind, with its penchant for assimilation, is scandalized at Her regard for distinction, and the existentialist sneers at Her "formalism," Her "creed," Her "static rigidity of outlook." For care of distinction denotes responsibility, and responsibility denotes commitment, and commitment denotes fidelity, but these they despise. Let them have their way and syncretism, moral, philosophical and theological, will engulf the earth, and chaos, confusion of all value, will annihilate man.

I was just such a syncretist. When my first wife, long before, had taken a lover, I had gone so far in these matters as virtually to adopt him. He had been my friend, and when the liaison came at last to my knowledge, I took him aside, and with a kind of proprietary paternal concern endeavored, out of the fund of my preliminary experience there, to coach him in one or two areas where I suspected he might find himself in trouble, in order that she and he, since they were involved in the thing, might realize it more fully. It was, I think, the only way I knew how to act with any conviction at all; the sort of thing my code called for. I proposed to be that rare man who, when other men would have exploded, genially blessed the inevitable and went about my concerns, not like a groveling cuckold so much at the mercy of a woman that she might wipe her filth on him just to see him grin, which was certainly not the case; but as a person who can meet the eventualities of his life with some measure of poise and dignity.

A sexual liaison, in our circle, was ranked as a kind of fatality. One accepted it, when it came, as blessing or calamity, but one hardly knew how to avoid it, on what principle, or by what criteria. We too, like the ancient Greek caught in a dangerous erotic situation, must yield to the imperious glance of Aphrodite, for to offend *that* Goddess was not to be countenanced. Such was our enthrallment that neither did we dare to "reluct from joy." Thus Llewelyn Powys, in that melancholy masterpiece *Glory of Life,* delineates something of the feckless attitude that inveigled my will:

> Sex is the backbone of all life, the pliable, beautiful, spiked backbone upon which the fair grace of the flesh is built. Except in its sadistic manifestations and where children are involved, we unhallowed religious should protect and champion it, forwarding the cause of lovers in season and out of season, natural and unnatural, licit and illicit. Nothing is more villainous than the way people of conventional habits endeavor to tame, correct and inhibit the wild splendor of Lust. Lust is nature's free gift to us all, and the hours spent in its consummation are beyond all

measure the most real and ecstatic hours of our life. "The lust of the goat is the bounty of God." Whenever mutual attraction exists between two people it is a life-disavowal to reluct from joy. A man's manner of approach to this sweet fountain, to this faery fern-shadowed pool, must depend upon his own disposition and upon his destiny. It is a personal matter and should, under heaven, have nothing whatever to do with other people, with one's family or with society. Mutual desire is its own justification at all times and in all places, and if our neighbors prove sulky, or our mother or our father, or husband or wife, or sister or brother, or our mistress or guardian, they must be deceived from cock-crow to cock-crow. Are there no feathers in the world to oil locks with, no back pantry door-keys, no hayricks, raspberry canes, apple lofts?

This was my code, and I preached it, and having taught such sophistry what could I do when the apt pupil, whom I had so assiduously prepared for my own defection, a defection which was never to come, should take, in her golden opportunism, the brimming chalice, and quench, and quench, and find it good? What was I to do then but bow my head like a reasonable man, and accept, and try to like it?

Try to like it! "Between the idea and the reality falls the shadow!" I took the young squire aside, and coached him most paternally, and gave the affair my blessing, and waited for it to wear itself out, to blow over, so that I might reclaim my own. For the stoic, when defeated, endeavors to yet wrest victory from the jaws of fate by remaining steadfastly impervious to humiliation. But it is one thing to wink at an escapade, and plan to triumph in the end by forgiving and taking back the contrite deceiver; yet when the situation gets out of hand, and one finds a stripling preferred, actually *preferred* to oneself, finds oneself sloughed off and deserted for all one's magnanimity, dropped like an unwanted appendage, a hamper under her feet, then, left with all that terrible nakedness of soul in a bleak universe, then indeed a man sings a different song. The genial blessing comes out the other side of his mouth—a curse. In the heart of such disaster, belatedly but emphatically, I exploded, and all the outrage and the anguish and the blocked suppressed human response of grief and shock and incredulity poured in on me. In that anguish I had crossed the line, and began to return to reality.

So this was the background, then, when at last, in another context, and with the seed of Christianity full flowered within me, I was unavoidably introduced to this old lover of my new wife, and I drew down upon a wholly altered frame of reference, and in the knowledge of person, of the integrity of person, took a different stand. As we shook hands, and our eyes met, I found somehow the right response given me, spontaneous and natural and direct, wholly outside all the old ambiguity; and in that full response of impersonal aloofness I excused myself in a moment and withdrew, and the peace that came to me as I dissevered myself from that situation was a very great blessing, the truth of it, the rightness, and the integrity. This man was an individual, this episode was a situation, with which I wanted nothing whatsoever to do; and I excluded myself from it by an act of human volition, based on a judgment of value, a sense of fidelity and a thorough grasp of distinction. I was no longer a mere ingredient in a fluxing complex of circumstances, attempting to maintain my dignity by a process of infinite adaptability. In the certitude of value I made a definite decision and took a definite stand, and rejected an unwanted consequence and repudiated an unwarranted possibility, and I was free. In that freedom I had found in marriage the root of living faithfulness, which is the root of responsibility and regard, loyalty and basic humility.

For if there was anything she had brought home to me it was the necessity in marriage of the true interior fidelity, a fidelity that drives below the levels of bodily association, or the commonality of convention, and becomes a dynamic and pervasive awareness at the center of the life. She herself lived it out with the acuity of the true principle, and I remember one of those lesser incidents, that have in themselves no great dramatic stature, but somehow stick in the mind, long after evoking in the memory the seal of an unqualified tribute, shaping the reference of that worth.

We purchased our weekly provisions at a store some little distance from our home, so that it was necessary to carry our supplies in large armfuls, and this we did together once a week. I preferred to carry the food in cartons, but she found this too awkward, and always asked that it be placed in paper bags. One morning I told the clerk at the shopping center to place our purchase in a carton, for I intended to carry it all myself; but she had not heard me speak, and seeing him begin she leaned to him and told him to please place it in paper bags. It seemed like a flat contradiction, and it took both the clerk and me by surprise. As he sighed and began to change containers I drew back in embarrassment, murmuring some disparaging concession, and visibly retiring from the field. In that moment the clerk and I exchanged a glance of profound understanding, a kind of momentary but unmistakable recognition of the plight of all men, of all long-suffering husbands, a tacit and mutually shared helplessness before the impervious domain of female intractability. Once more the brotherhood of the male had found its salute; in that instant he and I were bound by ties exceeding every affiliation; the marital compact collapsed from the union that transcends to the fetter that binds, the trap in which good men are forever shackled.

It is the kind of thing you encounter everywhere, mostly in jokes, in the cinema, on the radio, and especially in the innumerable and ubiquitous cartoons by which we resolve the doleful insufficiency of modern existence. As there evoked, marriage becomes the sad compact in which the sexes somehow find themselves, the thankless makeshift, while true fulfillment, the dazzling aspirations of felicity, lie remotely elsewhere. Even in the Catholic magazines you see it. In that effort to humanize their material they make dramatic the grotesque incidentals of married life, and in this emphasis merely join with the blatant glibness that everywhere cuts into the fabric of true fidelity. These are the skirmishes which Satan wins with never a blow. Out of them emerges the distinction of the sexes as somehow foredoomed to incompatibility, and when multiplied to constitute the prevailing social tone they make for an unconscious restlessness, a miserable squirming in the bonds of alliance, a divisive hunger for otherness that is most ruinous to the dedicated life. Between that clerk and me flitted the acknowledgment of life's most hopeless complexities, and bound us, strangers, fleetingly together in manifest identity.

She was hit, of course, torn between her own sense of misdemeanor and the acuity of the lateral wound that had in this divided us. It was a lapse, I must confess, in which I never found her. Rather, she adhered to the commitment with an instinct which, as I came to understand it and to see it in action, left me astonished at the fineness of its response, who had always drifted in that somewhat coarsened self-determination of the aggressive individualist. It was something so much more than the possessive attachment I first suspected, the clutching of a loved object. There was this possession, indeed, but as the relationship deepened it climbed toward superior regions, a matter of detached principle around which the action of her life could center. However I might fall into public error, and however firmly she might correct me in private, before others her interior allegiance never deviated. In her it flowed from a basic simplicity of attitude, something I came in time to recognize as inherently Christian, as wholesome as her sensible homemaking, her nourishing food. To me, who had made such a mess of marriage, it opened my eyes to the loyalty and the true security a marriage could mean. It was one other aspect of the fundamental disposition that more and more established in my mind the substance and the authority of the Catholic attitude.

But again I must say that if I have used the terminology of matrimony, it is done to render the psychology of the relationship, not to certify its validity. No insight into the complexities of familial accord, no adaptive skills of housewifery or husbandship, no sterling qualities of the responsible provider that mark the natural family man, nor the superb combination of affection and restraint which constitute the remarkable mother, much less the psychic splendors of erotic rapture, are the determinants of the authenticity of a marriage. Regardless how fast a race is run, if the meet is not official the winning time is never entered in the records.

For the institution of marriage falls under the mandate of Divine Law, and the State may support but not abnegate it. And although the Church claims no canonical jurisdiction over the unbaptized, Her role as teacher, expounder, and interpreter remains. For God, not the State, has established the terms under which matrimony is to be fulfilled, and the Church, not the Court, is the arbiter governing its function. Nor is this a later dictum of Her own; it has the positive attestation of Christ Jesus, King of Creation, Lord and Master of life, Eternal God. It is a stricture constituted not to oppress but to conserve. It ensures the personal rights of the individual partners, and the natural rights of the legitimate offspring. It conserves the delicate intricacy of the social fabric, without which the individual is coarsened and made narrow. To smash it on the plea of individualism is to make a society in which true individualism cannot be had.

And we have once more entered, I well know, that area where the unconditioned reader lays down this book with a sigh: the old appeal to authority again. He might have expected as much of the born Catholic indoctrinated from the cradle to the Church's peculiar creed, but he had hoped for more insight from an adult convert describing the psychology of conversion, more imagination, some clue to a mystery he finds incomprehensible. The appeal to an authority he cannot recognize because he has never experienced, slams shut a door, and he turns away in distaste. But as a matter of fact, it is the convert whom you will find appealing to authority, more directly and insistently, yes, more shrilly, than the deeply integrated, naturally and supernaturally mature Catholic, in whom the Creed was taken with his mother's milk to make the very stuff of his bones—you will find the convert appealing to authority on precisely those points of doctrine which he does not yet deeply understand. The problem may be seen in its crude form in the hysterical conversion among the enthusiastic sects: an intense psychological experience solidifying around it a host of unwonted beliefs on nothing more substantial than the dubious veracity of the raw reaction itself, pure subjectivity, yet all marshaled forward behind the sole authority of some scriptural passage wrenched out of context, fairly staggering under the exceeding pressure it has been made to bear. It is an attitude which you may see, occasionally, in Catholics, as you have observed it, doubtless, in me, but you will never discover it in the Church as a working principle. Regardless of what appears in actual practice, mere conformism has no place in Her conceptual structure. The convert, in his uncertainty, is especially prone to it, but its presence does not jeopardize his basic appeal to authority itself.

For authority is the principle by which conduct is governed in matters whose consequence extends beyond the individual's capacity to control. Yet this, in a sense, includes everything we do, and hence everything we do falls under the jurisdiction of either the natural or the supernatural law. Our acts extend consequentially into the vast areas of the enveloping mystery. No matter how much we boast of human knowledge we move every instant in a context of ultimate darkness. We can appraise, somewhat, the nature of effects, but the nature of the ultimate, the cause, the source from which all flows and in which its whole meaning resides, of that we know almost nothing.

The revelations God has made in regard to Himself, and man, and to the modes and means of human life, were made precisely because from the natural perspective they involve the mysterious, they are impenetrable mysteries, they are mysteries without the solution to which no man can adequately realize himself. To repudiate this knowledge because it does not admit of absolute experimental verification, because it has to be taken "on authority," and because the authority has been invested in a human institution and hence subject to abuse, is, psychologically speaking, understandable, but not really rational. And in this irrationality may be seen the source of our hysterical attitude to authority itself.

Physicists tell us that the hand we chance to lift affects in its transient displacement the gravitational tug of the remotest galaxies. As a matter of fact, the very processes of our thought strike into the vast web of being, but it is at the level of morality, the area of engagement of spiritual values in the consequence of human acts, that the complexity of relationships achieves its finest mesh. So dense is this mutuality that speaking in an absolute sense we can say quite boldly there is no such thing as a strictly private sin. Fr. Victor White, O.P., in his study "The Concept of Justice in Aquinas," places his finger on the quick of this matter. After discussing the character of justice in Thomistic thought, he goes on:

> Here we are introduced to sin precisely as *injustice*: a thwarting of the Divine order of justice precisely by the effort of the creature to claim *more* than is his due. Seeking to be as God, knowing good and evil and trying to be the master of his own fate, refusing to accept the "vertical" justice of God by himself usurping the Divine Lordship, the *Fons iustitiae*, man brings about inevitably a disharmony within creation itself, a state of injustice on the "horizontal" plane. The Divine order of justice implants a balance of opposites throughout the length and breadth of creation: it is impossible for one constituent to assume more than belongs to it without depriving another. The human will, by sundering its own proper subordination to the Divine Lordship and defying the Divine Justice, brings about a disorder, an injustice, a lack of balance and proportion within the *humanum* itself (*concupiscentis inordinata*), itself an unjust condition calling for Wrath from the Divine Justice, a hybrid automatically calling forth its Nemesis. This interior discord within man in its turn produces the disharmony of man and man (tyranny and slavery) and the unjust abuse of the infra-human creation with its painful repercussion on man himself.
>
> This broad conception of sin as injustice breeding injustice, *culpa* breeding *poena, poena* disposing to further

*culpa*—a sort of inevitable karmic process resulting not from some arbitrary decree but from the very nature of things as God made them—prepares the way...for a consideration of the requisites for the repairing of this injustice and the restoration of justice.

This immense complexity ought to teach us, if we can be taught, the staggering nature of universal interdependence, but we proceed emotionally as if we were the very darling of some supreme dispensation. The Enlightenment celebrated our individuality, our uniqueness, which is true enough, and most valuable, but it *implied* that we are therefore autonomous, and this is the damaging lie. This is the lie that leads us still to persist in the delusion that the uniqueness of our own impulse constitutes the final authority. We may agree to condition that impulse in deference to what we call "the common good" but we think of even that as a gratuitous concession accorded for reasons of expediency out of the warrant of our supreme mandate, much as an emperor might grant some concession to his council but never inherently forfeit his absolute prerogative. And on the other hand we will do what society forces us to do, but our *assent*, our uniqueness of judgment, we will never relinquish.

Thus we accept the authority of the specialist only because we assume that we ourselves, had we the training, would verify the same conclusion. We accept the verdict of the physicist on physics and the ditch-digger on ditches because it costs us nothing to do so, and we lack the time and the inclination to master these techniques for ourselves. But, accept though we do, we invariably reserve the right of repudiation. Our acceptance is always conditional. What we will never relinquish is the principle of our sovereign autonomy; what we will never acknowledge is the implication of our utter limitedness: that we are not the final arbiter in regard to even the merest things of our selves. We will support no end of mutually exclusive positions, and accommodate them generously in our souls, because we prefer abject unreason to the capitulation of our discrimination.

This is perhaps the common characteristic of fallen man. Certainly it is most characteristic of myself, and most instinctive, I think, with the generality of men I have known. It is not a symptom of merely intellectual arrogance, the pride of the rational man; it is not, that is, confined to the intelligentsia. I once worked on a pipeline in the San Joaquin Valley with an Oklahoman who, though he could barely write his name, in the areas of his own concern was omniscient. One point of pride was his knowledge of the opossum, and he claimed to have discovered what very few people know: the peculiar manner of reproduction of this marsupial, unlike that of any other creature of the woods. It was his positive assertion that the organ of the male is forked; that the female receives in the nostrils, where, presumably, the ovaries are located; and that after insemination she exhales the deposit into her pouch, where the whole process of gestation takes place!

Now, I had had sufficient experience with Oklahoma humor to circle this description with great gingerliness, but it soon became apparent that his version was held as fact. I was unfortunately too young to have acquired sufficient plasticity to accommodate the enormous latitude of human opinion, and I rose in defense of factual objectivity. A jug of wine was placed on the issue and the wager was taken. That night I consulted an encyclopedia. I discovered that the opossum at birth is very small and is transferred immediately to the pouch. This man, doubtless, had killed female opossum carrying these tiny, almost foetal organisms, and it was easy to infer that they had gestated there, and ingenious to deduce by what process it might have been accomplished. Certainly it was too good to abandon. For when I produced my authority and claimed my wager, he turned not a hair. All that was mere "book larnin'" and none of his people had ever stood by it. Very well, I proposed, come with me to State College, consult a professional zoologist, and verify the facts at first hand. Not at all. What did any of these city fellers know about 'possums? He wasn't born yesterday. Suppose, then, we find a government trapper of the Forest Service, a mountain man, raised in the hills, whose official capacity gave him some status of objectivity? This, he allowed, would be more acceptable, but in the event of an adverse decision it couldn't stand, for that would be only one man's word against another's. Besides, and here he turned upon me a glance of comprehensive pity, the ineluctable look of all wisdom bending down in its greatness to an ignorance unspeakably dense, and with infinite patience informed me that no Californian could ever really learn 'possums. It simply isn't 'possum country. To learn 'possums, really to *learn* them, mind you, you couldn't very well have come from any other place but Oklahoma.

We each kept our wine, and that night each doubtless drank a toast, the one to factual objectivity, and the other to personal opinion. It was the same with religion. I stood by enlightened pantheism and he stood by the Gospel, Four Square variety, and our judgments each retained that unimpeachable privacy neither dared relinquish. And I am afraid it is not confined to Protestantism, that much run-of-the-mill Catholicism is shot through with it. We proceed as though *we* had chosen a religion, and that makes it absolute. And once having chosen, once having identified the Church with ourselves, that makes Her holy! We have made our choice, and we stand by our own.

Thus it is that in such matters as marriage and remarriage, where the emotions and passions are so deeply engaged, the individuality of this impulse presides unquestioned. When people are badly matched, it is hardly possible to make them conceive of life together, and when they are happily but invalidly matched, it is hardly possible to make them conceive of life apart. In such cases the indissolubility of the formal marriage contract, especially in view of its contemporary legalistic aspects, is to them a kind of suicide. But this does not scotch the fact that marriage is more than a contract, involving not only man and woman but God, and that what involves God passes out of the domain of individual definition.

For a sacrament is simply a means of unification, a uniting with God. This is not the place to discuss the sacramental system, though it stands most crucially at the heart of the basic problems of this book, as indeed it stands most crucially at the heart of the problem of man, the life of man. But at least it must be realized that the sacraments are simply the means God has chosen to adhere man to Himself, make man of Himself, draw man up out of his created nothingness, and enable him to partake of the Divine. The modern instinct about this God-sourced but man-operated apparatus, this sacramental system, is that God, were He any kind of God at all, would not confine Himself to such dubious crutches, but rather by a singular and unique movement of interior illumination, He would so project His influence that the painful laboriousness of such human intermediaries as the sacraments, the hierarchy, the liturgies, etc., would have no occasion for being.

Well, it once was so. But there was a man named Adam, who was the first man, and who enjoyed those proclivities and who threw them away, and renounced them, renounced them for you and me as well as for himself, for we are his heirs; and like those earthly heirs who inherit their wastrel father's syphilitic curse, but not the fortune he squandered, so we inherit the liabilities of Adam, and his vast deficiencies, but not the least of his supernatural endowments.

But like a forgiving Lord who takes pity on the offspring of the wastrel, seeing their suffering He sends His Son, hidden under the form of their own kin, their very flesh and blood, who appears among them, and helps them, heals them, and leaves among them a means by which they may help themselves to an eventual full return to friendship, and to fortune, taking more delight in seeing them learn to support themselves with the means He has provided, than if He were to lavish once more the full sum of His regard upon them. So God sent Christ, and Christ instituted among us the interim means by which we too might gain that eventual participation—if we choose. This means is the sacramental system. These sacraments are the things we can do, the tangible acts we can make to once more restore ourselves to the wastrel's squandered heritage.

Childish? Ah, but beautiful. And no, not even childish. Childish perhaps, insofar as I have told it, but I have told nothing; the magnitude of the thing extends infinitely. It is inexhaustible in its implication once you begin the pondering of it, once a man has entered its hegemony and made himself of its scope. This is an aside. I was talking about a conversion, *my* conversion, but that's nothing. The heart of the matter lies here, in Him. Christ came. Christ moved among men. Christ was gibbeted. Oh, many men have been, but this one stood up afterward and poured back upon the fallen race the mystery of infinity. It has never been spent, that plenitude, and that's two thousand years. In Bread He perpetuates Himself, in Wine. As food. Food is replenishment, invigoration. Man may now come to God as directly as he comes to food, to bread and to wine. It is so eminently natural, the mode of this supernaturalism, the way He breathes His supernatural life into the human race, which, though left alive to the pulse of earth, to the pulse of God was dead.

And how, since this is Her function, can Christ the Church be anything less than total? If She is to be the Breather of Life, She has to be the receiver of all men, all peoples, all nations, all races, all cultures, personalities, temperaments. There are men so dominantly intellectual that the slightest manifestation of the subjective quickens their alarm. For them the Church can present the *schema* of reality as being so intricate and yet so consistent as to absorb the most astute minds. On the other hand, there are men who despise the intellect, hungering for the blind existential impact, for the realization of the preponderant flow of the Divine Source, and to these the Church offers pure Act in all its intensity, the Kierkegaardian leap given a true point of departure and an orientation the great Dane never possessed. And so for those who sneer at the Church's very universality, calling Her a trickster, out for all takers, spreading Her nets to catch the highbrow and the lowbrow each with his own bait—what can one say to such dissimulations? The true Church has to be the Church of all men, or no Church at all. She has to be the Church of the charwoman no less than of the intellectual; the Church of the executive no less than of the Congo tribesman. If the tribesman finds in Her the Earth-Mother of his primordial instinct and is hence fed, do you think the executive will be any less fed? Do you think the Earth-Mother does not survive in the emotional hunger of the executive no less than of the tribesman? Is this not what modern man is learning in his anguish? And where will he find an Earth-Mother in the world of today, among the neon lights and the telephones? Believe me, the Earth-Mother is dead indeed, but her need is not. Her need lives on in the soul of man, and the Church feeds it.

"Unless you eat of My Flesh and drink of My Blood you shall not have Life in you." God said that, the God-Man breaking the very flesh of His Body that men might eat of the Divine, and His words are for the executive no less than for the tribesman. They strike through the basis of the being, evoking under the levels of our sophistication a total need, a total response. "Unless you eat of My Flesh." Do you fear to eat the Flesh of God, O man? What fear is it you are huddling over, that knot in your belly, with your shrieking civilization, and your flight from life? What escape do you seek in your supersonic planes? What night of annihilation do you propound in the orgasm of your atomic bombs? "Unless you shall eat of My Flesh...." Come back, listen to your elemental heart, crying there for surcease in that riddled breast. When men threw the sacraments away in their fit of "reason" what did they throw away if not reason itself? What obscene gods did they propitiate in that violation? "Unless you shall eat...." Come back from your naked frenzy, and quench the hunger in your soul. Come back from that frenzy you call The Conquest of Nature! When will you begin again the conquest of the self? Eat, take up and eat. Be whole. In the Bread of God you will fill your flesh, and flesh and spirit will be one again. In the Sacraments of the Church and no other place will your body find its soul.

But we must come back to the essence of the matter, and face the complexity of issues impinging upon the marital state. Here, as elsewhere, the difficulty of the man of goodwill approaching the Church is that he encounters a hierarchy of valuation foreign to his whole way of thought. He commonly understands that the Church preaches the indissolubility of the marriage contract, and understands that this is based on Her concept of the supernatural mandate and the natural law. But he soon becomes aware that there are cases in which the Church does grant dissolution of one marriage for the purpose of remarriage in another, and this complication bewilders him. If marriage is indissoluble, then let it be indissoluble; that he can understand. "Hew to the line and let the chips fall where they may" is a good integral position with a kind of wholesome satisfaction in its very lack of ambivalence. In a world of shifting value he has at last found someone who really holds. But when he discovers that actually the Church does not at all maintain the absolute indissolu-bility of marriage, that She will dissolve certain licit marriages in favor of what looks suspiciously like Her own interests, for apparently no other reason than to win another convert or to expedite the machinations of some influential Catholic, then he is indeed bewildered. It smacks of straight religious political maneuvering, and revives all his suspicions of ecclesiastical wire-pulling. He draws away in disillusionment.

We see here one of the Church's gravest problems, not only in regard to those who approach Her from without but to Her own charges as well: She cannot arbitrarily simplify what is essentially complicated. If a given situation is morally or theologically complex, She cannot water it down or discount it to suit the prevalent mental or spiritual capabilities of those who look to Her, and if these persist in regarding Her capacity to hold distinctions as mere self-interest, mere religious politics, that is unfortunate. She Herself has to operate at the level of full moral and theological complexity, and then, and only then, can She indeed deign to "let the chips fall where they may."

The complexity here is simply that the fact of sacramental marriage interjects into the social synthesis an element which wholly transcends the prerogatives of the natural state. For there is a vast theological distinction between a basic licit marriage and a supernaturally sacramental one, regardless how much certain poets may confuse the issue in speaking of any fervent marriage as vaguely "sacramental." For though they correctly perceive its inherently sacred character, they are not to be understood as meaning anything more than its intrinsic seriousness. In speaking of sacramental sex, indissolubility is never contemplated. Apparently the very existence of such a precept is enough to drive the intrinsic "sacramental" character right out of the marital union. Sex is sacramental only so long as it is blithe, free and lovely, and not one whit longer.

But to the Church, sacramental marriage means an entirely different thing. Christ established the sacraments, the means by which the soul is assumed into direct supernatural relationship with God. One of these sacraments is that of matrimony, and it is its existence which complicates the marital situation. There is, first of all, the basic licit marriage contract, which has existed from the beginning, and which obtains between two unbaptized persons, and which, because it is based on a spiritual reality, does indeed remain indissoluble, in the ordinary course of events, until the death of either party. But since the Redemption there has existed true sacramental marriage, marriage between two baptized persons in a transcendent relationship with God. It is this relationship which remains absolutely indissoluble. The Church has in Her keeping, by divine appointment, the custody of the moral life of man; and the only marriage which She has not been granted the power to dissolve is this consummated marriage between two baptized persons.

But one thing should not be overlooked: in holding the distinction between the two types, or levels, of the marital status, we must remember that there has actually never been a merely natural state of marriage, with a merely natural permanent character, in the sense that certain animal species by instinct mate only once and for life. Animals mate, but only man marries. The instinct does indeed have its natural law, a law which governs the procreation of the species, and in man that law does of itself enforce upon the marital state a natural permanence due to the responsibility which the rearing of offspring and the cohesion of the social fabric exacts. But in man, mating was from the beginning endowed with a higher degree of mutuality, a compact of the spiritual order, true marriage, imparting to the natural permanence a special spiritual character. For since the creation of woman was out of man, in the marriage bond that indivisibility was directly asserted by God. In marriage they become "two in one flesh," a spiritual cohesion. And this spiritual cohesion is endowed between two people when, under the norms of their particular society, they accept one another as man and wife.

But such a preliminary pre-Christian state of spiritual cohesion was, as we saw, not yet truly sacramental, though it was indeed preparational of what was to come. God foresaw man's sin and Christ's redemption, and in human marriage established a suitable figure under which Christ's incorporation of mankind into the Mystical Body might be typified. Licit marriage joins man to woman spiritually, under a divine mandate, and is hence holy, and that is comprehensible enough. But the hard thing, the greater thing to grasp is the fact that sacramental marriage engages not only man and woman, but God as well. Indissolubility becomes not simply a divine dictate, as it was originally. It is an inviolate extension of the Divine Presence into the very fabric of the union itself. Union with God is of course the essence of all the sacraments, the thing they are made to do. But whereas the others engage a man to God uniquely, one to one, this sacrament engages him so along with another. In the mode of divinity these two are so truly joined that while each retains his mortal existence, there can be no question of autonomy. What is so joined can never again be isolate, can never again act as if it were not joined, as if no essential union obtained. For the nature of the join is love, God-love, *caritas*, and it is this which gives it its unique force; it is this which the Church refers to when She asserts the absolute indissolubility of the sacramental marriage bond; a focal force which cancels out the primacy of all the affective dispositions, the love in love consumed, the love in love transcended. It is the supernatural state, and in its term all natural love is meant to be engaged, and the sexual approximation transcended. To engage the natural sexual approximation outside either the transcendental sacramental marriage or the basic pre-sacramental one, is to render one of those deformations seen occasionally in nature, where things not intended have by some destructive force been yoked in violence. And that, essentially, is what she and I had created—a caricature of a holy state, a deformation rather than a union: the strained posture of two desperate hearts yoked in violence.

And though I now realize that both of us had hedged our previous unions too deliberately upon evasion and positive intentional disbelief to have constituted true validity, the matter does enter the consideration of the Church at the juridical level; She legislates not only for the individual fulfillment, but for the very character of the social fabric itself, and She refuses to jeopardize the "greater good" of the latter despite all the affective appeal of the former. Her grasp of the wholeness of the well-being of man is too profound to be so easily distracted. Given true testimony, true proof, She will indeed show Herself to be the most beneficent of mothers, but She will not imperil the consciences and the souls of many, that an occasional unfortunate might find a bit of earthly happiness.

As for us, She had only our record by which to judge, by which to estimate the claim of our sensibility against the claim of the broader social integrity, and the record was clear: two technically valid marriages, nor any scrap of evidence for another interpretation, saving only our personal attestation—and the attestation of ardent lovers has not, alas, proved of very great objective reliability. In our original unions we had each been free to contract marriages, but neither of us had given full interior assent. Her reservation had involved indissolubility: she no longer interiorly acceded to its supernatural character nor its divine mandate, its essential permanence. To this same reservation I had added that of procreation, the getting of offspring, prime end of the marriage contract itself. When it came to our own "marriage" she and I had indeed given to the contract full and absolute interior assent, without reservation, but we were by then not technically free to do so, and the Church could not acknowledge what had in fact no actuality. Our confused background was flatly against anything She ever taught or recommended. When one has made mistakes, the cost is usually of consequence, but none the less necessary. When the Sacrament of Matrimony has been thrown away, the Sacrament of Penance remains. And we took up our penance with a suffering joy, because through that suffering we had seen God.

As I conned these things in the new hours of our disseverance, calling back to my mind the great gifts she had revealed to me, I wanted, as I say, to make witness in a clear assertion, and in my verse establish the fullness of my debt. I remembered that I had written a series of poems to her when I first met her—a kind of contemporary Prothalamion, where the ritual is forsaken and only the intensity retained. It had the structure of a sequence, with two rhymed pieces for the opening and the close, and placed beside them two dominant sections, the first a kind of prologue, but the last the climax, the resolution, and between came the body of it, a series of lyrics that caught up the strangeness, the newness between us at that time. I thought now to write a closing sequence for counterpart. If that was the Prothalamion, the song before marriage, let this be the Epithalamion, the song after marriage, in a new and oblique sense, the sadness and the joy. My solstice poem could serve for opening rhyme and the poem of the Damned would make a prologue, for it was in terms of its threat that the action followed. I would write now the series of lyrics that would be its body. I changed the name of the earlier sequence to fit the new circumstance, seeing at last the full purpose in long perspective. I called it *The Blowing of the Seed*, and for inscription chose *the wind that bloweth where it listeth*. There was another sequence, written at the time of the fullness of the relationship, a sequence divided between great despair and great hope, and this I called now *The Springing of the Blade*, and for inscription chose *the cockle and the wheat*. So I would call this final sequence *The Falling of the Grain*, and I proceeded at once to write the series of lyrics that would make up its body, to grasp if I could the essence and the reality, the poignancy and the loss between us, but seen in terms of the thing we had gained, a gain that transcended and made whole the other sequences, for they had now become its antecedents.

And in thinking about what I should write, there came first to mind an incident from the very tag-end of our days, just before the actual hour of separation. We had had a previous invitation from old friends who lived in San Francisco, and we decided to keep it as our last evening out, but to say nothing of what impended. And it was a good evening, with relaxed sociability and agreeable conversation. In the course of it she began to read fortunes from a deck of cards, the sort of thing she could do quite well, with nothing occult about it, but a kind of imaginative insight as she probed the personality, and guessed what had gone into it, and created out of the guess what its future course might be. She did it with the others there, and we were all somehow caught up in the contagion of her imagination; and then she read them for us, for us two alone. It was a kind of beautiful symbolism that she made of it between us, with no one else knowing; but yet they sensed, I think, the sadness and must have wondered what it meant. But it had a way of balancing, of leveling away many unspoken things between us, and made for a depth of resignation and of reassurance that cut below the surface of what we had to achieve. We had been tense; filled, I confess, with the deepest anxieties; so that in the after-thought of this incident, in the aloneness of the house, I drew back into it, to render the essence of it in a poem; and wrote the lyric that was to stabilize the event, so that all it had done for us should not be utterly lost.

  iii. A Game of Cards

The black king fell.
"Sorrow for the king." The black queen
Fell beside. "Sorrow for the King
And Queen," you said, "but love—"
For the red heart rose. "Sorrow
For the King and Queen, but love...."

We read the cards for sport,
But how press back the tears at such an incantation?
You, in the prescience of the truly fated—
That was the thing in your voice, then,
When it rang in the room,
And sorrow and peace were at one in your face,
And you knew my grief,
Which was indeed
Joy.

*"But love, but love—*
*Sorrow for the King and Queen,*
*But love...."*

Most beautiful, wholly tender and true;
Sad prophetess, weep indeed in the soul,
But the smile redeems.

I shall forget many nights but never that.
The moon was out. The last train rested on its ramp,
And all the bridges home were empty of their fare.
The next day was the Lord's. Beyond it
Rose the immitigable week of His great word
Schismatic in our lives.

In the maturity of our peace, the pride of full possession, most regal in the new assurance, I had called us the King and Queen of California. And for amusement we used to affect the role, solemnly, in a grave mockery between us. It was caught up now to echo for the beat of the poem, the sweet and wistful punning of the fatality in which we moved.

That fatality meant death, the absolute cancellation of the self, the being's old determinant, its source of search, its cloudy objective. Now all its values, once most desirable, once held as goods, seen as true tokens of well-being, shock the soul with their wrenched misemphasis. And horror-stricken at the thing he was, at what his life was made, a man stares back along the path he walked in darkness, seeing with dawn the pits that gape on either hand, the long imperiled pursuit. *Will-o'-the-wisps*, they call them, false leads, fireflies of that fictional imagination craving a carnival of merriment out over the swampwater, a dance that time was not to designate, though death was there to keep.

And what is the self, that I turned to it, back in my beginnings, and asked it to lead me out of the morass into which I had wandered? What is it, that I thought it might take me forth onto firmer ground, where my feet might once again be set upon the right way, and those fogs of the fens outsped in my search for surety? Changeable, short-tempered, passionate and blind; indecisive, save in the hot decisions of the blood; uncertain, save in the blind persuasions of the nerve—are these the endowments by which one ever sets the estimate of a guide? And yet how I hung on it! Because it was most familiar and dearest; because it was most lovable; because it was easiest gratified and soonest asleep. Not, certainly, infallible, this I could concede, but what else is? For the self, at least, knows its own wants, that much is sure, and they are truly tangibles: revulsion and attraction, the two talismans of misery and delight. The issue, then, is settled. "Lead on, good brother! Most trustful and most true! Henceforth be my guide!" So shouts the reckless one, the soul, lost in the quagmires, and hoping for a path.

Thus it is that honesty, most salutary virtue, fashions again the betrayal of the self. There is nothing a sorrow feeds on with greater relish than its own lament; nor is there anything more voracious, more hopeless or more pitiable than a sorrow self-fed. It may be honest, a characteristic which militates against an insufficiency of utterance, but hardly against an insufficiency of direction. One of the marks of an age of relativism is that honesty becomes the sovereign touchstone. Honesty, which should be no more than an assumption, an initial guarantee that the speaker speaks in good faith, comes to be hailed as the absolute value. Can it be for this reason that the ages of relativism are also the ages of great autobiography? Having abandoned their absolutes, men can only cry out: "This is the way it is!" The earnest man, who has lost his sense of a final morality, reverts in his extremity to mere self-exposure. "I am at least honest," he will say, with that rueful lift of the head which is as close as he ever permits himself to a true heroism. But this is the point at which his honesty becomes like the greased plank to depravity, for he has in that statement achieved his finality, and there is nothing more in him to hold him in check. Whatever thenceforth he may do he can certainly say, "I am at least honest." This is not to forewarn of his injury to others, but of his injury to himself. Nor think it is to forewarn of his injury to his frame, his body. These may in no wise be involved, for as far as they are concerned one remains contained in the fear of men's disapproval. But there is a place where even that fear is incapable of striking, where even that fear may no longer protect one, and that is the soul. In the soul we are wholly free, and there may sin our heart's full, and never be seen. And it is there that the honest man, who is honest only, is utterly without defense.

Which leads to the disquieting recollection that the road to Hell is paved with good intentions. But there is a Justice, which weighs our conformities against our violations, and accords us our due. And there is a Redeemer, who assumed upon Himself more injury than we can do Him if we foul Him every instant of our puny lives; and rose unsullied; and waits for us, with such reserves of forbearance that we are forever incapable of offending Him more than He can forgive; and will forgive, if only we repent. But we don't have to. It is the simple choice that is asked.

And that is the lesson each who learns must learn for himself; and will look back after a time at his errors, as they lay in his path, like hazards he had to crawl through, with springes and catches, but not at that time known for what they are. As hazards then, let us regard them, and not strut in our scars as if they are the very badges of our worth. And if our honesty is to serve our art, let us be sure we reckon it somewhere near finality. And hope that the self, in its abject succumbings, reveals better than it knows the depths of its betrayals, and somewhat mitigates its guilts.

To us, the honest, the earnest but unprincipled, we who lived wholly contained in the veracity of the senses, the earth was all. Time, History and Reality were essentially processive, sequential. There was virtually no other aspect under which we conceived of them, because our gaze, the gaze of our mentality, the gaze, yes, of our mortality, was fastened upon them, and we saw them only in relation to ourselves, for from the perspective of the world there is very little else.

But to the contemplative, the mystic, this is not so. Reality for him is not so much sequential as simultaneous, realized in the ever-abiding instant of Divine Act. Time is virtually fictive: it exists, but is so deceptive as to radically transform the character of reality to the senses, unreal not in itself but in what it seems. In his gaze, every moment of time, like every segment of Being, is etched in instantaneity. As the light of the sun illuminates a great plain everywhere-all-at-once, so God's gaze fills the whole of reality, and constitutes the unspeakable preponderance of what things are. The contemplative knows, indeed, that what happened in time modifies what now is and what will be, but to him that is almost incidental. He knows that he too impinges upon time, and counts that as well a glory, but it is a glory utterly beyond consideration of what he can effect, which was our glory in the impingement of time. In the depths of his vision the mystic makes no move in terms of effect, as a man would move one thing to effect another. Everything is gauged in the great totality of the gaze of God, and its supreme aspect is that God wills it. Even if he puts hand to mouth to take food, it is not that he might thereby keep alive, but that God wills that he lives, and in such a way. For him, in the gaze of God, life and death are utterly equalized.

Thus the mystic in his vision teaches what time really is. His vision is not to verify his sanctity, but to demonstrate in the lives of men the nature of reality, for our time is the time of our senses, where, not in Being, but in Becoming we are wholly engaged in the consecutive, our mortal context, and our swift determinant, which is our love. It is our great blindness and the source of all our woe, that knowing ourselves only in time we love History as we love our lives.

Loving our lives, loving History, in that ignorance we are indeed pathetic. Pathos is the impact of our ignorance upon History. In the pathetic, our mortality asserts its uniqueness against the Gaze of God: we claim our own, which is a nothing, and which we will not relinquish, and what we will not relinquish is thenceforth torn from our grasp and cast down, and we cry out in the knowledge of our mortality, which is the cry of earth.

It is this, the instinct of its own mortality, which gives the earthly act its rending poignancy, and governs its pulse. This is the force that gives all earthly life its common identity. It is at the level of their mortality that the gopher and the swan, the eagle and the mole find their mutualness, achieve the stretched, imperious urgency which is their abiding impulse and their final undoing, the eternal voice whispered out of the mortal act which says: never again can this be. And the seizure implied there, as if only in that instant could the true identity of existence be fully certified, is the factor which gives the earthly act its impelling character of over-reaching, makes for the pathetic and the ludicrous, the desperate and the droll. And that hunger for fulfillment, which is the resolution of the earthly impulse in its own assuagement, becomes the creature's natural good, seeking to quell its nature there. Thus all creatures, swept up in this importunity, look across at one another and touch on revelation: all sensate things salute each other at the level of that leap. It is this for which they are prized. As we see posited in the exaggerations of the beast our own wrenched attitudes, twisted out of stasis, tipped forward excessively on impingement. Thus it is that the creature-beast in the instinct of its mortality, and the creature-man, struck from the vision of his own immortal soul, fill with the emptiness of all rapacity, feeding upon precisely those assuagements which are most mortal, most of the order of temporality.

But there comes a time when one beholds a new dimension, and the wistfulness has all to be shaken aside, no more to be savored. There is work to be done, spiritual work, the whole regeneration of the ruined and bankrupt world of the past; a whole change of heart and mind, a sea-change indeed, and no looking back. In his urgency one turns to the saints for verification, sees what they made of their lives, faced renunciations to brighten the hearts of such weaklings as we, and out of their very loss built triumph.

And how they stood by me in my need! How they hovered in my house, moved through my rooms, steadied me in my work, consoled me over my solitary meals, knelt with me in my prayers! There was my own St. Augustine, whose name I was to take in

Baptism, for my life had remotely paralleled his, save that I had not an ounce of that tremendous intellect, nor a smidgen of that sanctity. And the incomparable St. Francis, man of the heart's deep joy, who blazed through his age with all the heroic fervor of my own unreachable need, moving across his life's resistances with a declarative frankness I could envy but never approximate, who somehow even in his darknesses never failed to burn with an unclouded intensity. And there were those great saints of the Desert, in whom I saw renunciation carried to its absolute, who had lived out completely the hunger for solitude which I in my morose complicity had never attempted, and who proved its superlative uses in the spiritual emphasis. I felt the challenge of it now, the solitary as supreme contemplative, the challenge of a withdrawal deeper than my life could then support, having not the focus, the hard nugget of spiritual resolution on which to proceed.

And the inexpressible delicacy, the purity of those women saints who through my books moved into the ever-widening orbit of my understanding, teaching me by an incomparable fitness that was, in my separation, like a rare perfume, all the immediacy of the feminine instinct restored to its sheer perfection. I stood gape-mouthed, a dolt, dazzled by radiance: those two superb Theresas, the great mystic of Avila, whose knowledge of the spiritual life marks her near the status of Doctor of the Church, and her sister of Lisieux, out of whose photograph gazes the indomitable countenance of a spiritual Napoleon; the rare Bernadette; the luminous Gemma; the gracious Rose. In them I saw suddenly the terrible warped relationship to women, so twisted and so wrong, that had governed my life, made illuminate and true. Among them my own mother stood forth in my vision serene in her corrective light, all my rancid thwartedness dispelled, tall in her paramount dignity, and I could kneel and ask forgiveness, and pray of these her sisters the grace to purify, to make that warpage right. Beside her stood the women of my life, the two wives of my confusion, the first seen now as was my mother, serene in that clear correction, noble in her essential womanhood, freed of the damaging deformation my crudeness had imposed. The second, freed already as I knew her, smiling in their presence, the radiance of her own sweet sainthood, embryonic but real, that she even then was forging out of the very pain of her denial.

And the saints all sang. As I moved among them, I lived in their jocund company. They taught me of the things I must become in spite of anguish, *through* anguish. They taught me how I must learn the unfailing heritage that bound me back to the prime Renunciation, where the Cross-bearer hung up His strong life, that the weak might recover theirs.

### iv. The Quittance of the Wound

But God is good. Nor has ever, once,
In His keeping of this world,
Worked an evil in men's lives;
Not in all those losses, those takings,
The dark denials each in his time assumes and must ponder;
Nor in the great deprivations exacted of His saints,
When He would seem to have broken them in His bare hand
With His love and His wisdom—
Not once has He ever
Wrought an evil in men's lives.

Only the flawed of heart foul Him,
Only the blind, a fist pinched at the sky,
A mouth smoky with imprecation;
Or that sullen hutch of the heart's embittered brood,
Like the serpent's egg
Hatched out in the breast.

But as for these, His own,
These, who served as His saints,
These, in the luminous purity of their love
Knelt down on their deprivation,
And dipped the very wounds of self
In the painful balm of that compliance;
And let that piercing Finger
Probe to an inmost hurt,
Nor shrank to be traced.

These have taken the plight a trust entails,
And not doubted, and have counted
Every tremor of the soul,
And that long cry of woe
Shut back down into the cropped heart

> As only the cleanliest quittance
> Against the rapture of His face.
>
> And have put forth a hand to take up the loss,
> Though fear be with it;
> And the hand sustains.

No force, with the exception of the miracles, comes through to the expectant heart like the witness of the saints; no force lives so potently in the imagination as their lives live. The miracles, indeed, strike like lightning flashes, erupting out of another world, another realm of being, something utterly unthinkable in the mind's closed perspective, gouging through the substratum of the natural order in ruthless violation. A beneficent act of healing at Lourdes is actually as shocking to the natural reason as the frenzy of the sun at Fatima. Soon each is over, and in its going leaves a hole of incredulity gaping in the mind around the edges of the memory, fitful as a desperately remembered dream. The function of a miracle is to give hope, to banish doubt, to shake out of complacency, and these it certainly does.

But the life of a saint witnesses to a continuity that engages the power of belief at a wholly different level. Here moved a soul lifted out of the line of the ordinary by an unfathomable force, and its impact grapples by approximation. It is in this light that we compare ourselves. To the soul longing for liberation, ready to relinquish the fetters that ensnare it, dumb with the knowledge of its weakness and ardent for the activating grace, to such a one the life of a saint penetrates like a veritable beacon, a long far ray of hope. One perceives that it *can* happen, that it *has* been done, that we are *not* trapped, that this supernal freedom lies in the realm of the possible. And he starts to correspond ever so little, a new twist here, a stronger tug there, and bit by bit the way starts up.

To many another, however, the witness of the saint, the challenge of the saint, is a scandal and an affront, and he repudiates it as a lie, a blatant fabrication. Impelled in the preoccupation of the natural order, contained, inevitably, not only in its fulfillment but as well in its abuse, he is shocked by the gage of supernatural demand,

and he spurns that witness in an act of sullen fury or one of shocked surprise, of bland condescension or of cold contempt.

This capacity of the saint to drive reaction right or left, as the case may be, was forcefully brought home to me early in the process of conversion. Late one afternoon I was talking with a friend who had long been active in the radical movement, but whose interest, like that of many another, had been smothered out by the crushing issues of World War Two and the unfaceable demand of postwar politics. The Depression had receded in significance to the status of a mere historical episode; the unions were rich, well-placed, virtually another form of Big Business. Russia had long since sold out the Revolution, and with it the hopes of millions, and although my friend had been affiliated with an anti-Stalinist wing from the start, nevertheless the crushing, snow-ball effect of Soviet capitulation represented, across the years, a disillusionment too vast to withstand. He had in consequence become somewhat morose in his disappointment, and was endeavoring to reintegrate his life around his job and his family. His unconcern seemed impenetrable.

But not when I told him of my interest in the Church. He came to life, incredulous and aghast, and the inquisition was on. I could not face up to it, however, but pulled off in evasion, too tender for the stamina of rebuttal, too green, unsure, weak. I had no answers. Probing my armor for chinks, he discovered nothing but gaping holes. At last, suppressing in pity the lifting curl of his lip, he made some off-hand concession about still being friends in spite of it all, and turned to go. "I suppose," he said in conclusion, "it comes down at last to the exemplar on which a man chooses to model his life. For me, it's Eugene Debs. For you..." Here he paused, searching his mind for the precise parallel. Then his mouth pulled down wryly. "For you," he concluded, "it's Mother Cabrini."

I was stunned. I think no Catholic can fully experience the depth of intellectual insult buried in this remark. In the current collapse of familial loyalties the time-honored denominations of religious, denominations actually based on the soundest of human affiliations, are no longer equitable with anything but sentimentality and glibness. Brotherhood, Sisterhood, Fatherhood, Motherhood, insofar as they represent abstractions, were so sentimentalized by the Victorians and corrupted by the bourgeoisie as to become to later generations things of positive repugnance. My own father was a member of a businessman's service club, and he attended meetings wearing on his lapel a celluloid disk bearing the type-written appellation "Brother Louie"! Now, as a religious, I often encounter the suppressed ambivalence latent in these terms, the tear between what they stood for in themselves and what modern sophistication has made of them: to announce myself to my pre-Catholic friends as Brother Antoninus is to literally make their flesh crawl. Here for the first time I felt the impact of it driven like a demolition ram to the very center of my fragile sympathies. Mother Cabrini. In the mentality of my early conversion it had all the connotations of smothering maternal sentimentality, cheap piety, and sickening conformism.

I wanted to run after him in outrage. The exemplar of the Christian is always Christ, and he holds Him above every comparison. Moreover, there are scores of stalwart saints he will not hesitate to place beside any hero of the secular world. But this Mother Cabrini gambit was shabby and unfair. How dare he foist upon me such a weird apposition, which I had not elected, and could not concede!

It was too late. He had indeed delivered the knockout and sauntered away, and I shambled home through the late afternoon, a dungeon of chagrin. But as I turned the episode over in my mind, ingesting its complex of inference and implication, I began to recover myself. As a pacifist in World War Two, the name of Debs had always retained a powerful evocative appeal. It is one of those crystallization points in the consciousness of the American radical around which he integrates his closest sympathies. With my background it was no wonder the memory of the man was one to wound with, and the insight of my friend in employing it, to probe, in a word, the depths of my betrayal, was very shrewd. As to Mother Cabrini, I knew absolutely nothing about her. She was still in the news following her recent canonization, the first American citizen to achieve that glory, and it was doubtless no more than this that had brought her name to his mind. As to who she actually was, or what she had actually done, I was totally ignorant, and I dare say he was too. It was enough for him to inflict, and for me to suffer, that she simply be called "Mother."

Still, even so early as this, I had come far enough to be aware of certain distinctions. And as I mulled through the fags of my disconsolation, I had the sense to recall them. Mother Cabrini is a canonized saint. To be a canonized saint means that you have had at least four miracles to your credit, and that puts you in a category not to be approximated by the most superb proponents of natural morality. By the time I had reached home, having no more information about her than that, I had come to my decision, and it was one of the stepping stones of my life. "Very well," I said to myself, "I'll take Mother Cabrini. If the Church has chosen her, so will I. Not that I'm keen on this black-and-white, Debs-vs.-Cabrini, mutually exclusive equation, which goes to prove nothing at all. Eugene Debs will always represent in my mind something splendid, native and singularly American, wrapped up in a whole complex of basic loyalties along with the 'Gettysburg Address,' 'The Man with the Hoe,' and Vanzetti's 'Last Speech to the Court,' and I have no intention of relinquishing any of it. To my friend such an uncritical lack of differentiation will doubtless confirm me as a complete scissor-bill, which, politically, I dare say I am. But it's as far as I go. Beyond that I take my stand with the saints. Any saint. They're in a class by themselves. And, as the theologians say, 'We have got to distinguish!'"

But ever since then the two names have been inseparably yoked in my mind. They constitute a peak or cleavage, a break-over point of my sympathies. Their lives, I discovered later, are strangely parallel, being almost exactly contemporary. They had the same passion for the underdog, the deprived and the dispossessed. They moved in the same world of tenements and raw industrialism, factories and freight yards and foreigners. And yet how far apart they actually were! The one was motivated by natural social justice, the other by supernatural pity. Debs walked like a lightning rod through the social violence of his time. In the face of its manifest outrages he would not be silent and he could not be cowed. He caught up the conscience of America as perhaps none other of his generation did. His integrity was astounding, and it was at the root of his tremendous appeal. Now, in mid-century, it seems impossible of belief that in 1920 he actually polled nearly a million votes as Socialist candidate for the Presidency, while languishing in solitary confinement in Atlanta Prison for his World War One pacifist stand, and this in a country which only a few months earlier was throwing conscientious objectors into latrines! Truly, my friend could have done far worse than Eugene Debs in his choice of exemplar for the pattern of his life.

But Mother Cabrini, whose smile filters out of her photograph illusive and indefinable in its diffuse radiance as sunlight on water? She flitted with the hovering fragility of a moth through all the violence in which Debs was so passionately engaged, and the headlines of her time knew nothing of her. This is not the place to recount her achievements, and she herself would discount them. For all I know, every hospital and orphanage she ever built has been razed to the ground to make way for more gigantic, more modern, more ultra-efficient structures. But what she wrote on the hearts of her generation is ineradicable because it was written not on earth but in Heaven. She used people and money which any self-respecting anarchist would have spurned as corrupt, but those she helped with it, the lost, the homeless, the hopeless, the weak, the dead, scrawled her name all over the Gates of Paradise. Debs may possibly be a saint. Who knows? Perhaps, after he died, someone even prayed for his intercession, though given his views it hardly seems likely. But the aspirations that went up with the passing of the Little Smile, the evocation that thundered the silence of eternity, tells more about her, what she did, who she was, where she went, and the estimate of her worth, than a thousand testimonials in the daily press.

What the world does not understand about a canonization is that it is something forged out of the needs of multitudes. A canonization is not merely some kind of official ceremony in which the Church rewards, *post mortem*, for Services Rendered To The Cause, Her various worthies. Someone was on their knees. Someone, usually thousands of someones, suffering the whole frightening list of incurabilities and afflictions that beset the hapless race, were begging day and night for relief, begging it through the aid of an unquenchable spirit whom they knew in their hearts to be even then before the awful tribunals of the Most High. People in such extremities are not disposed to waste their time unless they have a consummate belief in the supernatural attributes that that soul embodied, and the absolute certitude that she is in a position to do some good. The Church generally requires the elapse of fifty years before a cause may be introduced. In the case of Mother Cabrini the limitation was set aside. Within twenty-one years she was beatified, within twenty-seven came the canonization. It was the work of millions, and they stretched from Canada to Argentina. I am afraid it is a testimonial which the Socialist Candidate from Indiana simply cannot touch. The two are in utterly different categories of being.

So it is that the witness of the saint drives through the web of human resistance, and makes clean a purpose, and burns the wistful wavering into a thing of certitude. But when the wistfulness will not wholly go, but recurs, in its waves of poignancy, as time deepens, drawing back and back, until all detail partakes of that luminous clarity the look of loss affords, each exquisite action of touch or response all mingling at flux in the strangeness of isolation, then the soul finds its way through new dimensions, new proclivities. So that in the times you permit yourselves to meet, bringing the spiritual solace which only the each of you can give to the other, in these times, then, the fullness of all the meaning, and the forsaken music, are somehow not forsaken at all, but only subtilized, harmonized, deepened, made pure and lowly, blown back through those blooming petals of the mind where all tears are laughter, and the laughter lives forever.

v. The Crowning of the Queen

So that you, too, whom I have loved,
Who have worn my name as wife,
Which was my pride in your wearing;
And I beside you, on these streets,
Knowing myself king indeed with such a queen—

You now have laid aside that queenship of the king
To take another kind of crown,
And I see how purity,
Assumed into the unrancorous heart,
Has lifted from your face a sorrow's cleft,
And made you radiant—a love
Greater than ever yours or mine,
Who in our humanity
Could but work through these meshes
Toward that wide comprehension
Where God keeps His own
In the grandeur of His own.

So do you now move through my mind,
And in your queenliness are still supreme,
Who have that gentleness
The deeply hurt but purely healed
Bring back to the world.

The hurt and the healed. And between us, most lucidly now in its tentative disclosure, like the faintly-sprung grass of Advent, that has tasted late-autumnal rain and now slits its crust, the subtlest trace of green in the gray, so too between us we bore already the trace of that divine affliction. And striving to regain, on some spiritual level, the approximation of a rare felicity our bodily presence had always ordained, finding out that the absence no similar poise perfects, our lives hung on in our own great need of such witness, this witness of the saint, in the knowledge and hope that we could forge from our weakness a taller resolve, see prefigured the rare air of a death that we perhaps, in our own witness, might one day be given to die.

For death indeed is a long coming, and a slow coming, and one never accommodates it. And to learn it by day, by night, hourly, by the minute, is as terrible a teaching as most blank deaths. In the death of a saint (the saint is she who has learned how to die) is achieved all the totality the scattering flux of inconstant life has never permitted. She has been made ready, daily; rehearsal, shall we say, after rehearsal; dying daily, dying in the look and the gesture, dying in the turn of the head, dying in the smile, the grave gaze of compassion, dying in the selfless unending heroic act that rises out of the iron trap when all within her cries to remain deep-sunken down on its old inertness—until, perfectly conditioned by that slow seasoning, groomed to the immaculate demand of the last great role, she moves toward the hushing darkness where Death, like an experienced partner, confident, awaits her, and walks with her out into the blazing arena, and turns to face her, the matchless insouciant protagonist, previous to whom all opposition has been mere by-play. This is the arena the world never sees, or rarely; but pitched about it the ranked hierarchies of Heaven circle it in. Above are the tall choirs of the angels, tier upon tier, stretching up out of sight, in the limitless reaches of the beyond; and near at hand, bending forward in their earnest intensity, their faces radiant and serious as they lean to regard, are the rows of all who have done it themselves, the calm inhabitants of Heaven, the ones who have their reward.

In this arena time loses its whole capacity to deceive. I think of St. Catherine of Siena, taking so many terrible weeks to die, and every hour of it erect before that celestial grandstand, fulfilling the last great affirmation, the final gesture of the beautiful drama that was her life in God. "In Thy nature, eternal God, I perceive my own nature. And what is my nature? My nature is fire." This fire burned her till she blackened, till she shriveled away, till "the skin," in the words of a witness, "rested on the bones without anything between." One remembers Job's "My flesh is wasted away, my skin cleaves to my bones, and there are nothing but lips about my teeth." Offering herself as a propitiation for the sins of the Roman people, who even as she died were plotting the life of the Vicar of Christ, she cried out to God in her intensity of prayer: "Invite them!...let their hardness of heart be ended!...punish their sins upon me!...Behold, here is my body!...let it be the anvil on which Thou breakest their transgressions asunder!"

I think of the maiden of Lourdes, racked on the gridiron of her immolation: "No, not consolation but strength and patience!...I am all flayed!...I am being ground as a grain of wheat!" I think of the Little Flower in her matchless agony: "Only a drop! My tongue is not parched enough!...O God, be pitiful to me!" I think of Sister Elizabeth of the Trinity, exalted in her nine day crucifixion: "O Love, Love, Love! Consume my whole substance for Thy glory!...I am going to Light, to Love, to Life!"

And all outside the convent the world of men moves through its web of finite contingency; time flows with hardly a ripple over the sunken rocks of their lives. The cities, vast clots of restlessness, focal points of a hectic kinesis, at dawn are plucked on the muted strings of their own awakening, blending at noon to a broad tonality, rising toward dusk in the swell of full crescendo, subsiding beyond sunset to slow-paced night and the long murmur of quiescence. Remote hamlets and hidden villages, webbed by the thin lines of communication, enact each in isolation the miniature pulse of that ebb and flux, and on the far-fallen farms the ploughman, incognizant, stoops in the brutal furrow. All these, element by element, in the thick uncomprehending dream of human life, all these devolve, sustained in their fitful shadow.

Even, perhaps, the convent itself does not grasp the deep engagement of that perfect role. A sister is dying, but there is nothing untoward about death in the cloister: it is all in the pulse of the actual. The nuns go about their tasks in the intentness of preoccupation which comes with time to constitute the religious mind. But under that roof and in that room this bed of inexhaustible anguish has become for a moment the hub around which it is all turning, revolving in a vast gyration, gaining pace as the agony mounts, faster, ever faster, until at last in the supreme intensity of its revolution, it achieves the floating suspension of a kind of divine stasis, as up from the center of a whirlpool the enormous walls mount skyward in fearful silence, hanging faultlessly in supreme expectation, while down in the deep pit of that death, at the excessive center, the mute face of the saint, white and death-drenched, stares up out of eyes blind beyond all recognition. Then, suddenly, surcease is given. The ineffable effect collapses in thunder, and she is freed forever.

    In such deaths as these the earthly mastery of the body achieves a new and essential function, the office of torturer, but it is not by election. This is hardly what the body has asked for, nor ever expected; not at all what it reckoned. The body has other needs, other uses, uses all its own, and all its own were its delirious engrossments. It has its particular version of Heaven, and it can never believe that this leads there. Screeching all its nerves in the terror of that intensity, it breaks itself back now into a dream of convergence it thought unachievable. We too, she and I, isolated in our bodies before their time, having touched out of season and been wrenched apart, punished in the wrenching for what they had coveted and indeed gained, we too could look toward the deaths of saints with a gathering comprehension. For us, it was the body that had led our souls into sin, and even now it was by the bodily deaths of countless unknown saints that the sin was lifted in expiation. And having come into the knowledge of such an excoriate interdependence, what can one do but take hold of himself to work a correction here, though he makes no more than the bare acknowledgment, speechless before the living torture his crimes have wrought?

    And so it is at last that the body, which has been so long a glutton and gone gorged, is taught now his proper place, taught in a stern teaching. The lord of the bone's marrow, having held the mastership so long, where now is his old dominion? He whom your thought played beast to in his salience, provoked in his slumber, and concurred in his claim, what has he become? A poor dog only, who heels when the voice sharpens. Until in that firmness of the voice great victories are daily gained with most astonishing ease, and one who had been a craven slave blinks his eyes at his masteries.

    In the sexual act, especially, this body had lain as a king, in whose lordly domain exulted the lavish rule of the senses. Once monarch of all that kingdom, now, despite his old eminence, he lives in exile, sullen and morose, brooding upon his past triumphs, his fallen glory. Made safe in exile, conquered at last and banished, let that claim of the body be given its due, and then be done with it. Serve notice if you must, in its final acknowledgment; salute the theme and the impress, and then, by God's transcendental grace, call it quits forever.

    vi. In the Ripeness of the Weed

And now it is summer,
And the strong weed
Shoulders the fence,
And the weak weed
Scatters,
And all things hold increase.

And the summer burns,
And I remember mornings
Risen one from another,
But must put aside that thought now,
Save maybe in rising
To note but the single
Print in the bed.

But there is a greater
Glory that one may come to,
Whence even that other glory
Gets its flame—
This we take.

Therefore do I salute that magic of yours
This last time in my poems, my wife—
We who clasped in the high try at holiness
Where holiness never could be;
And are now, since we must, at last content
To seek where it more purely is.

And the strong weed
Seeds, and the weak weed
Scatters, and I see in them each
A glory of God;
And am made grateful,
That of His help

> Can put down now the pride of the flesh,
> (Which had not, heretofore, been my ability)
> And am humbled,
> And not given to rankling
> (As I was),
> When the ripe weed
> Seeds, and the weak weed
> Scatters.

Quits it must be, indeed. And though this may suffice a man in the shaping crisis of renunciation, a great deal remains before the body can ever be said to have had its due. For in the erotic life, there is the tingling intensity of the teens, and this is founded on curiosity; and there is the muscular activism of the twenties, and that is founded on discovery; but the deeply-moulded physicality of the thirties is founded on experience, which is ripeness, and feeds on known needs, and the slow prolongation of custom, and its hungers move deep, and deep are its assuagements. So that those who renounce in the later thirties renounce to the depths, and the ache of that renunciation is the ache of the whole inner world.

And in the quietude of separation one perceives the finality of the thing he has gladly renounced, and knows the finality as the depths of its nobleness. In its essence of union all men, all women, perceive its seriousness; even as pagans we called it holy. But its true perspective does not end but only begins there. In complete Catholic wedlock, elevated to the glory of a sacrament, the union is almost supreme in the hegemony of earthly acts. Only the priest, in the Consecration of the Host, surpasses it, so essentially creative is it, the creation of a soul, so closely does it approximate the very faculty of Godhead.

There is a persistent, under-occurring attitude of Christian piety, in this country rooted in the psychological remains of continental Jansenism yoked to the native puritanism, which suspects sexual delight itself of being sinful, so that marital "chasteness" would limit the act to a kind of token performance, a sort of minimum fulfillment of the matrimonial obligation, in which while pleasure might accrue accidentally, to prolong or to savor would be somehow indecent. It is a view whose day, fortunately, is over. For to renounce sex, as a man fasts, cleanly, in full knowledge, for the sake of a principle, is one thing. But to nibble and be afraid, to taste and turn away, when the invitation has been accepted and the banquet is spread, why, this is mere meanness.

In the joy of His creation God does not stint Himself. Nor does the poet, in his great vision, renounce the fullness, the vivification and the impetus of his art. Rather it is only out of his whole intensity that the deeper art is fashioned. He fashions out of the magnitude of the abundance pouring through him, and if he so much as taints that abundance with his inhibitive scrupulosity, his very art will suffer. In this analogy, note well I do not speak of grossness, the savagery of the brothel thrown on the marriage bed, the coarse indignities of fornication and rape, the cravings of seduction, the lurid provocation of the thrill. But the sexes know each other only in the fullness of union; and in the family, where the whole future of man is formed, where there is not the fullness of this knowledge, the deficiency strikes deep. The husband who knows not the wife, in her deep quiescence, her intense receptivity, the naked depths of her soul and the slow poetry of her flesh, is a man who stunts himself in his capacity for fatherhood. The wife who knows not the husband, in the explorative liberation of his act, his range, his male penetration and the crowning mastery of his flow, bearing the God-given seed from his innerness to her innerness, is one for whom the meaning of motherhood will not be whole. These are the ignorances that damage the very psyche of the race, if not crucially (for indeed the knowledge of God suffices), then supplementally, surely; for the fact of children, of souls, in the intense and lovely seriousness that is God Himself in His creativity—this is true innocence. To fail in such recognition is to fail in responsibility, and at a fundamental level. It is to be content with mere sufficiency, and that, in the consequence of the children, is a kind of crime. Because they lack full knowledge of themselves they lack full knowledge of their children, yes, and knowledge of God. For God has given them this means, this freedom, to fashion in joy as He fashions, and instead they fashion but dutifully and shrink from the responsibility of the joy of all art, which is the joy of knowledge and of love. "I tell you not as servants but as friends." He Himself has said it.

Someone has noted the identity of the Hebrew words for cognition and coition. "And Adam knew Eve his wife and she conceived and brought forth Cain saying: I have gotten a man through God." Assuming the chronology of Genesis to be correct, one cannot help speculating whether if that significant event had occurred before rather than after the Temptation, our whole history might not have been different. Eve was not yet the thing she was meant to be. Was it that she did not *know*? Was it knowledge, the knowledge of being, the knowledge of the flesh, of love through flesh, she lacked? And in her insufficiency succumbed? At any rate, like Lucifer, she seized too soon what would have been given freely in time. But had she *known* Adam, really comprehended him, in the soul and in the flesh, might she not have scorned to have bitten such bitter fruit?

These speculations, if not theologically precise, are at least interesting, though no Catholic could maintain the act alone is the very purpose of marriage, its aim and its end, with children to be adjusted to the act, rather than the act to children, which is the modern view. But it certainly is the beginning of life. Everything we are is gathered out of this generation; even our souls come to us only through its focal energy. The Church Herself is born through it, eternally renewed through it. In marriage not to know it, not to comprehend it, not to love it, not to revere it, is to disdain one's origins, the gift of one's life. And disdain is the egg of lust.

The responsibilities of parenthood strike into the most remote areas of human accord, and in their consequences they are indeed fearful, but so are all responsibilities, equally inescapable. And as in any responsibility, fear vanishes in the way of faith. Between man and wife this is the way of openness, a consummate faith in the living God who has given them to each other, and through whom they give themselves. Their children will move in freedom, because they move in the atmosphere of deep accord, which is to say of understanding. Woe to them, woe to their children, woe to the race, if they draw back, refuse the joy with the justice, the magnanimity with the means, the generosity with the gift. In their infectious insufficiency they will breed a race of insufficients, miserable, runts of the self, whose souls have lost perspective, whose hearts are lame with fear.

Runts of the self indeed, cramped in its confines, but what of those who never learn its limits? The function which prudery smothers on the one hand incaution kindles on the other. Husbands and wives, dreaming through aimless hours at light inconsequential tasks, visionless, the body's stored capacities throttled on inaction, a technical age's paper existence, and the repressed libido deeply disturbed by the constant flow of erotic stimulation—these bring home to one another a suppressed unrest no intercourse can assuage. Out of their frustrate hearts they seek in each other a focal surge they have not learned to source, for they have not seen its term. There is no perspective. Marriage is discovery, slow growth, and these may learn it, but they waste years. And O the lacerations of those wounds, the injury and the anguish, the moaning and the loss! They overbear the abused faculty in their blocked contention, clawing each other for a word the mute tongues of flesh can never utter. The plunge for pleasure drives them beyond all bounds. Some of them, dreading deceit, feign passion, excite to lewd excess, that the marriage bed may slake and exhaust what is feared will flow elsewhere. Some out of mere boredom work up a holocaust, dredge between them a shuddering joy, rush on stupor. Some hate, slay each other with the violent act, strangle in the embrace, rend and dismember. Some plunder, force honey from the hive, grab the gift before it is given. Some cheat, haggle with their bodies over every ounce of affection, drive hard bargains, snatch by stealth what would gladly be free. Some indict, throw down their sex like a gage, a challenge, a leering affront. Some triumph, beat into brute submission, phallic subjugation. Some are suicides, would-be martyrs, enduring execution night after night, skewered on the turn-spit of delicious terror. Most devour, stanch the insatiate appetite, cramming their maws with another's flesh, to topple apart, engorged and replete. And always the struggle, the crafty plan, the feint and parry, the ruse, the forced advance, the alarmed retreat, and, at the crowning kill, the slaying, shuddering stroke."

Catherine of Siena, most delicate saint, watched them in their fitful multitudes blowing through Hell, saying, "I saw in particular those punished who sin in the married state, by not observing the laws it imposes, and seeking in it naught but sensual pleasures." And when her confessor inquired of her why this sin, which was not worse than the others, still received so rude a chastisement, she told him: "Because little attention is given to it, and consequently less contrition is excited for it, and it is more easily committed."

For the amoral manuals of our day indeed assure husband and wife that what obtains within married love may know no bounds, no act is vile, and so they rage with joy and fall, having not yet love. The impure heart fathers the impure act. The impure heart in the impure act revels in abandon, fights off reason and conscience, exults in its toiling conquest. These fall on each other spending their stored rapacity, or cower speechlessly behind their fascination, horrified, filling with the increase of revulsion their lacerated nerves. Then impotence palls them. They weep in the fine agony of incompletion, and midnight sees them wrenched apart, fitful in sleep, and dawn finds them crawling back toward the compelling abrasion that blisters and burns and never heals. The unsuckable wound.

Farewell, poor souls. I see you in your inner ruin, and know the remedy, but you have no heed, you will not be told. Suffer it out, most miserable, pale wounded warriors of the night, pale fitful fighters. Time is too much for you yet, life is too much. Break your pride on your own aggression, but learn! learn! When grace comes to you, seal up the crevice of those fractured hearts, and stand aright. I leave you.

For I too in the act of flesh, in the fleshly sin, had sought the engagement with that total intensity only God deserves, only to God is due. I had come to her after whole years of sexual segregation in the isolation camps of the government, and in my anarchism sought to strip from my mind every vestige of conventional inhibition that might spoil the free flow of my sensibility, release all the turgid eroticism, banked up and compressed in the thwart blockage of divorce and alienation, bitterness stacked on bitterness, cross-thatched, inwound, inter-threaded, the log-jam of outraged pride, and the raw reaction of the proud man cuckolded, and helpless to prevent his own debasement. She too had endured the outrage of repudiation, rejection and divorce, in a soul more alive to the exquisite torture of these deep familial equations than my own had been, and having emerged from Freudian analysis, with its positive sexual emphasis and its scarcely-veiled certification of the therapy of release, a certification actually, somehow, reinforced by the profound Catholic consciousness of man's predisposition to sexual sin, here too this blocked suppression, and this strong conjoined inducement, conspired when we met to fling us both together in an extravagance beyond the bed's capacity ever to purge.

Night after night, returning to each other, we took up our annihilation, pouring out the tidal onset of our want. Under that flood-rush inhibition after inhibition, dam after high containing dam broke down, spewed forth its wreckage, strewing the flotsam of those years. All the backwater brackish containment, the stale, stinking, mud-fouled estuaries of our past drained out, sucking back to the most remote bogs and sloughs of the cankered personality, exposing the festered creekmouths, pit-holes, tule-brakes of that corruption, all these sluiced out and burst in the wild spindrift flush of expurgation.

It was an outrush that could have but one conclusion: impotence. And when impotence struck, it struck with the swift crumble of a collapsing tree. In the folk-ethic of the bed a man has one prime purpose, one responsibility: to satisfy the woman. And when he fails his failure exposes to her and to himself the terrible depths of his deficiency. It had happened before in my life, but that was in conjugal intercourse, and I must say that for once the Protestant sympathy and gentle domestic equanimity with which the collapse was taken, the understanding and compassion, were something I can never remember without the deepest gratitude. But this spleenful Latin pride, this compounded Catholic violational sin, was stirred to the depths of its offended sensibility, unspeakably insulted. And when it unwound itself, like a snake coming out of its coil, the inculpating female tongue, laying about it with a fiend's invective, dissected in a kind of diabolical discernment the secret infestations of my pride, till there remained, when she had done, not a shred of tortured self-esteem unripped to tatters.

All this I say, seeing it in the long perspective, not in the least to her derogation. Not in the least do I indict the want of Christian charity, the lacked compassion that should, had it been proper marriage, seen to the terror of my plight, and out of that beneficent feminine intuition I would later know so well, heal the deficiency with slow love, gently restore the depleted energies, lovingly evoke again the desired response, and build once more the crowning consummation that was my primitive propulsion and her civilized delight.

No, the fitness of that vituperation lies in its precise proportion to the sin. Sinful was her anger, but more sinful was our lust, assumed to the stature of our whole attempt to make the sinful act usurp the very godly valuation. We were not worldlings. Rather we were two God-perceptive souls meant for the way of unifying love, but here we had engaged the carnal act outside the divine law, and plunged it to spoliation. We were two souls, endowed, each in our way, with the prime God-knowledge and the supremacy of the mystical attempt. Upon the very shelves of this sin-blistered room the writings of the saints stood by unheeded. Above us on the wall the Crucified shrieked from His nail-holes, twisting before the onslaught of our attack as every lunge of the spasmic loins riddled that badgered brow, our uncontainable violations conjoined to the total human sin that splayed Him there. No, in turning to spend on one another the supreme intensity of our owed acknowledgment we betrayed in fact the utter substance of our souls. And when she cursed me in the virulence of that sin, she sought out of her deepest knowledge to expunge the measure of her treason, and of mine.

For she knew utterly, in her most deep soul, that I was the instrument of her damnation, and in her ferocious insight she sought to brand on my every member the token of that recognition. She had thrown away her soul for nothing but my flesh, and my flesh was fickle. And proved in fickleness, proved in the seething depth of guilt, I endured the fitness of a kind of universal condemnation, lying there with my smashed face thrusted to the wall, incapable of flight, incapable of defense, incapable of any response save this flat and fathomless inertness.

*Incapable!* The word was branded on my being, written with a kind of hideous sulfuric lipstick everywhere upon me, across my back, about my loins, cinctured around my belly, scrawled down my miserable shanks to the vulnerable Achilles heel on which my stiff erectness had been founded, mocking the godlike angelism with which I had endowed myself. The whole indictment, the whole flaunting superscription, she signed with her cruel signature, proving to the world I was a fraud, and she a devil.

Judgment it was, and condemnation, and it was just. And the whip-strong tongue, that vocable of her seething brain, passion's seat, and the skull-piece of her Luciferian gall, that tongue rose to the relishing of its work. Unerring in its slithering delineation it flailed and blistered through the whole screeched wicker-work of my nerves, until my very bones absorbed the residuum of an anguish that was never theirs, took on a kind of rare articulated life, and living, howled. Her room became one walled-in hell, her bed a lake of fire, and I a tortured salamander, frenziedly crawling here and there among her fissures, a thing she would let live only until its flesh took on the precise hue of her condemnation, then she would kill it. The fierce line of her hate, umbilical, became the electric wire that whip-wraps roasting flesh in Texas lynchings, tying it to its fiery phallic doom. Criss-crossed on my frame, gaudy with sparks that feathered what her pitch had tarred, it lashed me. Wrapped round, mummified, layer under layer, cocoon within cocoon of my duplicity I saw all the constraining circles of my pride, charmed ruinous circles, those rings that self-deception year by year treelike had built in me, stand forth revealed. These fused at last to one, till like a piece of stovewood, kilned to a jewel-like rareness, there is disclosed within itself the very principle of its composition, perceived before it slumps to lifeless ashes and is gone—so was I too sustained, upheld upon eternity by nothing but my anguish, and her ire.

We died, that night, both of us, each to the other, I of abuse and she of abusing. We died, exhausted at last of either love or hate, eviscerated of the final frenzy of the self that had impelled us, but even such deaths as these do not redeem. Flesh-gutted, too carnal and too corrupt, not even such reproofs can slake the itch, when the prurient itch is on. The Damned will tell you. This death must seek re-killing fifty times, until the soul, like a drugged girl, waking in a stranger's bed and to a stranger's hands, looks up in horror from the thing she is, or has become. No, not even this could turn us in disgust from the engorged engrossment that egged us to such sickness, the surfeit of such sin. Like dogs drawn back to their own sour vomit, we took up once again the old engagement, seeking as ever to expunge the unexpungeable, gnaw out the ungnawable core no impotence can close. As even dogs must learn their vomit is not food, so in that wan resuscitation we learned that no kinesis of the venereal nerve conjoins the soul to its beatitude. The male, outpouring himself in the unstanchable female cusp till of his very marrow he is bled; the female, spread-eagled on the shattering male propensity till not one lone unoffered, not one last un-jabbed-at crumb remains—each somehow survives, corrupt but unannulable. Only the supreme God can feed this fury. And when the vomiting is done, and the soul, sick, depleted, gutted of the last reserves of its vitality, lifts up its face, and begs of the unsoilable Wisdom the boon of His forgiveness, then does that deft influxing grace, sheer, illusive as one solitary sunbeam strayed somehow through the skewed window-blinds that shade a whorehouse, animate within this shriven soul, which now has nothing left, His matchless hope.

Is this then all? Did God so construe the human soul that what is lost in lust knows no other end than lust, no other mode? Does degradation so despoil that no other use obtains? Some will say so: once a harlot, a virgin nevermore. But grace is more gravid. For the act is ordered to another end, and once reordered, regardless how late, resumes its order in that end. We learn. There is no cleanlier thing to say of life than this: it teaches. We learn. Even out of sin we learn. Even out of lust we gather a knowledge into ourselves. Aimed at beatitude, the truth-made soul, the truth-hungry mind, painfully puts down the gnarl of its disorder, heels from the onrush of sensation, rectifies. Out of such depths, such degradation, we too discovered how to put the act aside, stand free of it, look to a greater truth, and that was true teaching. But yet ere that, we learned a subtle and lovely thing, more sobering of the mystery, something of what the act was made to be. In the burning out of lust a love remains. In the quickening of grace a truth is given. In love and truth, governed not toward sensation but out beyond, toward childbirth, in the longed-for birth reaching up out of appetite toward true hope, through hope and into delight, to the final meaning of the incandescent act God gives to man to make in woman: that act of the bond; that act which makes two one; a meaning touching the summit of all tangibles. We saw through it to the very film concealing God, the nimbus of creation, saw to such aspect as no other glimpse can give; saw revelation; saw in this ecstasy of vision the universe knit in His procreative love, galaxies grasped in the blinding instantaneous glimpse, the far-flung suns of the primordial night known but as a sheen, a shimmer, flashed across His total insight of pure Love. And having learned through grace to know it pure, saw to the exposed revealment of the human soul, in act defenseless, naked, all self stripped from it, pure ardor, pure quest and utter gift, given in the act the purest testament a soul gives, because we had become God's instrument of true delight, of exquisite intent. We who had debased it saw it purified in the blaze of Christian hope, and worshiped the Christ, ourselves worshiped the creative Christ in the creative act, as Maker, who made Himself take flesh in the Virgin's womb, *non horruisti virginis uterum*, fathered forth, the Self-Begetter. We begged in that act the gracious Christ for the gift of seed to make our own loins fructify each other's, so clothe a soul.

St. Thomas, in establishing perpetual continence as necessary to Religious Perfection, seems to exclude the marriage act as a possible contemplative element as well. First, "on account of its vehement delectation, which, by virtue of frequent repetition, increases concupiscence," and there is a reference to the Third Book of Aristotle's *Nicomachean Ethics*. Second, "the use of venery withdraws the mind from that perfect intentness of tending to God," and the authority, quoted this time, is from St. Augustine's "First Soliloquy." Sex, it is believed, by its powerful influence, increases concupiscence, the disorder between reason and appetite, and distracts the mind from its supreme end, union with God.

For it must be noted, if the references themselves have not sufficiently warned us, that these observations represent not merely the judgment of St. Thomas; they are actually the summation of the whole thought of the Fathers and Doctors of the Church, from the beginning up at least to his own time; and not only so, but the best pre-Christian thought as well. Five hundred years before Christ, Buddha had written:

> The wise do not call strong such fetters as are made of iron, wood, or babbaja grass. But a love for jewels and ear-rings, and intense longing for sons and wife—such bonds do the wise declare to be the strongest. For they drag men down and, although loose, are difficult to break. Men who have cut asunder even such bonds, who have abandoned sense-pleasures, having become indifferent to them, go forth and retire from the world.

And two centuries later pagan Aristotle could tersely say: "In the act it is impossible to understand anything."

Pre-Renaissance Christianity emphasized this point of view so powerfully that modern critics, still in revolt against their formative past, have erroneously accused the Church of frowning on the sexual function itself. This is by no means the case. The Church has always strongly opposed any heretical sect infected with such a notion, insisting, on the contrary, that marriage is good, is indeed a sacrament, and that sex, the act around which the very fabric of marriage is made, partakes of that same indigenous worth. The position of the Fathers is simply this: sex is essentially beneficent, but the ease with which its vehement pleasure draws the mind down from the contemplation of God denotes its special vulnerability to the ravages of original sin. There is no question of *malum culpae*, a sin of moral fault, but only *malum poenae*, the evil of pain or punishment, a kind of innate liability, along with all the other infirmities resultant from the Fall, which does not actually destroy grace, but slows the man down and distracts him on his way to perfection. Their objection was not that the act was pleasurable, but that such intense pleasure binds the spirit. St. Thomas probably phrases it best when he remarks:

> Although this fettering of the reason through the pleasure of conjugal intercourse has no moral malice, since it is neither a mortal nor a venial sin; yet it *proceeds* from a kind of moral malice, from the sin of our first parent.

Now if the theoretical attitude is of ancient standing, as we have seen from the observation of Buddha, then the empirical or experimental verification must be far more ancient still. Over the course of history, man in his search for spiritual enlightenment and mystical union with God has come to a profound accumulated knowledge in regard to the liabilities of the sexual act in the spiritual ascent, and anyone who now seeks to revise the historical dictum, conferring on the act the high status of a true contemplative function, must be prepared to meet the virtually universal agreement of speculative thought on the matter. The Church Fathers, I suspect, would call such an idea madness, a symptom of our appallingly disordered modern world. To think that an appetite of the very lowest human order, a mere physical pleasure, should be elevated to the heights of mystical contemplation! That would be the mind of paganism as they knew and abhorred it, the aberration of dozens of enthusiastic cults, and to see its dangerous myth foisted on Christian spirituality would be to them intolerable.

For myself, I think the ancient tradition can be accounted for in two ways. First, by the relatively primitive character of human sensibility in ancient pastoral societies and its frightful disorder in ancient urban ones. And secondly, by the particular subjective position of the commentators. As to the first, Catholic writers have observed that in non-sacramental pre-Christian man, the sex appetite appeared to be sharply set off within the physiognomy, less assimilated and attuned to the spiritual emphasis, more insurgent. For many centuries Christianity itself struggled to absorb this crudeness of texture, and it was not until the Thirteenth Century and the first stirrings of the Renaissance that a new attitude toward the whole physical world was possible. Chesterton writes:

> The end of the dark ages was not merely the end of a sleep. It was certainly not merely the end of a superstitious enslavement. It was the end of something belonging to a quite definite but quite different order of ideas....It was the end of a penance; or, if it be preferred, a purgation. It marked the moment when a certain spiritual expiation had been finally worked out and certain spiritual diseases had been finally expelled from the system. They had been expelled by an era of asceticism, which was the only thing that could have expelled them. Christianity had entered the world to cure the world; and she had cured it in the

only way in which it could be cured....It was no metaphor to say that...people needed a new heaven and a new earth; for they had really defiled their own earth and even their own heaven. How could their case be met by looking at the sky, when erotic legends were scrawled in stars across it; how could they learn anything from the love of birds and flowers after the sort of love stories that were told of them....We know what sort of sentimental associations are called up to us by the phrase "a garden"...let anyone who knows a little Latin poetry recall suddenly what would once have stood in place of the sun-dial or a fountain, obscene and monstrous in the sun; and of what sort was the god of their gardens.

Nothing could purge this obsession but a religion that was literally unearthly. It was no good telling such people to have a natural religion full of stars and flowers; there was not a flower or even a star that had not been stained. They had to go into the desert where they could find no flowers or even into the cavern where they could see no stars. Into that desert and that cavern the highest human intellect entered for some four centuries; and it was the very wisest thing it could do. Nothing but the stark supernatural stood up for its salvation...they wrote across that great space of history the text: "This sort goeth not out but by prayer and fasting."

As to the second point, the marked subjective position of the spiritual commentators, it must be remembered that they were often converts, men in passionate struggle against an appalling pagan world that had once engrossed them. Furthermore, they were celibates to a man, for it is undeniable that celibacy is a vastly more propitious state for the life of spiritual perfection than is the life of conjugal union. But for the celibate the whole sexual problem is magnified out of all proportion to what it is in simple matrimony, for no force is so disruptive to the serene interior life as the sexual force, being at most a terrible torment imperiling the soul in its powerful deflection, and at least a nuisance and a very great bother. For him, one way or another it is an imposing problem. He can look on it as nothing less than a most vexatious liability in the path of his perfection.

But let us return to St. Thomas as we began with him, positing the objection that the "vehement delectation" of the sexual act increases concupiscence. His authority is Aristotle, but what surprises me is that the text he cites does not, if I read it correctly, support his thesis. For tracing it back we find:

> In an irrational being the appetite for pleasure is insatiable and undiscriminating, and the innate tendency is fostered by active gratification; indeed, if such gratification be great and intense it actually overpowers the reason.

How does the unchecked appetite of the irrational animal apply to the sexual activity of rational man? The conclusion of the quotation indeed supports St. Thomas's second point, the down-dragging of the reason, but his first point, that concupiscence increases with gratification, appears left without authoritative support.

At any rate, as empirical men in an empirical age we will hardly be inclined to trust Artistotle's rudimentary psychology, pro or con, so we must face up to the matter for ourselves, and ask if it is actually true that the common repetition of the sexual act in normal marriage fosters concupiscence. I dare say that the modern chaste Catholic man and wife would not agree—not only the conventional middle-class couple, whose analytical perceptions may perhaps be called into question, but married Catholic intellectuals of both sexes, aware of advanced psycho-analytical speculations as well as the principles of the spiritual life, readers of St. John of the Cross no less than of Freud and Kinsey. And in their negative reaction I think it is unquestionable that modern psychological theory would support them. Is it not the professional opinion that normal, moderately spaced sexual activity stabilizes and harmonizes the whole psychology, dissolves nervous tension, gives both the body and the mind tone and equanimity, helps relate the psychological and the physical into one smoothly operating psychosomatic whole? And in the modern view is it not precisely celibacy itself that increases the pressure, makes for disorder in the basic organism, leads to excess or preoccupation and hypersensitive reaction—all symptoms of imbalance the Fathers would tend to group under the liabilities of "concupiscence"?

I myself am certainly not prepared to go so far; these secular theorists have almost no experimental knowledge of supernaturally motivated celibacy as it exists in consecrated virginity, for it does not enter their offices. It is true an occasional fallen priest, some pathetic alcoholic or fornicator, finds his way there, and his example confirms, one suspects, the analyst's darkest suspicions; but the thousands upon thousands of sane and saintly priests, clerics, brothers and nuns who are the true refutation of the hypothesis never cross their thresholds. But I do believe the witness of Catholic married persons is important, and although I am unable to document it, I am confident as to what their verdict would be.

I doubt, however, that the Fathers would be convinced. They were contemplatives, and thought of spiritual perfection in specifically contemplative terms: the cultural values of the Christian society they created were contemplative values, and all the conditioning elements of that society were gauged to contemplative ends. Grouping all that psychosomatic "tone" under the heading of the merely natural they would thrust it aside, I think, and count any of the resultant liabilities as another ascetic element in a basic ascetic program. And having set it aside, they would go on to consider the supernatural state, and what was necessary to achieve it. As creators of a sacralist culture they saw the supernatural end in a different light than we do. Reality must have been more black and white. Almost none of the fine things of nature could have had too much concern for them, their attitude would be rather one of disinterested respect. Our contemporary Catholic spirit, on the other hand, conceives of sanctity as being achieved through the right exercise of natural goods, goods directed ultimately toward supernatural ends, of course, but nevertheless legitimate preoccupations in their own right; and it rejoices in them as gifts of God. That is the mark of a pluralist culture, the full realization of all natural goods, whereas sacralist culture is ascetic, repudiating natural goods not as evils in themselves but as so much diversion, impediments.

And I myself, rigorist that I am, believe that the sacralist emphasis, for all its oversimplification, is immeasurably the higher one, simply because it is the concomitant of the contemplative attitude. I do not believe the contemporary mentality, intellectual or spiritual, religious or lay, really grasps the acuity of the relationship between concupiscence and spirituality, simply because it has so little profound experience of contemplation itself. The Fathers understood the complexity and subtlety of the fact of concupiscence because as contemplatives they experienced its damage within themselves in a way no activist ever can. Understanding the heights of spiritual receptivity they knew how easily it can be destroyed. I think that contemporary spirituality clings to a kind of intellectual objectification of what the spiritual life, theoretically, is, rather than a truly realized spiritual life understood in its own right—or more properly I should speak of *contemplative* life, in this context, because much spiritual writing insufficiently distinguishes between contemplative and active spirituality. So when the Fathers thought of concupiscence they thought of its damaging effect on the contemplative life, where the modern religious, readily granting the theoretical problem, does not find it too crucial an issue. Concupiscence as it exists in himself has little deterring effect on his activist goals; moderate control suffices him. He tends to rank all that traditional asceticism as frankly naive; crude oversimplification of the synthesized body-soul complex. For there is nothing so unrealizable to the modern empirical mind as true contemplative qualities. Not only does it find itself unable to experience them, it literally drives them off,

With the disappearance, then, of the contemplative attitude in the Western world a whole new perspective, basically deficient in contemplative values, has come into being, just as with modern foods a whole new psychic and nervous texture has come into being. It has another kind of asceticism, this contemporary spiritual emphasis, the asceticism of "service." It readily denies itself whatever interferes with its active goal, and in its readiness to do so its own concept of heroic sanctity finds force. The old dichotomy between asceticism and indulgence is gone. The modern religious systematically dispenses from the entire ascetic norm which for so many centuries served as the chief guarantor of the contemplative life. He permits all legitimate (i.e., non-sinful) pleasures as necessary to maintenance of morale, that psychosomatic "tone" by which high efficiency in a technological world is developed and preserved. Flesh meat, the bane of all contemplative diet, becomes the nutritive staple. Sweets, stimulants like coffee and tea as well as tobacco and alcohol in all their forms; the radio, the phonograph, and now television bringing every variety of dramatic and musical entertainment; cinema, the theater and the concert hall; the vast wash of journalism and literary entertainment—all these are readily absorbed into the context of religious life as basic requirements. A religious may neglect every contemplative aspect of his rule, but let him avoid recreation and he is rebuked. Whatever the professional man of today employs to keep up efficiency and the qualities of his state, the professional religious employs as well, and efficiency, the pursuit of his particular goal, is his justification. He becomes impatient when accused of laxity by people who insist on judging him by the old contemplative norms. That, to him, is romanticism. He has relinquished the great and legitimate goods of marriage, freedom, and a bank account, and by modern standards that is asceticism indeed. It is more; it is heroic sanctity. It is, in a word, the asceticism of "service" and he can defend everything he has retained as contributory to its just fulfillment.

And I believe we deeply suffer from this deficient contemplative mentality; I believe that spirituality, in the sense the Fathers understood it, has become virtually extinct, so much so that I dare say they would hardly recognize the modern religious as being of the same spiritual stamp. There is almost no recollection, no recollected posture or bearing, no recollected speech. We hustle about, arms flying, pace driving, eyes roving here and there to miss nothing, ad-libbing over our shoulder as we proceed. Silence has disappeared. Monasteries are full of buzzers and intercom systems; lawn mowers snarl outside, wax-polishers whine within, telephones shatter day and night with their insistent bleat; even the cloistered contemplative orders have been invaded by high-power equipment, from bulldozers to threshing machines, with the abbot using an airplane on occasion to oversee the monastic holdings.

In this loss the great art of spiritual direction is also waning. For "mystical theology," which was, in St. Theresa's day, the concern of all "spiritual persons," when divergent contemplative practices were subjects of intense debate and experiment, is now the domain of a few specialists, writers who synthesize the utterances of the historic mystics with known theological principles. There was a time when the contemplative had to fear the ambitious director itching to mould souls according to his own pet theories; now the contemplative has difficulty finding a priest who will even take him seriously, and when he does he stands in grave danger of being psychoanalyzed. Despite the advantages that can be listed in favor of the contemporary pluralist emphasis, and I concede they are numerous, many thoughtful people feel that what we have is fundamentally poorer, that when the type of contemplative spirituality the Fathers envisaged was lost, and their remarkable insight into the depth and liability of the concupiscent factor in spirituality was gone, something superior to anything now possible went with it—infinitely superior; and I say it with all due regard to the greatness of modern saints, saints of a heroic and exalted spiritual impress, but saints nonetheless of a wholly different spiritual family. Mother Cabrini was remarkable, but she and St. Mary of Egypt, for instance, seem almost unrelatable, almost opposite species of a great spiritual genus.

Yet whatever its deficiencies the pluralist sensibility is the one we have. I too am a pluralist man, though I have very little use for the emphasis, as I see it in myself no less than as I see it about me. But having it, we may as well take advantage of its several virtues. I have heard it argued that nothing is more dangerous to the mission of the Church than the attempt to impose upon a radically altered mentality practices derived from a situation which has long ceased to exist, an attempt falsifying the spiritual problem and jeopardizing the role of the Church in the work of the world; that there is indeed a sacralist and a pluralist spirituality, but there is not a sacralist and pluralist *sanctity*, that they stand to it as means stand to end, sanctity being simply the adherence, through supernatural charity and in a degree manifestly heroic, to the decrees of one's duty, whatever the state of life or the spiritual epoch in which he finds himself.

Be that as it may, it is precisely in terms of this modern pluralist sensibility that I believe we can at last introduce a reappraisal of the sexual act as a legitimate contemplative element in the pluralist life of modern married people, and hence more deeply spiritualize that life, and elevate the temper of the family in a way perhaps not possible before. But in introducing this reappraisal I must insist that much of the older criteria does not apply; that what occurs in libertinage, for instance, is disorder from start to finish, and proves nothing. Neither do the deliberate misuses occasioned in marriage, for these too are sin, and destroy grace, and introduce disorder, and in no way constitute the even normalcy of the marital function. So too can be ruled out even non-sacramental marriage itself, whatever its virtues and however well-intentioned its aims, for without the use of the great sacramental aids the innate disorders of man will inevitably emerge. None of these conditions therefore or any findings derived from them, ought to be permitted to influence our judgment.

For it is only in terms of the sacrament that marriage, the sexual act, takes on its absolute mystical character, and in it we may look for a union higher than that of the most sublime natural sexual ecstasy. But obviously this mystical character does not thereby automatically protect it from its inherent liabilities: the same psychological factors prevail in sacramental no less than in non-sacramental marriage, and hence we must concede that the dangers of the act are true dangers.

In the initial stages, the so-called "honeymoon," the appetite is very inflammable, and seems insatiable, just as the appetite of hunger in one long unfed is inflamed by the taking of food; but under the sacramental efficacy it is always controllable, presuming there is no basic psychological disorder, no hidden neurosis to complicate the primary erotic situation. After a time the ardor cools somewhat, and the faculty is indulged with more moderation and conscious control, so that in the long later stages of matrimony its character of "vehement delectation" does not, I feel sure, merely by repetition, increase disorder, at least in terms of the prevailing spiritual context. It becomes rather a natural, adjusted moderate thing. Perhaps the threat remains, but it is one that lessens with experience, as Aristotle himself, a pluralist man, has noted: "It is easier to train oneself to resist the temptations of pleasure because these occur frequently in life." In any case, the liability exists only as potentiality, I think, not as concomitant. Thus it is that Aristotle can conclude:

> Hence our indulgences should be moderate and few, and never opposed to principle—this is what we mean by "well-disciplined" and "chastened"—; and the appetitive part of us should be ruled by principle, just as a boy should live in obedience to his tutor. Hence in the temperate man the appetitive element must be in harmony with principle. For the aim of temperance and principle is that which is noble; and the temperate man desires the right thing in the right way at the right time, which is what principle ordains.

As to the second main point of St. Thomas, namely, that the "use of venery withdraws the mind from that perfect intentness on tending to God," we have come, of course, to the heart of the historic objection to sex in the spiritual life. And as before, let us look first at the authority whom St. Thomas lists in support of his position. This time it is St. Augustine, writing in his "First Soliloquy":

> I consider that nothing so casts down the manly mind from its height as the fondling of women, and those bodily contacts which belong to the married state.

Everything that was earlier said about the subjective bias of the ancient commentators applies here with double force. We see in that one coarse expression the splendid drama of the conjugal join reduced to the drab frivolity of a pantry seduction. True, the *Soliloquies* were St. Augustine's first Christian work, written in the paroxysm of revulsion from his terrible attachment of the past. As he himself declares in the next breath: "It is even with horror and loathing that I call such things to mind." But nonetheless it was something he never really overcame. Years later, in the height of his sanctity, as a Bishop preaching in Carthage, he could declare from the pulpit in words literally wrung with anguish: "I suffer torture in my thoughts; I have to struggle against evil suggestions; my conflict with the enemy who tempts me is a daily one, well-nigh an unceasing one." Time and again one sees the mark of it on his work. I am always struck by the pronounced shift in emphasis occurring in his Rule, when, after warning against the various threats to religious perfection, he turns to the matter of chastity. The Rule of St. Augustine is read in the Dominican refectory every week, commonly in Latin, but once a month in English, so that one comes in time to know it almost word for word. And you listen agreeably to his gentle admonitions, his sweetness, gravity, moderation and control; until at last he approaches his old compulsion, and then his breath begins to thicken, the pitch rises, the language takes on a more electric urgency, and soon one sees the sweat upon that agitated brow. He seems in this never to have quite thrown off the traces of his old Manichean liability, and one wonders if, through his powerful influence, it may not have left its shadow on many centuries of Christianity.

And yet, laying aside the subjective difficulties, the speculative ones remain. Mystical theologians tell us that contemplation may be of two kinds, Infused and Acquired. Infused contemplation is God's gratuitous bestowal within the soul, and may not be self-gained. Acquired contemplation has to do with the means by which a man may prepare himself for infusion, dispose himself to receive the infusion when it is vouchsafed. We know that this infusion is first available to us in the Sacrament of Baptism, that it comes to us via the Gift of Wisdom, one of the Seven Gifts of the Holy Spirit; that its continual increase ought to be the line of normal Christian development; and that indeed it will be unless by our carelessness and self-love we fail to make ourselves ready or actually drive out with our sins such infusion as we have received. Hence the great danger of sexual pleasure, with its demand on the senses and its liability to concupiscence, which even if sin itself is avoided might well suffer sufficient misuse to coarsen the spiritual impress, and deaden the soul to spiritual realities. It was because of their profound supernatural awareness, their intense concentration on supernatural concerns, that the Fathers took so extreme a view of any passion that endangered the life of mystical infusion.

The quotations given above are from the *Summa*. In an earlier work, *De Veritate*, when discussing the gift of prophecy, St. Thomas has touched on the same matter. There he tells us:

> Some passions which are aroused from without interfere with prophecy. Thus Jerome says: "At that time when the marital act is performed the presence of the Holy Spirit will not be given, even though the one who fulfills the duty of procreation seems to be a prophet." Nor is this due to guilt, for there is not guilt in the marital act, but to the passion of the concupiscence connected with it....Strong passions of this sort draw the attention of reason completely to themselves, and, consequently, withdraw it from the study of spiritual things. Therefore strong passions of anger or sorrow or pleasure hinder the use of prophecy in one who has received the gift of prophecy.

Apparently, then, for a dispositive element to prepare effectively for infusion, it must quiet or allay the senses rather than arouse and stimulate them, so that the more spiritual aspects of the soul may be free for the supernatural influence. This, as we saw, was the great historic position of the ancient spiritual commentators.

Now in each of these cases, it may be noted, St. Thomas is not speaking of sex in itself, but in its relation to some other end, first to Religious Perfection and next to Prophecy. Would he likewise hold that *of itself* it possesses no element of divine ordination which might, in its own practice, aid the consciousness to greater awareness of God? He seems to say so, but since he has not specifically considered the matter we must be cautious. Furthermore, one's own experience contradicts this. On the basis of practice it appears that the passions do indeed draw the reason to themselves, but, commonly, rather than absorbing it to the point of "overpowering" it as Aristotle says, they seem to correspond to the will and achieve their own direction through that correspondence, going high or low as it does.

Thus if the reason conceives of sex as lust, and the will concurs and so ordains to use it, all the power of sex will concentrate the will on the violation of lust, as an end, a thing to be realized. But if the reason knows sex not as lust, not even primarily as an agent of pleasure but as an agent of love, conceiving of this love as a unifying element, a force whose function is to unite through its instrumental power, achieving together with another loved one whose power and whose love, joined to one's own, combine to hurl these two beings in love up the line of unification toward the end of all love, all unity, which is God—then does not all that previously suspicious vehemence of sexual passion become actually a terrific dispositive element toward an ultimate spiritual realization?

Everything in man seems to be determined by his use of himself, what he wills to do with himself, how he regards his act as end. I have looked at a magnificent landscape and been stunned by the Godhead inherent there so that I was forced to my knees in awe and worship, but the scientist friend who stood beside me saw it principally as geological structure. Again, two men conquered Mt. Everest together, one an Occidental, the other an Oriental. When asked how it felt to stand on that mountain the Occidental replied, "Damn good!"—experience evaluated in terms of kinetic reaction. But the Oriental said, "I thought of God and the wonders of His work"—experience evaluated in terms of the contemplative act. As a final, and, to me, crucial example, one might cite the case of the Christian penitent who uses even the passion of pain, of all passions the most destructive to the reason, as a dispositive element in his own quest for God, participating in the agony of Christ, the passion of pain impelling him up the line of unification, disposing, through the act of love it serves witness to, towards God's own infused bestowal.

Not only so, but if we have had to acknowledge an historical tradition of great antiquity and powerful articulation against the association of sex and the spiritual ascent, we can show on the other hand an equally historic tradition, of even greater antiquity, for their identity. What else do the universal fertility rites of primitive man indicate? And be it noted that the very emphasis of spiritual writers over many centuries argues so close a correspondence as to denote a powerful attraction of one for the other. Sex is the great pitfall in which religious enthusiasm invariably founders. The mystical element in the erotic act and the erotic element in the mystical act merge like man and wife wherever they are brought into approximation. It is their *misuse*, not their incompatibility, that the two traditions actually serve witness to.

And it is this which the history of my own life witnesses as well. I first learned of sex in the gutter, not one crumb of insight or aid did I ever get from home, and all through the impressionable years of adolescence sex kept its aspect of pervasive nastiness. My early sexual experience was stolen and sinful and I hid it guiltily in my heart, being too insecure to master what was virtually a compulsion; rather, I wallowed in it. But at the time of religious awakening, after the baneful years of my father's agnosticism, I discovered the work of D. H. Lawrence, and gained an insight into the natural mysticism of the sexual act. And it was the reality of this natural mysticism inherent in it, which I could experience and hence confirm, that sealed my belief in the existence of God. In spite of all the nastiness of sexual conditioning, a nastiness that struck back indelibly to my most formative years, the essential mystical purity of sex could not be hidden from my soul. It was in nature and in sex that I learned to worship. For years nature and sex were the only mystical realities I knew, and I knew them powerfully, and they kept alive in me the God knowledge and the God desire that brought me to the Truth. These things I find impossible to deny on the hypotheses of philosophers.

This deep sympathy between erotic and religious mysticism has been objectified by much powerful symbolism in man's past, and it has not failed to leave its mark even upon the ritual of the Church, which should serve, if anything could, to certify to the authenticity of the association. It is certainly not in conspicuous abundance, and one is thankful for that, for this is something of which a little goes a very long way, but it is more plentiful than many a puritanical Catholic ever suspects. The plunging of the paschal candle into the baptismal font, "the womb of the Church," on Holy Saturday is so powerful in its evocation as to shake the very foundation of the being, and the fulfillment of this generative movement, and its approximation to the deepest and holiest of our Christian impulses, achieves in this rite a deep and cleanly resolution. Something is made true in it, gathered up and completed and satisfied, and we leave the church fulfilled at a fundamental level.

And who can ignore the intense phallic character of the Cross itself,* the prodigious thrust transfixed by the prone line of the horizontal, male and female interlocked, pinned together by the compelling attraction each has for the other, Christ's passion purifying the basic generative symbol of the race? And in fact it is precisely in terms of such purification that the universally recognized mystical element in the sexual act can come into its own. It is in the assurance of a Christian Sacrament that the act may indeed find its pure mystical focus, protected against the precarious liabilities which imperil it through man's fallen nature and the intensity of its passion. Nor does the Church's insistence that consecrated virginity is the higher state detract a whit from its nobility. (St. Thomas teaches that it is only because of Original Sin that the virginal state is higher; before the Fall the conjugal state was indeed the state of perfection.) In fact, such certitude enables married saints to isolate from their act any corrupting psychological adulterants, purifying it in the ideal of the consecrated virgin, enabling them to use the act *as if* they were virgins, and thus make it their own contemplative means. Hence the act becomes purified, spiritualized, Christianized, and, yes, actually *divinized* in the exaltation of the sacrament, for that is what a sacrament does, it unifies with God. Thus seen, its fault becomes its virtue. Here, in the married saints, utterly gauged toward God, all that intensity will tell, its terrific vehemence launching two clinging souls, unified in a blaze of brightness, into sheer ascent. To consider it merely as a natural procreative function is surely to ignore its profound mystical character, its magnificent greatness.

For I sense a terrible oversimplification in the belief that passion, sensory intensity, is outside any integration into spiritual life, and hence, ultimately, mystical life, simply because it is capable of obscuring the rational faculty. (Actually that very obscuration of consciousness is itself a mystical phenomenon, one of the characteristics of the mystical state.) On the basis of experience it seems rather that the rational can through its superior intention direct the sensory intensity toward a corresponding spiritual focus, the will governing either for good or bad as it chooses, elevating high up into acute spiritual realms, using the very intensity as impulsion, or else collapsing and debasing into something subhuman.**

And indeed I have been shown an unpublished thesis, "Medieval Theology on Conjugal Love," by Fr. Fabian Parmisano,

O.P., in which this very relationship between passion and reason is shown as the formulation of St. Thomas himself, providing the philosophical verification for what was in me no more than an intuition. St. Thomas writes (*Summa Theologica*, 1a-2ae, q24, a3):

> The passions of the soul may stand in a twofold relation to the judgment of reason. First, *antecedently*: and thus, since they obscure the judgment of reason, on which the goodness of the moral act depends, they diminish the goodness of the act....

Here we have the heart of the ancient, historic objection to the sexual act as a constituent in the spiritual life, in both Occidental and Oriental spirituality. The power of the passion draws all concern to itself, obscuring the finer, more delicate overtones of intellectual and spiritual awareness that is man's noblest activity. No one who looks about him can possibly deny the truth of this observation. But that it is the *only* aspect, experience fails to verify. And to so confine it will be seen as an oversimplification, an abuse of truth. For St. Thomas goes on to say:

> In the second place, *consequently*: and this in two ways. First, by way of redundance: because, to wit, when the higher part of the soul is intensely moved to anything the lower part also follows that movement; and thus the passion that results in consequence, in the sensitive appetite, is a sign of the intensity of will, and so indicates greater moral goodness.
>
> Secondly, by way of choice: when, to wit, a man, by the judgment of his reason, chooses to be affected by passion in order to work more promptly with the cooperation of the sensitive appetite. And thus a passion of the soul increases the goodness of the action.

There we have it, precisely as experience confirms. St. Thomas was not referring here specifically to the relationship between sex and contemplation, but surely the principle stands. Nor was Fr. Fabian seeking to do other than defend St. Thomas against the modern charge of puritanism, yet I think I can find no more crucial support for my own concern than this paragraph from his paper:

I have used the term "imperating" as synonymous with the "summoning up" of passion which St. Thomas considers desirable in the pursuit of good, and I have used it with a purpose: in order to suggest, to those familiar with it, St. Thomas' doctrine on the function of Charity (*Caritas*). They will recall that Charity, according to Thomas, not only *elicits* supernatural love for God and neighbor, but also *imperates*, "summons up" our *natural* loves and directs them toward supernatural God. It is simply a particular instance of Thomas' general doctrine that grace does not destroy, but presupposes and perfects nature. Here in St. Thomas' treatment of passion in general we have a further particularization of that doctrine, and in his treatment of passion in the conjugal act, a further particularization still. Natural love, human love, passionate love can and does have a place in God's scheme of things as St. Thomas saw it—let but its object be good and Charity direct it into God.

As we regard this matter it ought to sober us, for here we observe how a position of great historical certitude, one verified by many acute spiritual writers and theologians and saints, even adopted by St. Thomas himself, is shown to be not definitive. Considering the sexual act as an *extraneous ingredient* in the spiritual life he was forced to reject it, for that was the only point of view from which he, in his historical situation, could regard it, judging it under its *antecedent* aspect. But all the while the principle of the operation of passion under its *consequent* aspect remained unapplied to this particular possibility, for apparently the mentality of that time simply did not consider the sexual response from such a perspective. And we see how careful we must be not to deny on abstract principle what native intuition, working on experience, asserts.

St. Thomas' great glory is his utter freedom in this regard. For often we see that considering a thing from one point of view he seems to arrive at a very conservative position, and we think the matter is settled, and suddenly he turns and looks at it under another aspect, and a new set of principles is brought to bear, and lo! from this aspect a whole divergent prospect emerges. Many a modern critic, Catholic as well as non-Catholic, has fallen foul of St. Thomas in this way, coming up with some impatient snap judgment, proceeding to construct thereafter a case of elaborate rebuttal; but when some Thomist gets to work on the problem, and synthesizes the relevant principles, knitting them together from here and there throughout the *Summa*, revealing the full breadth of reference behind the issue, then all the alarm is seen to be simply a case of a radically different perspective.

For St. Thomas was the inheritor of a remarkably coherent sacralist culture; he was, in the speculative order, its *term*, standing like one of those cathedrals which combines within itself all the converging values of the centuries which gave it birth. We, on the other hand, have almost none of that. We inherit rather an intensely pluralist culture, and each one of us stands as a kind of facet, almost a fragment, of the vast myriad divergence, all sensibility and no coherence. But if, as Catholics, we bring our pluralist sensibility back to that sacralist coherence St. Thomas bequeathed to us, filling out and amplifying through the very medium of our weakness the uncompleted aspects of that massive structural bonework, we will find the solution to many perplexities which now beset us, and we will as well give immediacy, texture, and nervous life to what would otherwise remain an unfleshed skeleton. So here, St. Thomas established the principle, which we as modern men perceive through the acuity of our pluralist sensibility, and gave us the foundational certitude, and the inherited sacralist coherence, by which we might proceed on our own.

And who am I to proceed on my own? No theologian, assuredly, but only a man with a little intuition in a highly subjective field. I detect in the sexual act three broad levels of response: the general, the particular and the transcendental; and because they all relate in some way to the factor of our intellection, our mode of knowing, of perception and comprehension, I assimilate them each into the total contemplative disposition, for they are very vital and very great. Even the most general, even the most lowly, the most rudimentary is great—that quenching of elementary hunger, that primordial satisfaction of corporal union, part groping on part, the tongueless flesh coiling in its depth of mutual immersion, soughing its own sigh of quest and solution, the meld of frictive adherence, regrouping itself on new polarities, the magnetic field of another's physicality, dredging between them the great carnal darkness of that domain, as teeming as black mud in the bottomless depths of its own stupration—this is very great, and one ought never deny it; only God can make it be.

And above the metabolic hunger rage all the convergent proclivities of the particular, distinction in unification, the basic attraction of soul to soul, mate to mate, as two things matched, made for each other. The shock of recognition that sees them in the closing act of fitness, fitted together; a generic psychic fulfillment each in the other, and it too is very great, greater than hunger, for a knowledge is here made known, a recognition and a discovery, an acknowledgment, and so exploring the knowledge given, discovery shivering in the join of flesh as two enquire together what the other is.

It is here too that all the bodily parts take nobleness, find their fulfillment out of this enquiry, out of the search: the maleflesh, erect, expectant, contained in its meaning of penetration and bestowal; the feminine chalice, lipped, receptive; the paired inebriating breasts, once pendulent in sleep, alert now, alive in their own intensity of apprehension; the flexed belly; the inter-crouching thighs; the deep inclusive loins; all the planes of the abstract back, so sculptural and sheer; below, the coiled buttocks made to drive; above, the swanlike neck bending the head that dips the mouth to make its compact. Even the hair of the body, tensile and electric within the context of total expectancy that is the pre-coitive state, the pubic hair an electric cloud, vibrant like tingling telepathic nodes, a nimbus about the pairing parts.

So do the sexes ask each other, ask in this act what the other is, of what each is made, what parts bear meaning, and what the meaning makes, asking and listening, asking and listening, and so conjoin. Each senses the fitness in the other, and the bodies are asking if the fit is true, can be, how matched, how deep the match obtains, whether indeed in the merge of the bodies the souls might merge as well; make, they hope, one soul in the fitting bodies, as the fitting bodies make one flesh. They ask and ask, listening through the bloodbeat of each other in that merge, the echoing blood to vibrate the message of communion into the hearkening soul—this too is great, very great, this comprehension of the inter-love in the fact of individuation.

For thus the souls understand each other, and it is by the merging souls, in love, through the merge of the bodies, with love, that their great meaning is made. Out of the rib of man was woman made, and now she is returned, and in his side is formed again, fused in the forked loins and the inter-listening blood—all he lost then through that division, the separation struck in himself by that subtraction, restored, restored to him, brought back to him, fused into him, and she fuses into his side, and is made his, and he hers, and they are. Christian writers have seen in the "deep sleep" that fell upon Adam a mystical ecstasy, related to the same "deep sleep" that later possessed Abraham at the great covenant with God. I see the sex ecstasy as a sign, or type, of that first mystical ecstasy. As Adam and Eve were paired in ecstasy, so are the man and wife, in each coition, rejoined in ecstasy. It is, in the physical order, the supreme embrace, as each enters each, the act of unification achieved at its total level, the tangibility of merging flesh achieving concreteness, the concomitant act of the unifying souls, unifying in their act of knowledge, their act of love.*** And because the intelligibility of such union, such knowing, derives from the vast intelligibility endowed in all things by the supreme Intelligence, it is in this that their comprehension becomes total. In the ecstasy of the sexual embrace the hiatus in the mind between existence and essence is pierced.

For over the plasmic quest hover indeed the higher natures of man, all his infinite gradations, his acute awarenesses, his intricate modes of reaction and response. It is out of these that such a singular response emerges, person to person, the bodily delight of the one in the other as beings of demarcated form, of an exquisite making, of something *shaped*, the shape given verve. And it is out of this again, the subtilization of comprehension that the two self-knowledges start to soar, to know love, the particularization of desire, cognition and electric appraisal, scrutiny, choice, a mode of decision, soul beamed to soul, a ripple of recognition: and the love gathers, in the knowledge and the revealment further seen, leading up and up, out of the particular and into the transcendental, the flutings of ever-refining insight, the unifying force.

For the act reaches up. And there comes a time when, in that upflight, level after level, tingling at last under the very hanging light of the supernatural mode, the high music of divine awareness, these souls conjoined in their own alertness wait for the upperness above them to drop, descend upon and seize, make a prey of them, consume and devour, and they hang in that hope, and are yet sustained, like two sparrows in the eagle's talons, that wait for the liberating beak to drop and grant them deliverance.

For love will not stay low; love lifts; love seeks ever above itself, seeks that Love that makes it a thing of love, evoking its love out of the illimitable Love that has it in being. It is *that love*, that prototypal intenseness bred in its realm of supernature, the aboveness of the awareness by which all soars, like a fire climbing its source of fuel, feeding up, ever. Can't you see what I mean? Two God-centered ones in their own delight can't stop at delight! The Aboveness demands! Two worshiping souls can't rest at the mere impulse to worship! This force lacks end in nature because human nature can't end in itself. Something else contains it, calls beyond, the vast Something toward which all its being is but ground, is but a beginning.

I have heard the objection that no one who experienced infused contemplation would ever mistake sexual intensity, however profound, for that divine participation. But mark well I have not said the presence of subjective intensity is the sign by which infusion may be posited. God's modes in the human soul may never be charted, from something so infinitely subtle as to be beyond any sensory response, and consequently any intellectual detection, to a violence more terrible than the most cathartic of natural acts. Truly the violence of God is a thing which no man who has been touched by it can ever mistake.

After the soul has sought Him many days, many nights, begging in its immaturity for some sign, some manifestation that its heckling incertitude may once and for all be silenced, that it might actually *know* in its consciousness the divine verification; coming back and back, begging, haunting the church, crying up its rosaries of invocation, until after many days it has exhausted itself, and it knows not how it may either stop or continue, its heart spent of hope, and yet the dry interior impetus driving it ever on despite its exhausted nerves and its numbed awareness—then suddenly, returning one morning doggedly to the commitment, it is pinned to the pew by a seizure that takes it in possession. And the tears pour down the face, the throat is strangled in its constriction, the body made rigid, sweat springs from its pores, the suppressed sex starts up in alarm, all the disordered passions of his indifferent years suddenly struck by a terrible hand, so that he may learn in this violence how reckless is his request, for he is not ready, he has not made himself fit in patience, in true interior purification, has begged without knowing what he has asked, nor its cost. And the violence of God possesses him, the dread hand of God strikes his soul, and all its faculties cry out in their clamor, jangled, the soul torn from the body by its living roots.

For out of the tabernacle upon the altar a black light, invisible, more powerful than any sun of the perceiving sight, or of the factual imagination, has poured into him the stream of its consuming ray. And there is no pleasure in it, there is ecstasy but no delight, there is knowledge, realization, comprehension, but no joy. This seizure is terrible with the terror of divine dread, this force, this furnace. But yet out of it, the Presence in an act of unspeakable love has possessed him, and he cries the inexpressible cry, in his pouring tears, the acknowledgment and the gratitude; for the pain is his own disorder unpurified, but the Love blazing through him is the quintessence of purity; and his impure soul screams in the anguish of its knowledge, seeing for once what it truly is, and comprehending the Love that waits for him when he can be made ready to come. It is the Sacred Heart; that much is given him to know. And never again will he ever really doubt; he has been filled. In that instant it seemed to him he passed beyond the conditions of hope and faith, for as hope is the expectation of what is to come, and faith is the homage of belief without realization, in this instant he had it, not the totality, but in his impurity all he could take, and more, and more, glimpsing beyond the outrage of the senses that were screaming down there in his tortured body, to the majestic Love that now again in an instant withdraws Itself that he might live, for this will kill him. And he will beg for help many a time again, but never for this. This is a purgatory, one that his senses, his nerves and his flesh, his electrified soul all flinch to remember. It is a thing no ecstasy of sex, no self-engendered dislocation of the senses, no transport of the natural faculties could remotely approximate.

And as for the gentleness of God, His divine solacings, neither here may the radiance of the erotic love form an approximation—he would never confuse the two. For the solacing of God is like no radiant woman's solacing love, ever. When in His own good time He deigns to bestow, to enter into His interior mansion, and resting there endow the charm of His presence upon the soul, which is His love; then does the soul come into its own, and taste of what it was meant to be, all its faculties, somehow, for that favored time made right and true, so that they are not sent scurrying off in fear, but are submissive, obedient, are fond and docile, and themselves come and make prostration. As even the ox and the ass at that manger did bring their bruteness into His orbit and there knelt down, so now do all the obediential senses kneel themselves down. And the man knows. And the tears well up again, not out of his agony but out of his understanding, for understanding is given him. And the blissful intellect drinks of His knowledge, for in that Love His knowledge is bestowed, and God communes with the soul through this knowledge, and the soul feeds on it, gazing deep and deep with the twin eyes of love, gazing into the abyss of love and knowledge that proffers before him the depths of that vastness. Who can speak? How long does this instant abide? Seconds? Years? He does not know. Time for him has ceased, its domain has vanished, the tortured years of his life have all vanished; his warped wrongs are gone; he suffers no guilt; he is made right, reclothed. His soul looks out of a new garment, as a bride, who weeps in her newfound self, weeping under the transforming Kiss, being now, in the Kiss, made other. Who can compare such profferings, such elevations? No act of man can earn them. No act of man can compare to them.

Thus the psychology of two distinct mystical states, but only the psychology, and the elementary mystical states at that. For anyone who has opened *The Living Flame of Love* knows the ineffability of what must lie beyond such fore-tastings as these. I say *only* the psychology because I know it is but the reverberation upon the imagination; infusion itself, a purely spiritual phenomenon, remains a thing above the whole imaginative context. And thus they oversimplify who say that one experienced in mystical infusion would never confuse sexual intensity with the mystical state. For the point is precisely not that it constitutes the mystical state but that it disposes toward it, that there is in the sexual act a natural mystical element, and this element constitutes a dispositive factor *toward* infusion, if God so desires to give. And furthermore, it is eminently fitting that in the procreative act by which is created the human soul, and by which Christ symbolized God's mystical union with the Church, infusion should be enjoyed.

No, not by psychological intensity can infused mysticism be recognized; rather, if at all, only by intellective depth, spiritual comprehension, a transcendent profundity of insight, the whole fact of supernatural charity bestowed and radiant in the soul. But it is the presence in the sexual act of a high illuminate insight, entirely natural but nonetheless sublime, establishing a kind of unspeakable totality, that compels one to acknowledge in it a profound dispositive factor. It is in its totality of participation that sensory impulsion plays its part, as ground-base, so that the spirit flings up, out-strips itself in the breadth of its delight; and in this delight, the delight of God, the true mystical enchantment, may indeed infuse and transform, supernaturalize the natural act, the souls themselves united in this mystical delight, which is God's own delight in His creation and His being. It is in such terms as these that the sad and lamentable "*malum poenae*" of the past may become the joyous "*bonum divinum*" of man's possible future.

And if we must seek further to know the true heart of its correlation, I think we could find no more fruitful approach than under the terms of the aesthetic act, participated beatitude experienced in the creative intuition; and it may be for no other reason than this that the perception of the poet registers its mystical character more acutely than, say, the analytical faculty of the philosopher, who has always tended to place it, by hypothesis, among the less differentiated sensory experience of the brute condition. And it is in this aspect that one may perhaps place a finger on the true nature of its dispositive function.

For just as in the aesthetic act the center of consciousness shifts back from the exterior sensory stimuli through the intricate mechanism of apprehension to their reverberation upon the center of the soul, that deathless spiritual substance where man is indeed made in God's image, that central silence where He eternally dwells and keeps all the outflung components in being, listening and regarding the hovering selectivity of its free will in the ever-arising continuum of choice; just as the aesthetic intuition perceives through the reverberating sensory mechanism that participated beatitude in the reality about it, and in the impingement of that beatitude upon itself, so too, I believe, does the erotic intuition. For as the aesthetic intuition is simply the comprehension of significance at deeper and deeper levels, so too is the erotic one, though here even the aesthetic is subsumed in its totality. In the sexual act at its most dense and complex integration man's whole being is totally engaged as no other natural act can engage it, more consequentially than any isolated sight, than any hearing, than any touching, engaged at the very basis of his being where all his faculties conjoin upon the intelligence, and are seized there in their totality of intelligibility. All its vehemence, its intensity, drives to the center of consciousness and is synthesized there, achieving form, significance, cognition, awareness, comprehension, understanding, revelation and beatitude.\*\*\*\* It is from this point of view that one dares to rephrase St. Augustine's judgment in direct opposition: No other act available to man under the terms of his own volition so carries him into the area of total participation, the area of total love, total otherness.

That it is not often so used is doubtless true. In fallen man the aesthetic act, indeed, all spiritual acts, may well be, had we the capacity to deeply discern, comparatively rare; though I myself believe that even the grossest man is far more spiritual than many another supposes, for I know my own ancient spiritual hunger, and yet none has been more gross than I. Be that as it may, the erotic act is indeed so complex that man can offer it in many ways: as an evil thing, offered in love of self, base lust, and this is sin; as love of another, a gift, and this is noble; and finally as love of God, and here we enter its highest domain, and this is worship. And to offer it in anything less suffices for many good things, suffices, indeed, for procreation, gratification, human generosity—but none of these exhausts its greatness, but rather, if restricted there, they cramp its greatness, waste its potentiality; and even risk reduction to humdrum function, made lurid by a guiltily gross animal pleasure, that which is actually a divine delight.

The great liability of sexual mysticism is that in its search for intensity it veers into the immoral, not understanding man's fallen condition. Outside marriage it is ruinous, and history proves it. And even within that safeguard its inherent limitation must never be forgotten. The great weakness of the sexual act as a contemplative element is that it cannot constitute the contemplative life; its end is not revelation, which, powerful as it is, is only incidental to it, but childbirth, and childbirth means care, concern, protection, provision; childbearing means the active life. A monastery for the married is unthinkable; their domain is unquestionably the home.

But there are Christian homes, virtual monasteries, real convents of purity, from which the pornographic world has been shut as emphatically out as from any cloister; and in *that* cloister, the guarantor of the nuptial felicity, in the sanctuary of the chamber on the altar of the bed, the act is worship, the act finds its great contemplative fitness. In it the chaste husband and the chaste wife gaze wide-eyed on God, drink of Him, a music slow and sublime, a creative transport, a loving contemplation, a mystical poem, a soaring canticle. The pure touch of the husband and the pure response of the wife, how sure in its delicacy, how exquisitely tuned! The maze of the somnolent being awakened, gathered together, every agent of response, a sublime orchestration, all quickening, too full for surmise, a great up-gathering, a sacrificial holocaust. And on its eminence, tumultuous and vast, all the Himalayas of the soul stand forth revealed.

No one who in the altitude of the act, at the sheer crescendo, held at the hurricane's heart, no one who so gives himself to God through her, the wife's own total gift, no one who has heard the wife cry out to God to make her bear, cry out of the insuperable intensity that has her in possession, lifted beyond the confines of demarcated life, crying the greatest hunger of the human cry, no one but a dull unfeeling clod, I swear it, will doubt. She would not flinch to be torn in shreds on that instant so long as God quickens the begging womb, the quickness passed to one soul other: a birth, a burgeoning.

Beware, eminent Doctors, how you mark it down. A million married saints in Heaven will prove you wrong, who came to know God in the true practice of this vocation, made it their own regarding act, their contemplation. *Canticle of Canticles* is their text, and they will quote you chapter and verse, and silence you with Scripture.

But there is a greater glory, are greater givers, and these are the virgins; greater because they give more, renounce the true joy, the splendid pleasure, the deep stability, the bodily calm, the broad sanity, the elemental physical poise of the marriage state, to assume the crucifixion of the nerves, the taut frustration, the instability, the insane babblement of sensory unfulfillment, that are the haunting liabilities of virginal consecration. Why? Because a supernatural offering made in despite of the natural context brings, in the total supernatural context to come hereafter, incalculable recompense. These are the ones who carried their thirst unslaked, and through the heat of the day have not touched water, and brought the epitome of their desire straight up through the narrow gate to the single Fount. These bind themselves by vow, giving to God alone a gift they could have shared in splendor. Christ is their spouse, and none other, and they save themselves for Him with all the purity of purpose and holy expectation with which the bride saves herself for the groom. This the Church declares. And though I have sought in these pages to redeem the conjugal act to its contemplative fullness, the loss of which I believe accounts for its terrible misuse and its wretched fitfulness today, yet the superiority of the consecrated state is unquestionable. I hope to celebrate contemplative virginity in the greatness of its claim, but that is for a later writing. I had only begun to live it. Too late in my life to be a virgin, I yet sought the grace of a virginal heart, a mystery that Baptism, despite the poor body's lost integrity, will certainly confer.

\* \* \*

\* At the time of writing I was unaware of the basic feminine character of the cross symbol, a distinction, however, which strengthens rather than diminishes the force of the erotic parallel. C. G. Jung, in *The Symbols of Transformation,* comments: "It is clear from all this that the cross is a many-faceted symbol, and its chief meaning is that of the 'tree of life' and the 'mother'. Its symbolization in human form is therefore quite understandable. The various forms of the *crux ansata* have the meaning of 'life' and 'fruitfulness', and also of 'union', which can be interpreted as the *hieros gamos* of the god with his mother for the purpose of conquering death and renewing life. This mythologem, it is plain, has passed into Christianity. For instance, St. Augustine says: 'Like a bridegroom Christ went out with a presage of his nuptials into the field of the world. He came to the marriage bed of the cross, and there, in mounting it, he consummated his marriage. And when he perceived the sighs of the creature, he lovingly gave himself to the woman forever.' *Sermo Suppositus,* 120. 8. The 'woman' is the Church." I am happy to offer this sympathetic recognition by St. Augustine of the beneficence of sex to ameliorate the strictures I have posited against him elsewhere in this book.

\*\* Louis Lavelle, *The Meaning of Holiness,* p. 4. "The mark of the saint is that he always lives at the limit of his powers. There is no one whose life is so close to the spontaneous movements of nature. He seems in a way to surrender to them, to find in them the source and spring of all his action. We may indeed think that he fights against these natural impulses; but it would be more true to say that he directs them all to their final end, to the point at which they bring him perfect satisfaction and fulfillment. In the process he is obliged to transcend the limits of nature, in order that nature may achieve in him the end towards which it aspires. In like manner one sees the mathematician, using the concept of limit, press to infinity a series of terms and so transcend the concept he is using. So too the saint never brings into play and never suggests the use of any save the most familiar sentiments. No one is more accessible than he. But of these same sentiments he makes a most extraordinary use; for he manages to give them their full power only by forcing them (in order to fulfill their aspiration) to transcend the uses to which we had previously consecrated them. At the moment when they seem to approach fulfillment, they appear to give way or to be transformed into something of a wholly different order. And so in the saint we recognize all the impulses of nature, and yet in a sense we do not. It would be a mistake to think of him as always engaged in a relentless war against his natural impulses, for nature also comes from God. He transforms nature into the supernatural. He rediscovers its origin, its destiny and its full significance."

\*\*\*  "Love is the immaterial super-existence in which the beloved is or becomes, in the lover, the principle of a gravitational pull or intentional connaturality by which the love tends inwardly towards existential union with the beloved, as towards its own being from which it has been separated, and thus loses itself in the reality of the beloved." (Maritain, *Existence and the Existent*) Is it not in the actuality of the sexual embrace that the material principle is incorporated into this union, that the unifying force achieves incarnation, that the "immaterial super-existence" attains concreteness?

\*\*\*\*  This summary, made on the basis of intuition alone, finds a kind of corroboration, I think, in the following passage from Josef Pieper's *Fortitude and Temperance*. He writes:

"The sense of touch, according to St. Thomas (and Aristotle) has a special rank among the senses. It is not a sense among other senses, but is the 'basis of the other senses;' 'all other senses are based on the sense of touch.' In this sense of touch there is contained principally the entire essence of the senses in general. By the sense of touch, above all, a being becomes sentient—*animal*; where there is no sense of touch, there is no sentient life. — This is the first point.

"Second: 'Among all sentient creatures man has the best sense of touch.' 'There are animals which see more sharply or hear more acutely or smell more intensely than man. In the sense of touch, however, man differs from all other sentient beings by having a much more acute perception.'

"And third: 'Among men themselves those who possess the better sense of touch have the better power of cognition.' 'One might suppose that cognitive talent should rather correspond to the excellence of the sense of sight than to that of touch, as the sense of sight is the intellectual sense and best perceives differences in things.... But one must say that cognitive talent corresponds more to the excellence of the sense of touch because the sense of touch is the basis of all other senses. Therefore he who has the better sense of touch has consequently simply a more sensitive nature and as a result a keener intelligence. For the excellence of sensitivity is the basis of excellence of intelligence. But from the fact that one has a better auditory or a better visual sense it does not follow that he is simply more sensitive; at most this is so only in a certain respect.'"

This passage, it seems to me, puts the sexual act, in the hegemony of human acts, in a position of unchallengeable pre-eminence, for nowhere else does the sense of touch come into such total engagement, and hence nowhere else are the broadest and most deep resources of the intelligence so completely evoked. In the sexual act, by virtue of man's exercise of his most sensitive faculty, he becomes most characteristically human rather than, as is often implied, most characteristically bestial. It becomes more and more clear why Christ symbolized His relationship to the Mystical Body, the highest of all relationships, under the figure of the marital term. Be it noted, however, that this elevation of the sexual act to such unprecedented importance cannot be used to alter the Church's defined doctrine that consecrated virginity is a higher state of life than that of matrimony. The definition has to do with *states of life*, not specific acts within those states of life. It is quite possible for the sexual act to be man's highest natural act even though matrimony is not man's highest state. Under the vow of celibacy one sacrifices the present earthly good for a future celestial good that is even higher—a sacrifice made on the basis of supernatural faith alone.

---

Josef Pieper, *Fortitude and Temperance*, trans. Daniel F. Coogan (New York: Pantheon Books, Inc., 1954), pp. 95-96.

\* \* \*

And the time drew on to when I could lay all burdens down in the full quittance which is the supernatural assent. It was mid-July, the blaze of summer, the year at its height, all day long the sun pouring down its rotund vocabulary of fire, the fruit trees in the backyard burgeoning with life. The apricot, sterile in my two-year's sojourn there, now burst into plenty, like the new life of my soul, and littered the ground with its gold harvest. The apples shattered the dead stillness of night. They dropped down the dark, thudding through leaves and branches. I picked them up and held them in my hands; they were like my own hopes, like my life, that had to fall to the ground to die, that had to be lifted up and exalted. The rampant blackberry bore all along its runner clusters of black juice, leaf-smothering the rearward fence in a wild splendor. At night the moon hung lucent, potent and feminine, rich with a received influx of life. Far off under the west of the world the sun still bathed it with light; in the absence of the sun the moon took on glory.

And at last the time for Baptism had come, for the great reception into the Church, because the three months of catechetical instructions were done. There were eighteen or twenty of us in that class, and for the most part all would be entering, though here and there would be one who could not yet come in, touched, somehow, enough to stay through the course, but untouched enough to make the assent—some lack of clarification deep in the soul imposing its obscure denial. But for the rest of us it meant the augmentation of our tempo of preparation, as we began to make at last the actual arrangements. But even as the date was established, there remained unsolved the problem of a sponsor, a god-parent; I could think of no friend who called the Church his own; and I began to realize that she who had taught me, she who had brought me in and left me to go, was virtually the only Catholic I knew.

As I pondered this fact I became more and more astonished. What did it mean about the Church? I had thought to enter into something I had heard called The Mystical Body, and where was it, where had it been, and of whom did it consist? I had met hundreds of people, spoken deeply of serious subjects with scores, but this one person, who was to be the instrument of my conversion, had been the only Catholic I had ever really known. Even yet it astounds me. I must have moved among hundreds of them, but there was nothing about them distinguishable from the horde of merely secular Americans in whom they mixed. St. Chrysostom, speaking in the third century under conditions approximate to our own, had declared from the pulpit:

> Yea, the believer ought to shine forth not only by what he hath received from God, but also by what he himself has contributed; and should be discernible by everything, by his gait, by his look, by his garb, by his voice....

It doesn't happen today. Many an American Catholic adopts the protective coloration of conventional behavior, almost as if to prove to the world that he is indeed of its own definition. The only vigorously demonstrable enthusiasms he permits himself are those shared by his non-Catholic fellows, and patriotism is his specialty. In a world of political insecurity he exhibits that strained anxiety to be as tough as the toughest which confirms in his neighbor the already firm suspicion that there is something essentially fascistic about the Church Herself. This he truculently denies, but his truculence hardly serves his adjuration. And as for his true distinction, the real things that set him off sharply from the men beside him, the profound things of his affiliations and the deep things he can show, of these he is almost secretive, if not to say actually ignorant.

I remember how in those days I wanted to wear my faith as a living badge before the world; yes, a defiant badge which I expected the world to despise, for I had been of the world and I knew what the world thought of it. Sometimes on my walks through the city streets I held my rosary openly in my hand, visibly saying my prayers. I think I shocked no one but the Catholics, though among them I must have left behind me a veritable wake of wrenched sensibilities, almost as if I stood guilty of some unspeakable sacrilege. So too in Church, kneeling for the Prayers at the Altar after Low Mass, I spoke out with that ringing clarity which comes of new conviction, from the first pew where I ensconced myself. But I never failed to sense behind me in that discreet congregation the pall of a pervasive embarrassment, as if I were trying somehow to usurp the role of the priest, as if the part of the congregation is to remain forever repressed, forever inert, forever tepid.

This intensity of conversion which demanded of me the character of pronounced public witness set me off from the people about me, and I entered the Church filled with a great loneliness, in a middle-class parish which I did not understand, among parishioners I neither knew nor understood. The motives of the convert are often impugned as one who seeks security and consolation in the herd, but I never felt either. I was never so alone in my life. To me it seemed that an uncrossable gulf had dropped between me and my familiar past, and that nothing at all, on the human level, had been gained to compensate for it. My loved one, and the deep fulfillment of marriage, its psychic and its sexual equilibrium; my friends, whom I learned in this how much I needed, and how needfully I loved; my way of life, evolved over long and mellowing years, the old established habits of my hands and mind—all these I must now, in this single act, reckon as a loss. And what had I gained? The Church? What was the Church? I could see Her only in the throes of contemporary existence, struggling to shape some suitable equation between Her venerable traditions and the onslaught of a technological age, administered, often enough I suspected, by people more in tempo with the age than with the tradition, so that many a time, in my raw reaction, the sight made me sick.

Pondering these things, as the experience began to slowly cut into me, testing me, in my weaker moments I was shaken to the core. Come, I would say, answer: What is the Church, with Her slick suburban churches, sprung up like mushrooms out there in Suburbia? In my hunger for the ancient life how I hated those edifices! Possessing the invariable lurking atmosphere of the fabricated object, conceived on some architect's desk high in a San Francisco skyscraper, drafted by men whom I suspected would never pray in them nor anywhere else, thrown together on a production schedule of break-neck compression, a creation of transit-mixers, jack-hammers, acetylene torches and automatic saws, I could find nowhere about them any trace of a little love. The padres did better with an improvised plumb-bob and a tribe of Indians. They did better because they knew the earth out of which they built, and loved it, created, as they well understood, from all eternity for the use of man's worship, and therefore holy. They did better because they were *in* their tradition and not outside it, that great baroque tradition of which they were the final exemplar, a tradition of supreme spiritual passion, a tradition integrated into their heart's blood and the pang of life. They were men in whom experience was still direct and immediate, undiffused by a thousand baffling deflections, who could walk from Mission Dolores to Mexico City in the line of duty, and for whom the associations of honest sweat were not confined to the tennis court. Pondering these things I would square away in disgust, and ask whom, besides myself, at my age and with my background, did I think I was fooling, and how lightly did I gauge my affiliations?
But then I would shake myself free, and tear loose from the bite of that devil, whose realm is the imagination, where he lords it over the images of the deep unconscious, and plays upon the antipathies of the heart like seductive magic. For well I knew that the truth I claimed was more permanent than those svelte new-fangled statues which like movie queens bless the admiring congregations, more crucially articulated than the "imprimatur-fodder" which crams the vestibule rack; more commodious than the Fords and the Cadillacs purring like metallic panthers by the curb, more adorable than the mink so modishly draped on the half-naked shoulder of the woman

beside me; and infinitely more abundant than the harried liturgical insufficiencies of American parochial life, where on Sundays the Masses must go like clockwork, the congregations change in shifts, and woe to the inept young priest who lingers in love, failing to clear the church and parking lot before the next contingent arrives— beyond all these, and above them, but somehow, for the better and despite the worse, sanctifying them, even them; beyond all these the thing I claimed was the Christ, Jesu, the Logos, the pure creative Principle. Him I had sought, and Him I had found, and from Him I would not be deflected. For in Him I had learned the secret of Love, and it has no limit—I, who had loved two women in the extremes of passion, never had loved till I loved the Christ. Fastened on Him I could grind away on my beads through all the streets of the city, and sing out my thanksgiving after Mass full-voiced, though I might skitter the whole furtive congregation!

For Christ is the Church and the Church is the Sacraments, and these are the breasts that will feed me. The Sacraments are the teats of the Great Mother, by which the flow of supernatural life is passed to the unceasing generations She brings into the world, which She nourishes and sustains, out of the milk of Her life force, Her sacramental strength; and once I had taken these living teats never again could I starve. I was like a ravenous suckling dropped in the teeming litter of life, and I was famished for life. What did it matter if the rest of this brood were not exactly to my liking? I had found the teats. Would I have preferred an earlier generation, one of the Mother's ancestral litters, born out of Her body in a more primitive era, under more earthy, less fussily hygienic conditions? Did the historical circumstances really make the difference, whether I came to [the] Light in the electrically heated incubator of today, the reeking sty of the High Renaissance, or the makeshift hutch of the Apostolic Age? I had found the Sacraments, the teats. And if the Church Herself in Her earthly members were to become externally venal; if the Church Herself, who in Her temporal ministrations is today more pure and unsullied than perhaps [at] any time since Constantine, if even the Church were to become externally corrupt, sunk in the mire of the worldly pig-sty, and reeking of the dung of worldly engrossment, let me never be deceived. Let me hold to the teats and suck. Weep for Her (if that should happen), and pray for Her (if that should be), but never relinquish the life-giving teats, the strength of whose Milk cannot be diluted by any foulness of the worldly sty.

Cling to the teats, and suck milk, suck life. And if, through my own indigence, I slacken my jaws and slip into the mire, then like the famished suckling let me crawl to the Mother, crawl back to the teats, and suck, and suck, and find my fulfillment.

And if you who prize the Church are shocked that I speak of Her sacramental teats, be still for a moment, and understand the thing that I would drive down to. For there are many levels of existence locked in a man, and they all need light. If he is going to be met with truth he will have to be met at his level of sustenance, and then fed there, the level at which, for him, all consequence truly engages. You have to show how the Church heals and accepts at that level, at every level. You have to show that the Church leaves no part of him out, even his most base part, even the depths of his carnality. Sometimes a man, caught in the mechanical abstractness of civilized life, has so great an elemental hunger howling within him that only through the most gross, earthy, four-letter concepts can he truly "engage." Sometimes a man sees himself as a pig, and his mother as a sow, and the rest of humanity as an unspeakable litter. You have to reach him there, heal him there, let the Church heal him there. If the only way such a man can come to the Church is as to a sow, then you have to show him that *this* sow is holy. You have to meet his carnality at the level of its own impingement, and lift him out. And if you draw back through an offended taste, if you impose your own scrupulosity between his hungering soul and the movement of grace, then believe me, every iota of that scrupulosity will be burned out of you in purgatory to the precise measure that it prevented souls from meeting their salvation. You will be like one of those wretched missionaries who have to hustle a pair of factory-made pants on a heathen before they can bear to let him breathe the name of Christ. I know these things because they are deeply in me, no less than in such a missionary. All the scrupulosity is there, the finicking conformism, the squeamishness, the picayune nose-wrinkling disdain. But the carnality, the swinishness is there as well. There is a part of me that is gross pig, but the Church heals it, feeds it. The Sacraments pour life in it, make it pure and great, give it dignity and grace. There is a fallen part in me that sees mankind as grunting, swilling swine. To that man in me, to the suckling in my soul, I sing Her panegyric. For She is divine.

And in my nearness now to the elemental Mother, the Beautiful One, who is no sow, but the Mother of many children, whom She warms in the bosom of Her breasts, and sings to sleep in the peace of Her presence—in my nearness now I longed for the sacramental breasts; but before I could taste them, there did remain the problem of the sponsorship, and who would be my god-parent.

And then I remembered the friend to whom I could turn, one of the few Catholic poets of San Francisco; I had made her acquaintance two or three years before, after I had come down from the North; and I was heartened and made glad that I could have one there who understood both the impress of my past and yet herself shared my new allegiance. I wrote her a letter and of course she obliged, and I made arrangement with the priest of my parish, and the Baptism was set for a Saturday afternoon late in July, and in the little Baptistry of the parish church I received the Sacrament. And when it was over I walked home alone through the sun-filled afternoon, the spanking breeze clean off the Bay to speak to me of the clean thing I had become. And next day, Sunday, in the nearby chapel of the Dominicans, I walked up between the choirs of the men in white tunics who all unknown to me then would one day be my brothers, and received my first Holy Communion. And I knew that *she* had come, and across the chapel at the other side of the sanctuary she too had received, and we bore back to our separate places the one God within us. That God bound us, a binding that had become our whole reality. And the following day I returned again for Mass and Communion, and all the days thereafter, and at week's end I entered the confessional to receive the Sacrament of Penance, the third Sacrament of my inception, in order that my venial lapses of the week might not go unabsolved, and that I might receive the great healing movement of spirit this Sacrament affords. And so I began at last the basic regimen which constitutes the true way of life in the Church: daily Mass and Communion, and weekly Confession, the unshakable supports upon which the way of perfection stands.

And yet, faced with the actuality of this event, this Baptism, which mind and faith tell me is the paramount event of my life, prior to which all facets of existence can only be counted as insufficiencies, my account of it here is almost shamefully bleak—inadequate not only in terms of the sheer grandeur of the thing, quite beyond the telling of the pen, but no less so in terms of simple dramatic resolution. Everything I have heretofore described has been merely preparational. This is the culmination of the prodigious thrust, and surely any sense at all of formal fitness demands some recognition of its great resolving character.

But the pen hovers in hesitation. The whole Sacramental System is, theologically speaking, intricate, and has been precisely defined. It is the acute work of specialists, and one hesitates to bungle the sublime. Grace is something which the natural imagination of the poet can make very little of. True, the Church has evolved a convincing ritual which symbolizes at the level of action the underlying supernatural reality, so that to narrate the action is to expose the principle. But for the poet the difficulty is that often the ritual itself has with time lost its elemental character. The baptismal rite, for instance, has through adaptation to the needs of infant baptism become so compressed as to bear little relation to the great drama of the soul in its rebirth. Even the sequence of the Sacraments has been altered. The full meaning of Confirmation lies in its proximity to Baptism, which should immediately precede it, but since Baptism is no longer confined to Eastertide, and since obviously it is impossible to have a Bishop on hand for every occasion, Confirmation is generally postponed. I did not receive it for another six months. It is true that as now commonly practiced it does perform the needful function of a puberty rite, but this only emphasizes the fact that for me to achieve here any true insight into the complex of the initiating Sacraments would take almost a separate disquisition, quite apart from the manner in which I experience them, something I am not able to do.

Still, this scanting of what is actually of such fundamental importance may not be denied a certain psychological relevance to the situation today. The convert, sufficiently instructed in the theology of Baptism, but receiving little specific preparation for the symbolism of the ritual, goes through it in an uncomprehending abstraction. His instructor, who has, as a Catholic, all his life been conditioned to ritual, and who is, as a priest, daily living in its context, underestimates the depth of ritualistic divorce from the lives of those nurtured outside the Faith. Nor is this so much his own personal oversight as it is the collapse of all ritualistic meaning in contemporary life, so that even among the clergy, for whom it might be called a basic tool of their work, ritual is apt to be taken not quite seriously. It is almost as if, in the Church, ritual is maintaining itself through this unpropitious age in virtually residual form, kept alive by Her legislative power until such a day as men may recover their senses, and learn to live again in the great flow of life and of nature, and can salute again in these primal acts the majesty of being; and when they do, the ritual which the Church, great mother and protectress, has preserved for them will be there at hand with its unquenchable reference, to assume in its slow resolving meaning the deficiencies of our earthly incertitude, its meaning as ancient as earth itself, man's life on earth, man's seasonal existence, prime with earth meaning and the vast poetry of nature. But we live in bad days. Like many another convert I had received the great initial Sacrament in a kind of numbness, my spirit aching for a liturgical sufficiency that was not to be.

On the other hand, it cannot be denied that certain of my difficulties were clearly of my own making, or at least inherent in basic human misunderstanding, whatever the ritualistic deficiency that might be urged. In the Baptismal rite for instance, as the priest touched my nostrils in that symbolic action by which is purified the senses of man, I was prudishly scandalized by the smell of tobacco on his fingers, and the shock of scandalization shivers like a wave through the sea-caves of the imagination, dispelling any more lofty synthesis in its echoey boom. For fifteen years I had been a heavy pipe smoker, but the preceding Lent, on the eve of the separation, at the razor's edge of conversion, steeling myself in the apprehension of its obscure approach and desirous of making some renunciation that would prove at least to myself the earnestness of my air, I had laid the engrossing habit aside. It was, somehow, not hard for me to do, and I discovered the freedom in being quit of it, and rejoiced in a liberation that faith had brought me, as if to prove that right renunciation does come easy. And it was a sign, I accepted it as a sign, and looked to the greater renunciation with full confidence, for this had stood as token. And now I was scandalized that a priest should indulge it; for since I, not yet in the Sacraments, had forsaken it so easily, surely a man of God, a priest, ought not to remain entrenched in such practices. For does not St. John of the Cross say that although a bird be tied only by a trifling thread, until that thread is broken the bird cannot fly up? And the shiver of scandalization shook through my mind, disconcerting me with the delicious egotistical complacency the smug mind breeds, preening the ego in that obverse self-congratulation by which we feed on the imagined shortcomings of somebody else. These comforts of the self drowned the rich symbolic meaning in their fictional deceit.

So too at First Communion. Speaking from the point of view of its surface psychology (for indeed in the depths of my will I knew powerfully what I was about), I was more aware of her presence there, whose face in those days was the one ineradicable image of my mind, than of the magnitude of the occurrence. Or rather, the magnitude seemed in my mind to gather its greatness from her nearness, the drama, one might say, of that powerful juxtapositioning in time, Christ's sanctifying heart contingent upon our own, and ours on each other's, caught up now in a ritual of real sufficiency, as about us the Dominicans, habited in their metaphysical black-and-white, fell upon the choir-forms in the plunging act of abasement by which they acknowledge the forth-coming of the Host. I do not deny that our togetherness there was good, a holy participation—that ineluctable Bread hovering at her lips and mine, the same God in the same Rite, the same Light in the same lives, the same Love in the same loss, and the same unreckonable Gain—what fool would sneer at the mystery here between us, two who stood on such thresholds, who had crossed such reefs?

But as for me, and what obtained in my soul at that first coming-in of the Eucharistic life—the unspeakable transformation, the total resolving change that made me one with the Divine, exalting my humanity, my basis of being, my weak will, even the physical deficiencies that riddle the human frame, all these swept up into the transcendental level, as the Christ-God makes the faith-following man a thing of God, in God engulfed—what natural good, what poignancy of human drama here, but shrivels to insignificance! What human passion, human love, human comprehension, but falls away to the delimitation of the thinly superficial!

But I? What did I see? I saw her face. And what did I feel? I felt her presence there, far across the chapel, and a score of communicants between us, the God in the golden vessel borne majestically from mouth to mouth, from her expectant mouth to mine—of all the possibles of spiritual response, it was her presence that I felt. Not, thank God, the erotic thing, the old magnetic sexual force that once had fastened us together; rather say the maternal presence, as far across the crowd-choked plaza the lately lost child senses in its sure instinct the mother's presence there and is drawn, brought back to the breast, so was I drawn. As Dante filled his gaze upon the face of Beatrice, there on the lower rungs of Paradise, in the last long looking, before she smiled and pointed Up, so I filled my consciousness with the nearness of her soul. It was in her nearness that I took the Bread. And torn between those sensibles, the woman and the Bread, I rose, and the Bread, mismanaged, clung to my sleep-parched palate; I had not been warned to moisten the mouth and keep down the tongue; and this accident distressed me. I struggled to expedite the difficulty as I found my place, discomfited and cross-purposed. What should have been the consummation of a long chain of magnificent effects, dissolved in a series of utter irrelevancies.

Sanctifying grace is an experience, indeed, if we understand its influx as a stupendous occurrence in the soul, but it is not a sensation, and the imagination, that synthesis of the senses in which we mostly live, can make nothing of it. In the strike of grace, whatever might be recognized as concrete experience most probably relates to phenomena of but strictly psychological origin. The convert, however, is not above susceptibility to a more dramatic expectation, and when it fails to occur he can only console himself with the comforting allowance that charismatic signs have no essential relation to sanctity! The soul knows not what to expect, and so expects everything. It is swollen with spiritual sweetness of a highly transient and heady kind, and so raw is it in its reaction, and so indeterminate in its expectation, that it can hardly tell what it is to do. It hates vanity, but is very vain. It hates gratuitous display, but breathlessly waits at the communion rail for the Host to leave the fingers of the priest and plummet to his lips! From now on, it can only overcome its inconstancy by a true constancy of application, and that will take time. But time irks this soul; it wants everything now, on the instant. It wants passion and fulfillment. It would gladly be torn to pieces in order to lose itself in God, but it cannot. The one thing that is wanted of it, it wants not to provide, and that is patience. The zeal of conversion is more terrible than puppy-love, but it is not unlike it in its blindness.

Puppy-love! That riot of sensuous demand, unsupported by any conditioning experience, the impact of powerful bodily instinct upon the exposed consciousness, striking below the levels of its controls, riddling its frail structure of stability and its tremblingly tenuous norms of response; infatuation, the vivid imagination elaborating in a sublime frenzy around the instinctual core, its breathless romantic vagaries stimulating the thought to richer and more hectic dreams; excessive deductions soaring out of improbable hypotheses, the insatiate craving of the heart that has had no factual foundations to ground upon—puppy-love! In my adolescence I had lived it through, and I do not despise it. Never had I seen moonlight until I saw it then about our love-struck heads, that girl whose perfect love I knew, lips that in the kiss pledged their unendable trust to mine, the flowering mystery of touch, lighting the smoldering depths of unawakened being into sheer beatitude. I had liefer lived that truthful madness of the convinced heart in all its ache and all its paralyzing apprehension, than schooled to a thousand rational adumbrations. I was nearer then to true wonder, the beautiful condition, the God-condition, His own inexhaustible wonder in the unfolding instantaneity of what He is, as now in the vast expectancy of my conversion I was nearer to wonder and to truth, than many a later prudent circumspection would ever bring me—but each had to go; they can't be kept. It will be, actually, by many a setback, many a rude blow and heartache, and many a deprivation that stability will come, as the soul learns that it cannot grasp all its desire at once, and discovers in the check and counter-check to let the timelessness of God's will work in it.

It is never long delayed. By the time I wrote "the binder's poem" the resignation had indeed begun to deepen. Once in Communion the resignation could truly begin, and as I daily wrote my verse, or printed on the great handpress, or bound what I had printed, the slow days settled one upon another in a steadying accord. The making of books, too, had been a common thing between us, and this was the poem that caught up that area of our experience, and consummated it in the greater thing, which was transcended again in the greatest Book, which she had read to me so often, to draw us bit by bit into the universal orbit of its claim.

 vii. The Burning Book

 Now it may happen that one
 Who is himself a binder of books,
 Sometime, too rough with the needle,
 May pierce to his hand, and by chance from that pierce
 Let fall his blood in the book;
 Then does he, seeing it,
 Cast out that leaf as blemished,

Because there is blood on it.

But in the book I bind for you
Rather do I now take up that leaf
And bind it in; for as our blood
On the leaf of this life is surely no blemish to God,
So do I trust that my blood in this book
Will be no blemish to you.

For it is by blood that we are made dear.

It is by the blood of Our Lord each day in the Mass
That we are perfectly endeared to God;
And therefore will it be by the mingling
Of His blood with ours on the smutched page
Of our life, that we may hope to see endeared
The smutched page of mankind in that otherwise
Blemishless book of His Works.

And as my blood is alone on the leaf,
So on the leaf of this life
Must it also remain alone from yours.
Yet do I pray that in the broader Book
May these mingle, and be altogether
Quenched in that brighter Blood,
Which burns, and is the true
Letter of life,
And pure on the page makes up the rare
Rubrication of the Word.

And now I had written out the lyric interlude, and it was time to face the writing of that poem serving as tent-pole, as roof-tree, the high humped water-shed by which a sequence achieves the tip-over, to all break forward, descend again to the levels of its source. This poem I now faced, and groping down into the complex of the aesthetic response, I sought its focus. What came rose up out of the whole pressure of an element which heretofore I have only referred to, but which from the beginning was all about me as a troubling presence, an area of unrest, and a deep anxiety. I mean the attitude of my friends.

I was never a man too closely bound by such attachments, and consequently I was not finally dependent upon this friend or that for the crucial decisions of my life. But I was nevertheless dependent, as are all men, upon the respect and affection of those people whom I admired. In matters of principle I had always acted independently, though here too I suffered sharply if the issues were deeply drawn, filled with self distrust, often torturing myself with doubts. In entering the Faith I cannot say that I had to endure the scenes of savage renunciation which have accompanied the conversions of so many, but still the incredulity, the bewilderment, and the genuine pain existent in my dearest friends was unmistakable. It would in any case have been bad enough; but the separation gave it an impact which produced something like outrage in those who had a real interest in my well-being.

I had never been able to adequately communicate the concatenation of psychological impress, nor the deep spiritual trend by which the revolution occurred. The very interiority of it almost precluded utterance. The poetry I had been writing, which one would have expected to lay bare the deeper drift, contained hardly a hint of what was moving till the full magnitude of conversion opened with the plunging commitment of *Triptych for the Living*. Nor do I know how to explain this inarticulateness; was it simply that I resisted on a surface level my own interior trend? I dare say that my friends saw it simply in terms of subjectivity, a reaction explainable purely in terms of the marriage, and I dare say that she who was accountable received a good deal of behind-the-scenes vituperation for having beguiled me from the deeps of humanistic sanity to the shallows of impressionistic religiosity. Nothing much was said to our faces before the separation; doubtless it was hoped the drift would wear itself out; and indeed it was not believed that I could sufficiently lose character as to bind myself to so unlikely a commitment. But there came a time when this all had to be faced, for after the separation friends must be met who could not mask their feelings, and who had to speak their minds.

And still, no matter how I tried, I could not meet their minds. I could not, for one thing, delineate the process of the change. There are certain elements which, intellectually, one simply cannot divulge. "My wife has some records of Gregorian Chant, and after listening to these I have decided that the Catholic Faith is true." It sounds silly. Or, "Having studied a book of the portraits of the Saints which my wife owns, I have come to understand that my old beliefs were incorrect." No one would confess to such a thing. He wouldn't be thought sane if he did. Yet the fact remains that Gregorian Chant is one of the most powerful contemplative elements the Church has created. To be exposed to it week after week is to be penetrated at a level which all the facets of the discursive intellect can make nothing of, the inherent *force* of an attitude and a life, a spiritual commitment and a hierarchy of values that lay the soul bare in a way it can never be otherwise touched. And to behold the continuity of sanctity in the faces of the saints, the visage of holiness made manifest across long epochs, and seen in all its multiplicity, transforming the natural countenance into the veritable mirror of divine manifestation, is to lay hold of a witness that, for me at least, not only could not be discounted, but was actually the kind of witness that counted for most. These things are evidential, tangible; if not true proofs at least powerful signs, proclaiming in their immediacy the conviction of proof. And they strike through layer after layer of acquired misapprehension (what had I actually known of the Faith, of the Church, of Christianity? nothing at all). But nevertheless, these are things which cannot be spoken, for at the time one does not know them, has not assimilated them. One stands mute, in a kind of anguish, seeing the counter-anguish, the bewilderment and the pain, the bafflement and the incomprehension in the faces of his dearest friends; and he can say nothing.

Not that I was actually confused. I was indeed unsure on many profound issues, but I was truly serene before the kind of objection I commonly encountered: a cluster of rather pat formulations clotted at the front of the consciousness serving only to keep the deeper problems at distance. Sometimes I would gasp to hear an objection which, to one who has begun to acquire the basic attitude of religion, drops across him almost painfully obvious, thrown down with what was meant to be an air of devastating finality; and I used to wonder what people thought had happened to my mind if such objections were still beyond me. I had forgotten that it was not so long since they were my own whole stock in trade. But I was never able to begin, the event was so vast in my mind, grounded back on such slow interior transformation, and the objections so hopelessly wide of the mark, that there appeared to be simply no basis of rapport. I knew, of course, that these blatantly superficial objections were not really fundamental to the opposed position, a matter of greater dignity; what we were up against was actually a profound cleavage of attitude, the hiatus between two radically divergent points of view;

and in the emotional context the smoldering resentment crackled out around areas that seemed too glaring for credulity. They should have reflected that if these details were so obvious, there must have been some reckoning made of them, for in truth it is easier to ridicule the Faith than to refute it. The hard thing is to start making concessions; to concede to the truth at any place along the line is, consciously or unconsciously, to start the way in.

    I was restive in this state of interior trouble, with its suppressed anguish and its psychic instability, disturbed in the tension of strained relations I felt about me, and I determined to make the center-piece of my sequence a kind of justification of what had happened, to give the final summation of how it came to be, and why; to answer these objections, and to lay the old claims [to rest]. It is in a genre I had never before attempted, and does not fully achieve what it endeavored to do. It emerges more as a picture of the mentality of the conversion period than any conclusive defense of the act itself. I had entered the Faith by the intuitive rather than the analytic approach, and I lacked, as I still do, the knowledge and intellectual training to make a really integrated defense. Apologetics is a science, and a cool one, and there is neither science nor coolness here; but as a mirror of the impact of conversion on the mind, the poem may be read. It is necessary to the sequence, and indeed gives a clue to the shift of feeling, the merging hostility and the yearn for understanding it records. I was hurt that my friends had not understood; I loved them, and needed them deeply. I felt naked and exposed in the rawness of my new social orientation, where everything I encountered was gauged at a cultural level chilling to my soul. I turned back to my old friends with that hope of momentary release, to enter again the old accustomed association where nuance and reflection were spontaneous and acute, and found only the blankness in the air. Actually everything had changed, and it could never be the same again. I could not be both the old man and the new. But I am afraid it threw me back on my pride, and there is the mark of hurt pride in this poem, a mark which went into the making of it, and must stand as long as it does, ineradicable.

    The poem begins with a brief introduction, to catch up the underlying areas of response, to make the mood, before it proceeds to its business.

viii. From the Summer of the Flesh

I

For summer swells,
As the age, swollen,
Out of synthesis and into dissolution,
Summer's magnificent contradiction,
Brings forward within it a new
Winter of the world.

Who also, in the summer of the flesh,
A burgeoning pagan matrimonial,
Watch through to a frost, renounce;
To the wonder of a spring, and then
That limitless latitude
Beyond the swinging of the sun.

II

And many there are, struck by the strong
Extremeness of our choice, many there are to say:
Religion, making the threat that God
Breaks man from woman, in this alone
Will certify the naked falseness of its claim.

No justice ever enforced
Twin souls to separation
Merely to keep allegiance to a dead
Tryst of the past, a tryst
Utterly done and turned from,
Renounced long back in pain.

The Church convicts herself
Upon the human injury she would exact;
Blightens the very sacrament
She would exalt.

She speaks of love,
But here is love rebuked;
She talks of truth,

But here is truth suppressed;
She pleads by reason,
But here is reason choked.

When did a wrong repeated
Ever make a right?
When did a wound reopened
Ever heal a hurt?

You call this kindness?

Is this the merciful predicate
That brings the world from woe?
Is this your mild word
Leading the lost to light?

This dank taboo,
Conceived by the guilt-compulsive Jews
Who loathed the carnal tribes of Asia,
Become a fierce fixation
In the medieval-minded Church,
Forever forced?

What is a priest,
That he can take the measure of men's hearts?
What can he know of you, the eachness of you,
That touch, that tremulous hovering of love
Calling between?
What can he hope to know
Of such an earnest immanence
The man and wife compose?
What croziered Bishop, what Pope,
Clean out of sight in Rome,
Claims insight sufficient into the quickening touch
A natural marriage grounds on,
That he in conscience can intone:
"Anathema sit!"

Surely there is a nameless fascination,
Rooted in something evil,

Which draws you down,
Submits you to its smoky offices.

Break out!
Walk forth in the existent world,
Where living men and living women meet,
And trust their simple joy as earnestness enough
Beyond the blooded dogmas of the past!

Outside the church,
Across the cemetery plots,
The dandelion looses its hapless seed upon the air,
Vibrant and quick and free.
The Church can't hold it.
The cemetery wall can't keep it back.
Off with the blackbird and the jay
Raucous beneath the leaves,
It sifts and eddies,
Never to be contained.

Time like a cataract
Rushes in torrent to the indelible grave.
We have, between the double darks,
All we will know of laughter
And of love.  Let us now
Clasp while we may in the high
Camaraderie of bodied being,
Graceful and blithe and free,
And pass on, when we must,
Into the grainy earth,
At least together.

    III

So have I heard it said,
So have I said myself,
Back there, those passion-darkened days
Of ignorance and disdain;
So did I learn it at my father's knee,
The old agnostic, shrewd with the raw
Sagacity of the world.

His generation gauged its rebellion
Carefully at God, but gave to mine
The double-bladed knife
To cripple authority wherever it crossed us.
For us, the heretic was the saint.
Not that he stood in error,
Of this we took no care,
But that he stood alone.
To stand alone!
That was the ultimate,
The unexcellable thing!
Oh how we twisted on the stakes of history,
Gritting defiance while the flames licked up!
The past and its outrages
We made the weapons of our servile crimes.
"The truth shall make you free!"
Such was our purloined cry,
(Trampling truth meantime with our callow feet),
"Conscience supreme!"
Thus the rebellious will,
The deified self, made absolute,
Thrust forward into the very gaze of Truth.
Conscience we seized on, yes,
And shook it like a club against God's face.

For conscience is truly supreme:
More so, alas, than we had ever
Chosen to ponder. A man may err, may drift,
Go down the deserting lanes to desolation,
And nothing to keep him back.
Only the weak will, and it,
Left to its own, goes spineless;
Shunning the Godly voice
It turns, and takes up its temptation,
And finds at last its conscience
Terribly supreme. The great fatherly hand
Has given us that gift and will not make it less.
Nor jeopardize that high
Prerogative of choice that makes us men.
But fixed on the richer
Vision of a humankind

That freely might cater sin
But spurns it, as some
So spurned it—the saints,
Magnificent company, those free-born
God-determined souls, who begged
The gracious gift, and gained it—
Those Few, that we, as possibles,
Might know the perfect side of freedom
And the reason it was made.

For conscience, righteously vested,
The reason's purest gift,
Is clearly anterior to truth,
And must subserve it.
But this we would not reckon;
This we refused to see.
Truth, lost in the speculative
Errors of the past,
Had ceased as absolute.
We were the scrawny heirs
Of those mulish dissenters,
For whom the Angelic Doctor's limpid gaze
Was mere myopia. Straightway
They jammed the rudder.
Behind them rose the passionate
Pinch-browed schismatics,
Who quit the smelly Ship
To jockey each his incontaminate skiff
Beneath Her lee;
And riding out the break
Could not afford to probe
Their costly-purchased prize
Too closely. That ancient rupture
Truly served us well,
For we inherited the full
Impact of their mood,
If not their ruinous theology,
And, set to splitting every moral code

In the raw quest of appetite,
Proved conscience our lucky out.

The free! We called ourselves the free!
Poor liberated pawns of circumstance!
Shaken in the muzzle of untruth
We tossed from trap to trap,
And made our futile rushes,
Shrilling our freedom,
The veriest dupes in Satan's witless chain gang,
Slaves, and could not recognize our slavery.

Truly we were the free.
For though the prejudicial world
Imposed its irksome order on our lives,
And fear could keep us,
Yet in our hearts—boundless.
Our hearts were lawless as Dachau,
Where we might try
Endless experiments in degradation.
There we could plot our dark
Expiatory murders,
Seduce the merely timid,
Or ravish the merely proud;
Keep incest with the soulless
Daughters of our dreams;
Govern all but ourselves.
Strange lewd perversions
Hulked beneath our ken,
Hungering for entry.
Somewhere within, the rapacious ego
Whispered in terror and would not be still.

And everywhere about us
The sad disordered world
Staggered and drove on.
Deep in the darkened cinema our hearts
Restored the jaded rapture of the wish.
Each night the newssheet
Roused us afresh to some new
Cyclone of sensation, whose passion

Hurled through the cities,
While the black vacuum hidden in its head
Smashed a thousand hopes
In its erratic rush.
Huge were our hearts,
Which so loved the human,
Which is but to say the self,
That all it might manifest
Earned from us each a breathless fascination.
    Lord! Lord!
    How may we fare!
    The ample-spirited, all,
    The large abundant minds,
    The lofty ones!
    How may we fare
    When the strict Word
    Cleaves our divided hearts
    And judges us on justice!
    Not that we had no mercy;
    Truly our hearts were fat with mercy!
    But that we had no shame!
    And not to see the shame
    Is not to see the Glory!
    And not to see the Glory—
    What garment will we seize on in that Hour
    To hide our nudeness?
    What leaf, huddled about our loins,
    When the transcendent Light,
    Thrown through us,
    Opens our inward eyes,
    Shows us the things we are
    Measured against that Might!
For what we despised at heart
Was purity, however principled
We tricked our passions out,
However we held that earnestness alone
Licensed us to folly.
Purity we praised,
But kept it a kind of vague
Purity of motive,
A general spontaneous joy,

An upward gropingness,
Blithe manifestation of the outflown self.
It we called pure,
And it we worshiped,
And where it led us
There did we wish to go,
And frolic the vernal pastures
All our years.

And there, alas, we went,
Loud in our proclamations.
The dead hand of the past
No more to bind!
This was the Liberation!
Ours, the unshackled goddess
Whom none had dared to free!
And so we flung,
We flitted between the absolutes,
Where all was quick,
Fervent and alive,
No conscience-curbing precepts
Fenced that glade,
And the booby-trap Temptation
Was not made.

But Purity, that pricelessness,
That lodestone, that light,
Purity would not come.
Somewhere about the time
We tried our first exhilarating crossbreed
Purity disappeared.
Shy as the little child
All innocent of heart
Who would not stay to watch,
It left us.
As would my little brother,
Before my boyish depredations,
Lower his eyes and leave, so Purity

Left us to our feckless lot.

For Purity excludes.
Purity withholds, denies, rejects;
Is single; resists admixture;
Burns out the insufficient
And the residuum of dross.
Purity hurts.
It chastens and subdues;
And of its ministry
Much is demanded.

But we, what we desired was *all*.
And pillaged right and left
To prove our claim.
History we tortured.
Morality, we skinned it inside out,
And gaped to see its strictures drop like hail.
Did Purity desert?
Then let it desert, the miserable fraud,
For here it revealed itself
The sleazy thing we all along suspected:
The drab piety of spinsters and rural deacons,
And treacherous as well.
For look: shadowed, under the cast
Of its pale shibboleths,
There does the cankered Inhibition lurk,
And the dread Neurosis,
Ominous and old,
Twitches its spotted skin and breathes.

So Purity and we at last fell out.
The very source by which we justified
Our lofty rupture with the past
We now rejected.
And then, it gone,
Quite suddenly we had become
One with the past we spurned.
We took on something of its paltry lusts,
Its snide equivocations,
Its double words.

Not old, not even middle-aged,
To these in fact we were as yet the young—
But to the truly young,
For whom the sharp gradations of their lives
Run by the year, the season,
Those breathers after the burnished absolutes,
Who, as has been said,
Forever demand the heroic—
To these, already our lustre looked
The tell-tale tarnish of capitulation.

And so we made the break backward again,
And took our place
With all the paltry generations we despised.
Nor would we clean confess it,
But scraped up reasons,
And fell to plain dissimulation;
Made now no loud triumphant attestations as before,
But quietly slunk back into line
With some commodious lust that we had got attached to,
And couldn't bring ourselves to quite relinquish.

So what we had at first merely declined
We came in time to hate.
For Purity would not stay out,
But stood there,
A little distance off,
Under a tree perhaps,
Or down the road,
Or even gazing in at the window.
And just as we prepared for some
Truly magnificent feat of the appetite,
Some marvelous *tour de force* of real temptation,
Then would it stir,
And we'd look up,
And see it there,
With its sad compelling gaze,
And the trouble in its eyes.
That bilked us.
From then on it was war.
We sought to do it harm,

And lent its name to scandal and to filth.

And crowed to see its dearest own
Apostatize: the cloven hoof
Peeping beneath the cassock,
The immoderate oath
Black on a maid's mouth;
And gleaned from some antique text
The weak, too-willing nun.

Oh how these made us whinny with delight!
The ripple of bawdy laughter
Gusting along the spine!
Roiling the somnolent juices of the blood!
How splendidly we danced!
How earnestly we had no care!
(Till care came to us)
And kept no moral absolutes
Until the day the Absolute
Smashed in the door
And found us jiggling there—
Ripe for a ruin!

IV

No, my good friends,
My friends, I did not fall in panic
On my Faith, folding, as you have it,
With the frightened herd,
Creeping beneath the snug authoritarian roof
To dodge my own decisions.
Rather was I beaten;
Obstinate, I resisted.
The compelling Fact
Shook me. I hedged,
Tried it half-way,
Squeezed to escape,
Could not; was brought
Face up. It broke me down.
And when I entered,
I was not dragged

A-whimper by the heels,
Nor for mere certitude
Hugged up a crucifix
To keep from thinking.
I walked in upright,
In the full choice of my will,
And His,
And knelt down at His holy place,
And tried to quench that pridefulness of heart,
Before the glimmer of a God
Great enough to worship.

Nor may you mourn the human injury:
There is none.
For what is rightly done,
And in the full knowledge of righteousness,
Can never injure.
What's rightly done,
And once done, held to,
Assumes the blessing of the cure.
There is a rightness in the heart,
Which knows, before the face of God,
Across the mesh of human consequence,
Where hurt and heart-break
Hold, like handicaps, their principalities—
That rightness knows the way which must be walked,
And marks, and shows no judgment
Ruled and held and counted as a loss,
But counts a greater gain,
Out of the loss restored.
This in ourselves we prove.

And as for them, the patient priest,
The gentle Bishop and the saintly Pope,
They had no need to know
One inkling of us.
They mark no judgment in our hearts.
They only ask
Whether our actions fit with the constants of the Faith,
A faith that we, as they, are free
Either to take or turn from,

# PRODIGIOUS THRUST

Just as we choose.
Nor do they ask
Whether we burned, avid as animals,
Or whether our natures in a holy tryst
Touched in the quick of piety.
God knows it.
God knows alone.
He, only, judges.
And of our love,
What holiness was there
Will be our merit in the after-time,
What grossness, our regret.
God never asks of man
What he would have Him do,
Now hot, now cold,
Indulgent today, rigorous tomorrow.
Rather does God declare,
And for the good of man
Only declares, and for
No other reason.

There was a judgment of the Lord's,
Far back, deep in the human ancestry,
And never countermanded: *Thou shalt not
Put away thy wife and take another.*
Mankind has never proved it wrong.
All his vertiginous experience,
Centuries, the peeling civilizations,
Seamed with error and the failure of its faith,
The long waywardness of human degradation—
Mankind has never proved it wrong.
But in his anguish, and bitterly,
And in his blood, and in the hurting of his heart,
Has proved it right, has proved
It right.

We erred. We sought in each
What only God can give.
The tenets of the Faith
Which proved the past,
Prove now the present,

As this age sickens:
Divorce, wherein the union
Of the highest selves in solemn compact
Is ruined to knock those twinned souls
To their doom: the hapless child forlorn,
Stranded along the tepid backwash,
Where passion's ebb,
Runs out its rush,
Stagnates and stinks;
Willful sterility, a soul
Denied its frame, a child its kin,
The loveliest act of man with woman,
That mingling, that merging
Of the flesh in flesh
To make a furtherance of flesh,
For one end only: the child! the child!
The new soul clothed with flesh!
But now the thrusted stoppage strikes,
Onan's ancient crime blightens the mystery,
And the indigenous appetite,
Made monarch, thwarted from trueness,
Rushes unguided on the pales of fate!
>   Oh pity the doomed of life,
>   Who will not hold their hands out to its gifts!
>   Turning the frightened eyes
>   Down from the Lover's gaze!
>   Who will not face His face!  I
>   Late, as the pale of heart are always late;
>   Would only know the tingle of His touch
>   But would not bear His weight!
>   Who shrink behind the drapes that dusk the room
>   When He comes forward with His faultless tread
>   To lift the bridal veil,
>   And lead them inward to the vested Bed,
>   And quench forever in the gravid flesh
>   The mortal Maidenhead!

We erred.  Blinded by pride
And the ego's loud lament,
Our reckless choice assumed.
Off there, deep in remove,
The rightful husband and the rightful wife

Invest their ways.
Those marriages, in fealty made,
Were ruined in distrust,
Draw Hell's imperil.
Founded on fornication,
Reft in adultery,
Abandoned to the black monsoons of self
They split and perished,
Never to be resumed.

But she and I,
Now in the rich felicity of faith,
Freely confess the rush of guilt
Under our importunity,
And ask redemption,
And rather like kin-folk
Enter in His Church,
To find an equipoise
From all that onslaught of the self.

God finds the heart,
And of His finding there is no mistake.
It knows. Almost like seed
The planting is,
That stirs and grows.
The intemperate self resists,
The root strikes down;
The green branch lifts its frond;
The soul, split open by the lively Root
Exults; the inordinate self
Shudders before that Godhead
And succumbs. The soul exults;
The revolution of the heart
Is won.

Stormed, the old intrepid kingdom falls in flames
And wallows in its ash.
Out of that ruin rises up the resurgent soul
To meet His Church,
Where God confirms His weakest ones,
And makes the captive-proud

His highest hostages.
A Church built of the bones of sinners,
Purged of guilt.
They sing there.
They stumble in the rows.
I reach them, arm in arm.

Church of the Eucharist! Hardly
Can I enter Her door!
Hardly can I kneel at Her altar
So clumsy is my soul before the Host,
So helpless am I made!
How spell the dignity, the mighty worth?
How ponder the consummation of such love?
I see what weakens in the Church
Is only of my own, the human thing,
The human insufficiency.
But the worth! All that is God's!
The very hand of God
Clears in Her, keeps Her firm!
I see Her in Her past,
And am made proud,
And in Her present,
Yes, and am proud;
And see Her in Her future,
Her vast potential,
Wombed, the matrix of the Saints,
Where the human destiny
Shapes toward its sheerest pitch;
Am quenched up in Her scope,
Seized in Her wide embrace;
I move in the knowledge
That She cannot fail!

Universal Covenant!
Each instant of the earth,
Assumed in the hallowing of the Bread,
The hallowing of Wine;
Each instant of the earth
Assumed as Body for these asking ones,
These penitents, thronged to Her altars.

Under the crucifix the Host subsumes;
That glory blazes within the hand,
Blazes upon the up-thrust open lips,
Pours to the heart.
We rise, drunk with enlightenment.
We stagger to our place, each one
Cups of the Incarnation,
Each swept up in the strong
Intoxication of His trust!

Souls!  The myriad,
The many-millioned!
Rife with the charged capacity
For sanctity or sin!
Now for a time
The virgin and the vagrant
Are as one, wholly contrite
And stainless, exalted in His grace.
Deep in the nave
That Power smoulders,
Inexhaustible.
Under the candles,
Under the vestment drapes,
Under the tabernacled crown
He waits forever for His wanderers;
And draws them home.

We did, in parting,
No other than we should.
Little enough, though hard.
Little enough, though grave.
Little enough, though such a cost of pain—
But pain, not injury;
But lack, not loss! not loss!

Nor are we now alone,
Though in our distant habitations we recline.
For we are knit together in His love,
Clasped in His close embrace,
Twined as the children twine,
Who in His hermitage

Have made their glorious bed,
And under the bright Rooftree
Rouse up the exalted head
To meet the mercy of His gaze.

I have from her the memory of one
Most beautiful and wise,
Who brought me to my faith,
And laid her hand across my life,
Healing my hurt.
In her a graciousness of God resides,
Who is my adoration.

And in that vibrant Hour
Beyond the tolling of His bell,
We will be there;
And lay aside these masks that make the world,
And in the suddenness of that transcendent birth
Leap up together;

And wake, and watch,
And speak the praise of Him who made us be,
That man and woman we might see
Out through the other's eyes
The vaster vision, and the larger destiny.

And in that hushing of the heart
The turbulence, uplifted, is made free.

And the heart is freed. And the long days, and the nights, freed, all freed. What was our past between us, but one final consummation? What had we bestowed on each other unused in the final revelation that teaches what the long intentness never could have known? We were parted, yet joined. We were separate, but together. We had shared and now were spent. And the heart of this juncture asks no questions, replete with the gift born of the sacerdotal plenty. There was not a smile ever exchanged between us but worked to the wonder that we came to see.

So the poem that had begun as an objective disquisition had by its conclusion been turned into an undisguised celebration saluting again her whose influence had been so great in my life. That is no more than fitting, in a sequence devoted to her leave-taking; but it is the last. Not so much by diminishing interest as by fitness, I with this poem terminated the salute to that attachment of the past, and began to turn resolutely forward to the things on which I had staked so much. The summer was past the full now, and perhaps I felt my life was too, but I took up the things of summer and of God. In the earlier sequence, *The Springing of the Blade,* after the climax of the center-poem, I had concluded with a short off-trending lyric that led to the resolving music of the final rhyme; for there the whole purpose was to take the series out of the electricity of the initial encounter and to lead it forward into depth, to deepen the relationship, and in the deepening, flow forward to the richness of the life to come. Here, however, since this series introduced a disseveration, the final pieces are gauged to quite opposite an effect. The function is to pass out of the lesser relationship and on to the greater one; and in the wide summer world, the magnitude of seasonal growth and incipient autumnal change, I swung free, and forward, fastening my eyes ahead, to never again take up my pen in celebration of her who had evoked from it so much.

In this sequential ode which introduces the finale, the personal reference is not to her. We were never in the North together. It is rather to those old associations who had shared the years of trial up there, the Waldport years, and indeed to all my friends, everywhere, all those colorful, unconventional, anti-conventional people, who had shaped my thought and shared my misfortunes, good fellows all, comrades and associates, now estranged from me in the unbearable cleavage my act had introduced. Had we not suffered the same exile, borne the same curse? Had not the village urchins pegged at us the selfsame stones? Had not the frowsy waitresses snubbed us behind the same lunch-counters? And so I gathered them together in my poem, and spoke to them as earnestly as I once could, in the simplicity of the things we loved in common: shore, sea, sun, season; and tried through these common touchables to lead back to the heart of the thing that had happened to me and to hope thereby for their understanding. For they were dear to me, and very close to my heart; and my mind was with them much in those days. They had meant so much to me. They had given me much, both of love and of knowledge, and I owed them much. They were the best people I had met. And each day I gathered them into my prayers, and prayed that they too might be made to see what I had seen, and to come as I had come. And I can ask it yet, not only in the worth of what they would receive, but in the worth as well of what they are. For having known them truly, this I know for certain: they deserve nothing less. In the magnitude of summer, then, I brought them all together, and in my poem spoke as I could not elsewhere speak, spoke not of our differences, but in the emphasis of what we each well knew, and, knowing could unquestionably affirm.

   ix. Past Solstice

Past solstice; not yet the length of a month past;
And now to leave, to go forth from the house,
Aware of a first lack in the light
Where nothing but the light had sprouted.

So. That autumn edges? Days go short?
Is it not of God's hand, all?

As in the North, remember, at the year's
Change again toward its final quarter,
After the somnolent summer held sustained its peace on the sea,
Then would the autumnal storms be blown in at night,
And we picked our way down to the shoreline at dawn,
And the eastern light, strong at our backs, stood out to sea,
And threw a different face on the sea;
And we saw how the inswell of storm,
That had troubled the face of the water far out,
Disturbing those listless nooks of the tide,
Those eddies, where all stagnant summer the sea held to its
    hoard,
And now brought forward, shells, bottles, glass balls, pieces of
    wreck,
Many wonderful shapes, many wonderful things of the drift,
Dead legions of the life of the sea,
Strewn flotsam gifts of the ocean-going fleets,
All there, all to be touched—but at next tide
As solemnly gone, quite taken,
That glittering beach, far as the sight fell,

# PRODIGIOUS THRUST

    Picked clean.  Even the gulls
    Gone.

    And yet the sea was the same.
    The sea was the source in which all tides were manifest.
    It was the sea we went to.

    So God in His seasons.
    And the God-seeker, the man God-loving,
    He will not worship entire opulent fall, nor sparse winter,
    And will let frolicsome spring go its own way for once.

    But will look rather to that eternity *within* the flux,
    Where the Source of all the seasons holds them back at His
          mighty Heart,
    And breathes on them in their order.

    For the seasons seen are only the things of time,
    And time seen is only the order of things,
    And all things will fail.
    But the Source of all things will never fail.
    For the nature of things lies in their being apart,
    They may suffer reduction;
    But the Source of things is not fashioned of parts,
    And may not be reduced.

    And we, being things, love things and the sequence of things.
    We love the seasons.  But what we seek of the thing
    Is that greaterness within the thing
    Which keeps it in being.

    Therefore praise autumn, praise opulent autumn,
    And breathe the white breath of winter,
    And revel with spring.

    But love what autumn will never succeed,
    Nor winter curb, nor spring survive;
    What even summer, the tall triumphant summer,
    Will never surpass:

    Love Him.

The final rhyme came late. The year drew down to its great liturgical close, the first of my experience. Time after Pentecost ran out its final weeks, disposing of sunken centuries, and the rise and fall of many civilizations, and the abundance of much ancient wisdom ordered in its span. And the rains came out of the close sea before the cold set in; and in the last of the warmth the seeds set down their roots, and the slim blade stiffened. And it was Advent, the seasonal close but the liturgical beginning, the cross-flux that catches one up then, for all the sensible world is indeed closing, but the spiritual world is but beginning. And this magnificent symbolism caught me up also in the whole story of my anguish and assuagement. And I wrote the bare poem that would bring this sequence of love to a close, a love great enough to part with for a Love greater still; the love that knows how to release when the time is meant. I had been taught that love. Now Advent was to teach me again, over, what the year had taught so well. I could not regret one instant of it; it was so final and so serene, so deep in its resolution.

x. Advent

Fertile and rank and rich the coastal rains
Walked on the stiffened weeds and made them bend;
And stunned November chokes the cottonwood creeks
For autumn's end.
And the hour of Advent draws on the small-eyed seeds
That spilled in the pentecostal drought from the fallen cup:
Swept in the riddled summer-shrunken earth;
Now the eyes look up.

Faintly they glint, they glimmer, they try to see;
They pick at the crust; they touch at the wasted rind.
Winter will pinch them back but now they know,
And will not stay blind.

But all Creation will gather its glory up
Out of the clouded winter-frigid womb;
And the sudden Eye will swell with the gift of sight,
And split the tomb.

So the year waned, and I thought that I had the mastery of it, and in a way I had, but in a deeper way I had not. For in all my zeal in the Faith, whatever the psychic anguish I had felt, I had never been crushed. At no time in the long event had I been truly crushed, and that must be before I came full circle. Now Christmas drew on; word arrived from her people that they were coming up from out of town for the holidays. They had welcomed me into the Faith but had not seen me since, and arriving they came into the house, as we had all commonly shared it on their few vacations in the old days, and again we were all together, save her. We made to have a great feast on Christmas Day, and her confessor did not object to her coming. Near noon she returned to that house she had left eight months before, and so much had changed in us. But she walked into the house, and in those very rooms, where we had loved so deeply, and learned so well, she looked into my face and smiled. And the beauty of her smile, so sweet, and so glad, so filled with consequentiality, struck through all the shells of my mind a great blow. I turned from her into another room, to escape, to seize hold of myself and master the thing that had sounded in me. And she saw my distress, and came after me, and touching my arm looked in my eyes again, and smiled that meaningful, questioning, ineffable smile; and suddenly everything in me collapsed. I had to get out. I could not shut down my sobs. I broke forth coatless into the Christmas sunlight, and ran into the street, and ran till I found the little church, and there on the altar rail where daily I received the Body of God, I flung myself down. And for the first time was given me the towering stature of my loss.

Later her brother found me and brought me back. I regained my composure, and the day, which for all had been shattered, resumed its gladness. But the thing that had happened put the finality upon an episode that otherwise would never have been complete, would have somehow remained, on the human level, abstract and unfinished, lacking true resolution in the imagination and the soul. It was a purge. And it was, as purge, a comprehension, a way of knowing, that must be learned in the basis of a man, in this life or the next, before he may ever find Heaven.

# Epilogue

# I BEG FOR DELIVERANCE

> *See then, my very dear father, that I want nothing in me to be hidden from your eyes, I who not only disclose to you my whole life, but so minutely make manifest my individual thoughts. And for these thoughts I beg your prayers, that long and last, unstable and fickle as they are, they may sometime stand fast, and after much tossing about may they turn to the one, true, certain and enduring God. Fare thee well.*
>
> Francis Petrarch

IT IS MIDSUMMER, 1955, and once again I stand in the cloister-garth with the young night about me, and the summer stars far up their lucent altitudes, remote gouts of fire burning their cores out in the long instant of their life. Over the roof of the monastery comes as ever the muffled vocabulary of the city, a babble of traffic, torn by the ragged wail of its sirens, the doleful mourning of its trains, a vast and murmurous cacophony, disquiet and intense as the whisper of a psychotic. The monastery is dark, almost vacant, the priests scattered out to their summer assignments, and the host of Student Brothers sent north to the new retreat house in the Oregon Cascades—only the Lay Brothers to maintain the buildings and a handful of priests; the chapel by night voiceless of its pulse, unresonant of the Chant, by day bereft of the Liturgy, empty, an emptiness hung like a pall on the once-full choir, the silent-standing stalls.

There has been, since that other time I stood here and conned the Prologue to my book, little outward change. I am still a Dominican, still a *donatus*. I wear the same Lay Brother's habit, the garden is unaltered, the monastery keeps its peace. But between the shaping of those words and these resides an event so powerful in its reverberation as to separate the before and the after into two virtually irreconcilable phases. That event was a whirlwind attempt at the Clerical Novitiate, an impulsive bid for the priesthood; an attempt which in six excruciating months saw every vestige of motivation eradicated from my soul, and saw me at last flung back like a repulsed thing into the category out of which I came.

Up to that point every phase of my life in the Church emerges in retrospect as a distinct advance: the solitude following my conversion, a whole year of unprecedented creative activity; that first retreat with the Jesuits and the recognition of the religious life; the fourteen purifying months in the Catholic Worker movement; the discovery of the Dominican intellectual apostolate and the rapid crystallization of religious vocation; the first painful but intoxicating months of advance in the religious life; the final luminous dream of the priesthood; the move to secure the necessary dispensation; the actual attempt; and at last the swift and staggering collapse of vision, blow after terrible interior blow, and the crippled retreat back here to the House of Studies.

For six months I wore the white scapular of the Dominican cleric. For six months I chanted in choir the Divine Office, learned the subtle and complex inflection of Gregorian Chant, pored over the history of the Order, studied the Liturgy. For six months I moved about the altar, assisting the priest in the august mysteries of the High Mass. For six months I escaped my old position on the periphery of the Order and moved to its center; and saw it as a future priest might see it, from the center; and was instructed in my every move in terms of the center. For although there are Orders in which the conception of the Brother exists on a parity with the priest (neither the Benedictines nor the Franciscans were originated as clerical institutes), in the Dominicans it has always been the priesthood alone which constitutes the superior grade and which determines the center; St. Dominic lives on as the embodiment of the Christ-like priest. And the Lay Brother understands this; the Lay Brother is content in his supporting role, for it is indispensable, and his reward will be very great.

But having acknowledged so much, what may be said for the *donatus*, a layman in a religious habit, a layman with a religious name, living on in the heart of the monastery, neither fish nor fowl, an anachronism, caught up in his painful ambiguity, his life one long frustration in his search for center? For that was the passion which was uncontainable, and which swept me in. And for that little time I was integral to the center; for that little time I touched it. But yet, throughout, the gradually gathering darkness, crisis upon crisis, the blackout of the soul, collapse of the vision, the utter cancellation of the dream, to end at last in that horrible shambling retreat back here to the House of Studies, the stripping off of the white scapular and the donning of the black.

Dark night in the cloister, black night in the soul; void of the spirit; painful suspension of the faculties; all the caverns of the senses emptied of their store. Everything I have touched hangs on unfulfillment, misshapen and grotesque, my life half done, caught on its forty-third year, sputtering away in incompleteness. The *Great Psalter* is long since abandoned, passed off as a fragment to be fronted up by another printer, bound by another hand; the handpress standing down there in the cellarage untouched. Nor have I set pen to poem these many months; they blow in pieces about my cell, littering, the unread leaves of the sibyl. The story of *the thrust* remains half-finished, cut off at the conversion, truncated; its conclusion, which was to narrate the search for vocation and the spiritual ascent, remains unwritten, the hand that should write it impotent with complicity, shaken by indecision, drained of all purpose. *Thrust* will itself have to go out unresolved, indecisive and unconvincing, mocking me with its flaws—its raw gaucheries, its shaky apologetics, its indiscreet disclosures, its brash unseasoned certitude. And so much to be said. And so many better ways to say it.

And I ponder again the implacable darkness that is driving me out of the Order. I entered it on the strength of a genuine commitment, of that I am certain: *veritas*, the search for truth, the abiding quest of the knowledge of God. As an artist I perceived in the Order the deep fulfillment of the creative man, the rectification and sharpening of the productive faculties in an intellectual context gauged toward a superlative end. I saw its essential freedom, a liberation of the spirit which I felt to be crucial to the line of my own development; and I entered, and that spirit pervaded me, and I saluted it as a vocation which, in these respects, must surely be second to none. I made no mistake.

But the contemplative claim in the apostolic end will not abide diversion. The contemplative claim burns its votary free of all diversion, the apostolic end seizes him up in its crying compulsion and will not release. The onslaught of spiritual darkness has forced me to undergo not the bloom of the talents but their remorseless cancellation, the roots of the faculties cauterized in an interior fire until every vestige of aesthetic response has been seared away. I subsist at last only on a kind of bed-rock motivation that has apparently nothing to do with my conscious life. I am here because God wills it; it comes to that. As far as its earthly existence is concerned, the soul in this extremity seeks one thing only, to quench the darkness that rages within it, and that has no end.

To quench it by a more perfect conforming to the divine exemplar, which it cannot see, but the forces of whose demand it feels everywhere upon it, a magnetism of such intensity as to leave it agonized in the glare of its limitations. Its deficiencies are its torture. The least freedom fills it with apprehension that it may capitulate. It hates its free will because that exercise may tempt it to deflect. It seeks a context which will never let it deviate from the invisible force that has filled its being. It gropes about it for every means of maintaining itself against the recalcitrant energies subsistent in its nature. But the spontaneous acts and movements it once loved to do, acts that seemed to impel it towards its goal, impulsions of love, fond mortifications and denials, penances heroic in their intensity and lovely in their proof, intoxicating achievements over its nature—these now become to it as absurdities, incomprehensible, their spontaneity all an illusion. It huddles concentrated within its elemental being incapable of gesture, gazing mutely and with anguished fascination up the torrent of implacable justice that pours into it, burning it out.

Its need for stability, for an impervious context to match its interior demand, has become a passion, and like all passion it spends itself. The enthusiasm of vocation set down in my Prologue has been swept from my heart, the residuum of affective and even intellectual affiliation has been stripped away. I long for a starker emphasis, a more ruthlessly concentrated spiritual atmosphere, a harsher poverty, a fiercer contextual asceticism. The Dominicans, acute theologians, have taught me to distinguish implacably between pure grace and any variety of psychological intensity, whether of sorrow or joy, and however extreme. But it is a teaching which the onslaught of spiritual affliction has canceled out with everything else. In this tremendous ineffectuality I am beyond such distinctions.

But I do see that in the spiritual life my error has been to seek only that which I could relate to my enthusiasm: the Order, the Church, even God; to reckon spirituality in terms of reaction. But now in the night I am brought to see that no kind of enthusiasm can hold. Neither the Order, nor the Church, nor God will sustain the soul at the pitch of its own demand. Such exultation feeds only on the roots of its primal disorder. It was not made to last, and in the not-lasting one broaches the realization that everything he once reckoned as an affiliation is, quite simply, no more. The thing it was has vanished. Something is there but he no longer recognizes it. He becomes the supremely unaffiliated man. Confronted with its aloneness the soul can do one thing only: pray. By day and by night I beg for deliverance.

I beg for deliverance, but from what? I plead release, but to where? One thing I have discovered: imperfectly, confusedly, but still a discovery—that I am helpless, impotent. In a general metaphysical way I knew this of course, but I had no realization of the levels within me into which the helplessness extends. I have been moving on illusions, dangerous illusions. I feel I am still moving on them, that for years I will be moving on them, out of them, all my life moving through the illusion of what God is, while He remains something unspeakably other. The reality of Him will be forever withheld from me, is something I will have to die to discover, and then spend the split second of all eternity in the titanic grip of discovery.

And I see that despite all that enormous hunger of mine I never understood my own good, never construed what I needed, never accurately posited the merest ingredients of my own happiness, had utterly no grasp of its essentiality. Of myself, I see, all I can do is err, and that is human. But this suffering is divine, and in it lies my safety. Sometimes for a moment the naked darkness is pierced and in the ray of a jewel-bright disclosure I know that its totality is, in its depths, something obscurely of my own making, something I have actually chosen. That it is, in fact, the fundamental thing I had asked for, all unknowingly, back there at Baptism, when I asked for the Christ. This death, this annihilation is the real answer to my request, the gift I truly desired; the boon I would beg of God if I were big enough, could see enough, had vision enough to open my arms and embrace it. That it is, in fact, precisely what Baptism means, the faintest incorporation into the mortal dereliction of Christ. For though I cannot conceive how I ever could ask for this, yet I know in the profoundness of my faith that I have got abundantly what I asked for, and that this must be it. Now it edges on with an inexorability that leaves no doubt as to what it means to bestow. Its term is nothing less than Golgotha, the Skull, place of earthly death.

For truly the Church assumes in man's life the instrumentality of Golgotha. Not, as the skeptics have it, the institution of intellectual destruction, but on the contrary, the context in which the purgation of saints finds its consummation. Outside Her hegemony surges pain, a universe of pain, the nightmare pain of chaos. Inside Her domain there swells another universe of pain, as comprehensive and as inescapable, but it is the purgative pain of incipient order, and its reprieve is divine. Outside Her, one suffers with the animals; within Her, one suffers with the saints. It is a pain made holy in Her head, the God-Man who proved in His death its immense uses, and taught us to prove in our own the function it serves for others.

For the Church is not a heaven; She is a purgatory, the earthly purgatory of man's elemental cleansing, and Her pain is pure; that is why men flee Her; but Her pain, if acceded to, completes itself in Her life. Only within Her dispensation does the soul really begin to suffer with exactitude, and then the suffering gathers upon itself in a beautiful concatenation, the orchestration of a sublime anguish, pure function, pure purpose. It is this which makes it beautiful. The passion of Christ re-enacts itself in the deeps of the soul, and makes the soul the vessel of divine commitment, the instrument of the universal music, a kind of supreme lamentation of the life of God in man, melodic and sublime, resonant of the conformability of Christ's perpetual pain, His precious endowment to the Christian soul, the soul of assent.

In Him we suffer. Soon, in Him, we die. In Him, of Him, we ask no better thing than so to suffer, nothing more perfect than so to die. The Christian, the contemplative, fastens his straining eyes on his death, the point of his unification. He lives out the straining nerve of his soul in the hope, the sublime expectation of that death. Oh, indeed, he flinches and fears; his flesh cries out, coward that it is; it *knows* its fallenness. But it is aware that on the Cross the baseness is burned out of it, like malignant fever burned out of proud flesh. *Burn, O Mind Divine! Burn, Thou vast Intelligence of God!* In such vast intelligence all imperfection is consumed, because it is consummated into the universal order. Show an area on earth where there is blind fortuitous pain and some Christian saint will appear and make it holy. That is the function of the Church, the Christ-function in Her; it is in this pain that She becomes Him. This pain-action is what He does in Her, like a marvelous poultice which draws pain to it, absorbs pain in it.

And as we become of Him, in Her, so pain comes to us, the pain of many others, of many wounds, many anguishes, all these are drawn to us and we absorb them because we are of Him in Her, and that has become our function. Thus the Christian serves the world, saves the world, brings it to be back from itself and into Herself, the Bride who assumes and assuages the passion of Her Beloved, and makes it be, and from the passion pours forth much fruit. We walk encompassed in Her glory, enfolded in His pain. And though we try indeed to flee, He will never let us escape. For He knows this, and we must learn it, the secret which, though the instinct of our flesh struggles to reject, our souls must never deny: in His pain sounds our peace, the tranquillity of true order. When we assent to His pain, we assume the universe of peace. And in this comprehension His pain, His peace, that ocean of immutability, closes over our heads.

# In Situ:

## The Making of *Prodigious Thrust*

### An Afterword By ALLAN CAMPO

*"To this you must resign yourself...in the life and work of every man lurks some undone remnant; this is the lot that we all must bear."*[1]

DURING THE LAST YEAR AND A HALF of his life, William Everson attempted to put the finishing touches to the "undone remnant" of his long and productive career: finalizing his material for the scheduled publication of *The Integral Years*, the third and concluding volume of his "Collected Poems"; laboring to advance *Dust Shall Be the Serpent's Food*, his autobiographical epic of which five of the projected ten Cantos were in print, the sixth in progress, and a seventh glimmering in the wings; bringing forward "The Tongs of Jeopardy," his unpublished book-length meditation on the assassination of John F. Kennedy, written nearly thirty years before; and giving renewed attention to the most long-standing portion of that remnant, *Prodigious Thrust*, completed in July of 1956.

In 1963, Everson had written a new introduction for *Prodigious Thrust*, appraising it several years after his transformative "breakthrough into the unconscious," which had occurred immediately upon the book's completion. In the fall of 1992, he produced yet another introductory piece—this time taking into account both the effect of the drastically changed Catholic ethos that resulted from Vatican II and the fact of the book's unpublished status all those many years. This latter introduction evinces an unevenness attributable to the ravages of the poet's Parkinson's disease, then in its sixteenth year, which had rendered him incapable of sustained writing, a process so laboriously slow that the train of his unimpaired thought simply outraced his physical ability to keep pace. The following year, he contacted me in the hope I might yet have a copy of the typescript from the re-typing I had done thirty years before, since it had turned out that the typescript housed among his papers at the Bancroft Library was itself not intact. I did, and sent him a photocopy.

Not long afterward, pneumonia and its severe complications hospitalized Everson for a time; an uncertain recovery restored him to his Kingfisher Flat home for a few months, and there he died in the early evening of June 2, 1994, at the age of eighty-one.

Now, some forty years after its completion, the book attains William Everson's long-held hope—publication. And what is striking, what must be kept in mind, is that, in spite of the passing of four decades, the book remains as it was when Everson finished it in 1956. And that is how we must regard *Prodigious Thrust*: within its original circumstances of composition and completion—*in situ*.

\* \* \*

Over the years, those who had occasion to read *Prodigious Thrust* in typescript generally reacted with varying degrees of discomfiture—the Brother Antoninus revealed therein not the man they knew: that straitlaced Catholic convert with his often tendentious, sometimes self-righteous attitude; his unwavering adherence to the authority of the Vatican church; his solidly foursquare defense of the Catholic positions on such matters as marriage, sex, contraception, homosexuality. But, of course, they were reading the book from a different perspective than Everson wrote it.

Vatican II had made the early 1960s a watershed moment in the long history of the Catholic Church because, beyond the myriad and even sweeping changes it wrought, what it most radically accomplished was to enable the previously *sotto voce* Catholic diversity and dissent to become the open exchange of public discourse. When Everson wrote an Introduction for the 1982 reissue of Victor White's *God and the Unconscious*, originally published in 1952, he made this point in a statement that applies no less truly to *Prodigious Thrust*:

[T]he Catholic society this book confronts today is a radically different world from the one it was composed to engage, something that should be borne in mind on opening its pages. The tight ship of Pius XII is no more.[2]

If *Ecclesiastes* is to be believed—"There is a season for everything"—the 1950s were the season for *Prodigious Thrust*. The succeeding decades rendered it passé, if not positively anachronistic. Hence the unease of those who read it in years past. Hence, too, the pointlessness of rehashing the Brother's earnest discourses and elevated rhetoric in an attempt to render their orthodoxy palatable to the contemporary reader—even if such an attempt could succeed. Pointless because what ultimately matters is the book itself, the inner dynamics of the work that give it an estimable stature regardless of seasons.

In any event, within the book's own pages, in addition to acknowledging the problems orthodoxy may well cause the reader, Antoninus frankly admits to its shortcomings, calling it "indecisive and unconvincing," confessing to its "raw gaucheries, its shaky apologetics, its indiscreet disclosures, its brash unseasoned certitude."[3] Nor does he spare himself, even going so far as to score his monastic demeanor as "fake medieval attitudinizing." There is no need for us to add anything further to what Antoninus has already conceded.

The fact is that, when we enter the pages of *Prodigious Thrust*, we enter the scenario of the "hero's journey," the timeless world of myth as it impinges upon the substance of what we like to call *reality*. Joseph Campbell summarizes it for us:

> The standard path of the mythological adventure of the hero is a magnification of the formula represented in the rites of passage: *separation—initiation—return*: which might be named the nuclear unit of the monomyth.[4]

This adventure begins with what Campbell terms "the call," which comes in various guises and serves diverse purposes. Often the herald, the carrier of the call, appears as an unworthy, even unsavory figure; and the call itself, among other possibilities, "may mark the dawn of religious illumination."[5] It takes hardly a moment to see the relevance to Everson's Christmas Eve conversion: "I saw the sheepherder in the shepherd, and the shepherd came alive." The call to conversion *took*. And he entered the opening phase of his journey—*separation*.

Separation it was: first, left to himself in the house he had shared with the woman, his wife, who had provided the circumstances for his conversion; then, moving to the Catholic Worker House of Hospitality in the pariah-world of Oakland's Skid Row, ministering there to the down-and-outers; and finally, the most profound move, his entry into the Oakland monastery of St. Albert the Great, the Dominican House of Studies for the Western Province.

Fittingly, Antoninus frames this book of his time of separation by his presence within the monastery's garden, the "cloister garth," a form of the *temenos*, the sacred and protective precinct of ancient origin, wherein the work of separation could be carried out. What that work entailed we find specified by William James as he discusses the phenomenon of conversion in his classic study, *The Varieties of Religious Experience*. At one point, as he recognizes that conversion partakes of mystery, James essays to delineate it in this way:

> Neither an outside observer nor the Subject who undergoes the process can explain fully how particular experiences are able to change one's centre of energy so decisively, or why they so often have to bide their hour to do so. ... All we know is that there are dead feelings, dead ideas, and cold beliefs, and there are hot and live ones; and when one grows hot and alive within us, everything has to re-crystallize about it.[6]

*Everything has to re-crystallize about it.* Precisely. The work of Antoninus' period of separation was nothing less than a total reshaping of the beliefs and attitudes by which he lived and the perspective within which he viewed the course and events of his life:

> When I entered the Church my values, the whole emphasis of my mind, underwent a rapid and profound alteration. I left behind the vision of the end as purely natural balance, and struck out for the end as supernatural extremity, the absolute attainment beyond all the limited attainments of life.

If Everson seized the moment of conversion through his inner kinship with the cthonic shepherds, it was left to Antoninus to pursue the labor of assimilation in kinship with the Magi, the intellectuals. This would be no easy task even to begin, for, as he writes with regard to his early espousal of pantheism, "I did not claim to have worked out my position with care: I hardly concerned myself at all with formal philosophy. I was too distrustful of the rational faculty for that." Distrustful or not, but aided by the intellectual atmosphere and contacts within the Dominican monastery, he took up that "rational faculty" in order to grasp and articulate the prime interests of the Catholic magisterium—faith and morals.

This, then, is the first level of the dynamics operative within *Prodigious Thrust*. It is quite along the lines of what Carl Jung denotes as *auseinandersetzung*:

> This untranslatable German word means having it out with a thorough discussion of every aspect, airing all the pros and cons, always with a hint of eventually coming to terms.[7]

If the intuitive approach and the "episodic" method of the poet are, as Antoninus indicates in his Preface, at variance with the reasoned continuity of narrative, they form the essential mode throughout the book: from experiential encounter and intuitive perception to discursive extension, as Antoninus takes his cue from whatever comes to hand—whether mundane grocery-store incident, human interaction, scriptural account, or doctrinal issue. Furthermore, it is often enough (though not always) the poet's way with language that rescues many a discourse from what might otherwise be impassable turgidity.

The manner in which the book was composed is relevant and worth noting at this point. Antoninus described the process in an interview some years later:

> This autobiography I began to write about the same time that I began to print the *Psalter* [i.e., 1952]. I was writing poetry through here too. I was not writing when I began [the autobiography] in a very sustained way. I just began something that would be a kind of sketch. Then I would

write something else that would tie in. Then the first thing you know, I would say, "Well, maybe I really ought to try to organize this material into an autobiography of some kind."[8]

What matters here is that, beyond describing the episodic composition, the account confirms the impression that Antoninus wrote the book concurrently with the outworking of the conversion process. Consequently, as we read his book, we experience his substantial effort of coming to grips with Catholic doctrine, even as we experience the sometimes discomfiting effects of his tendentiousness and stringent orthodoxy—unaffected by those ramifications ensuing from his psychological breakthrough and unmodified by any later inclination to accommodate the revisions effected by Vatican II.

Furthermore, as Antoninus continued his writing of *Prodigious Thrust*, he was also entering that phase of the spiritual ascent known as the Dark Night of the Soul—"the interior purgations of the religious life, a process mysterious and profound, to be starkly experienced, but hardly to be described." For though, except in the anguished Epilogue, the book does not attempt to express the Dark Night experience (an attempt that would be the substance of the later *The Hazards of Holiness*), that experience resides as pervasive background. For the Dark Night experience is not at all some ethereal reality that proceeds apart from the everyday demands and circumstances of the individual's life. Whatever was transpiring within the soul of Antoninus was also an integral part of the painful setbacks he endured during this period: the poetic drought, the untimely halt to the printing of the *Psalter*, the failure of his attempt at the priesthood. In point of fact, given his commitment to the spiritual life, Antoninus had to learn in the desolate suffering of 1954 to 1956 that he was not yet fit to go forth into the world and display the works of his talents and his aspirations. Before his *return*, there would be an *initiation*; and it was the labor of *separation*, delineated in his book, that would get him there.

The intellectual stock-taking embodied in *Prodigious Thrust* was itself one aspect of the Dark Night—designated as the "purification of the intellect" in the literature of mysticism. Yet, even as he carried forward this necessary work of the intellect in the service of his conversion and spiritual progress, Antoninus was bedeviled by a conflict which forms a deeper level of what is at work within this book.

\* \* \*

William Everson was quite emphatically one of those converts who "have startled and still startle the traditional Catholic by their inability to unbend."[9] He describes himself as he was in the early time of his conversion:

> I remember how in those days I wanted to wear my faith as a living badge before the world; yes, a defiant badge which I expected the world to despise.

The finding of his vocation and his entry into monastic life seemed only to intensify this attitude, for he took up his new life as Brother Antoninus bearing as his charge "the terrible attempt to be the most monastic of monks."[10] He tells us in the present work:

> I entered the Order like a clenched fist. My spirit was knotted upon an intensity of commitment to which I directed my entire force. In that intensity...[I] have been the painful exacerbation of those around me, whose charity sustained me through my violations, whose forgiveness absolved me in my spirit.

Obsessed by the unyielding persona which dominated him, Antoninus was wont to call attention to the least deviation from the monastic "ideal"; consequently, his day by day "exacerbation" made it a "drag" to be around him, as one of St. Albert's resident priests of that time recalled, going on to say, "You couldn't do some innocent thing without him moaning and reminding you that you were corrupt."[11] Probably every Dominican who spent any time at St. Albert's during those years would have his own "Antoninus anecdote" to tell. No doubt his fellow internees from the conscientious objectors' camp at Waldport, Oregon, where he spent most of World War II, would have commiserated, perhaps chuckling as they did, recalling how Everson, early on in his internment, had been dubbed "One Long Moan."

Such behavior sprang from what Antoninus pointedly describes as "the taut constriction of attitude which from the beginning was my focus in the Church"—an attitude that, as he points out later, went toward confirming him "as the complete rigorist, an attitude accountable, I am told, in terms of my particular past, and forgiven with it." Forgiven, it may have been. Resolved, it was not.

His expressions of self-deprecation punctuate *Prodigious Thrust*, a *mea culpa* counterpoint to the elevated religious perspective and earnest discourses. Unlike the stereotypical "true believer," Antoninus remained in open conflict within himself. He lived out a tension: the polarity he perceived between the monastic persona which governed his book no less than it did his conduct and the flawed person who contaminated both.

This observation brings to mind what Everson had written in the Foreword to a projected collection of his final pre-Catholic poetry, as he attempted to explain the underlying movement within his earlier verse:

> We behold a soul endeavoring to achieve resolution by the willed imposition of extraneous elements; imposed because the interior truth was unfaceable, serving on the one hand as a mask to conceal the real dilemma giving it birth, and on the other striking an attitude or stance, an artificial resolution, a bid for formulated coherence, the attempt to contain the interior demon in the cage of verbal structure. And yet the exorcism was never complete, the demon was never expelled.[12]

He continues his explanation with the comment that "the crises of life (war, sexual betrayal, divorce, new marriage) demolished the mask, cracked it open."[13] He was mistaken. The "game face" he had donned in his effort to be the "most monastic of monks" was but a variation of the mask. Its creative embodiment was now his book, as earlier it had been his poetry. That tension between person and persona, genuine as it was, was but a symptom, as the book was yet another "bid for formulated coherence, the attempt to contain the interior demon in the cage of verbal structure." Nonetheless, these remarks should not detract from the high accomplishment which *Prodigious Thrust* represents, for such is the intrinsic complexity of motives and influences within human endeavors.

Indeed, it would take the full act of the book's composition to accomplish what all those prior years and works could not. It is critical, then, to recognize that *Prodigious Thrust* was not an outrider, simply marking time until the poetic drought ended or vocational adjustment was attained. For it is axiomatic that Everson invariably wrote his way through crises, just as he explained to an interviewer:

> I generally write out life crises and use the poetry as a way of resolving difficulties I find myself in, objectifying them and universalizing them.[14]

With the poetry temporarily in abeyance, as the crisis of his religious life intensified so did his efforts with *Prodigious Thrust*. During his stay at the clerical novitiate, he was, as he described it to Ruth Teiser, "throwing myself into it. I was throwing all my creative energies into the writing of this autobiography." And when the priestly aspiration collapsed, sending him back to St. Albert's in an emotional and spiritual shambles, "I kind of sustained myself through that crisis by pouring myself into that prose work."[15] But before the instrumentality of his book reached its full effect, Antoninus arrived at the point of impasse: "I had attempted exterior observance and I had no inner freedom."[16]

\* \* \*

That "inner freedom" was straining to be born. Take, for instance, his question midway through the book: "And are we not invoked to the imitation of Christ?" The incongruity of citing a spiritual directive following his self-confessed ineptness in attempting to use commercial metaphor as Christ had done so effectively is jarring. The intimation that there is more at issue here than the use of rhetorical devices is borne out by his answer:

> Let this be understood: no kind of imitation is Christian. ... It is the Christ in us, not our pallid imitation of Christ, which must be brought to bear.... And we become Christ by being in the most exigent manner the wholeness of our individuation, which is all our perfection is.

Carl Jung—who would become Everson's psychological master, as Robinson Jeffers had been his poetic one—could hardly have put it better.

Antoninus concludes his exhortation: "'To thine own self be true' strikes to the substratum of the Christian faith." The shift from an outer paradigm to an inner one and from the Christ to "thine own self"—unobjectionable as theological scrutiny would show it to be—is not only a departure from the prevailing Catholic consciousness of the time, but, more significantly, it betokens the unachieved resolution to the dilemma engendered by the attempt to be the "most monastic of monks." The ability to follow his own directive was contingent upon the achievement of that "inner freedom," which, for the time being, remained beyond his reach.

Further on, he proposes a liberating admonition, directed to the poet, but no less applicable to the person:

> In the joy of His creation God does not stint Himself. Nor does the poet, in his great vision, renounce the fullness, the vivification and the impetus of his art. Rather it is only out of his whole intensity that the deeper art is fashioned. He fashions out of the magnitude of the abundance pouring through him, and if he so much as taints that abundance with his inhibitive scrupulosity, his very art will suffer.

Here indeed is a statement that rings true to the Everson/Antoninus of common knowledge—a statement which, like the previous injunction, breaks through the constrictive persona so dominant throughout *Prodigious Thrust*.

What may be allowed a Ginsberg, a Ferlinghetti, a McClure (to name but three from among the writers of that Beat Generation with which Antoninus was linked in the late 1950s), or a D.H. Lawrence or a Henry Miller for that matter, was no less allowable to a Brother Antoninus: the freedom of the artist to pursue his aesthetic vision. He had, for instance, already made forays into erotically infused religious poetry with "The Encounter," "A Savagery of Love," and "A Canticle to the Christ in the Holy Eucharist"—not to mention the baldly violational "The Cross Tore a Hole," left unpublished in its proper time.[17]

In the aftermath of his psychological breakthrough, Antoninus was better equipped to carry out the dictum he assigned to the poet; and, having espied "the mystical element in the erotic act and the erotic element in the mystical act," he pursued his "massive exploration of erotic mysticism" (as he terms the effort in his Afterword to *River-Root* in its initial publication) and his penetration into sacred violence with such poetry as *River-Root*, "The Song the

Body Dreamed," *The Rose of Solitude*, "The Last Crusade," and "The Tendril in the Mesh" before his Dominican years ended.

The truth of the matter is that, as a religious in the mystical tradition, Antoninus found a breadth, and with it a boldness, that the constricted poet of *The Residual Years* never touched. Something of this latitude of the imagination appears when, late in the book, he draws upon the metaphor of a sow's teats to express the spiritual nourishment proffered by the Church's sacramental system. To deflect the objections of readers whose religious sensibilities might be offended (certainly more likely then than now), he points out that "there are many levels of existence locked in a man, and they all need light"—a fact he himself would soon discover beyond his current awareness.

Nor may we ignore his daring exposition of the sexual act as containing a disposition toward the contemplative act. However painstakingly he pursues the rational orientation of his disquisition, assiduously marking his trail with citations from Thomas Aquinas and others, the real basis for his insight is intuitive, expressed in that segment of the discourse wherein he probes the physical-affective experience itself—moreso by far than the discursive approach indicated by such a statement as "I believe we can at last introduce a reappraisal of the sexual act as a legitimate contemplative element in the pluralist life of modern married people." What we witness is the situational use of the rational in the service of the poet's intuition. And, for good measure, we may note that it was the experiential segment which he cited later as "the theological underpinning of the sexual act."[18]

In such instances as these we see the Everson/Antoninus who—so emphatically present in his poetry, his readings, his personal encounters—seems so largely absent from the pages of his earnest book. At the same time, they enhance our grasp of that tension out of which he wrote, signifying for him and for us the liberation he sensed and desired, but did not possess.

\* \* \*

We come now to the pivot upon which the book, considered *in situ*, turns toward *initiation*, having been the means by which Antoninus articulated his *separation*. The tension inhering in *Prodigious Thrust* has shifted, moving from the disparity between persona and person to the impasse between "exterior observance" and "inner freedom." The net result, as he stated it in his mid-1955 Epilogue, was "the implacable darkness that is driving me out of the Order."

Given the difference between the sequence of the book's composition and the sequence of its final arrangement, the turning point is not obvious. So we start with what we know. And what we know is that Part Four, well over half the book, is principally comprised, on the one hand, of the poems making up "The Falling of the Grain" (including the otherwise unpublished "From the Summer of the Flesh") and, on the other, a variety of discourses regarding sexuality (contraception, homosexuality, sexual mores, the nature of marriage and marital sexuality, and the contemplative element within the sexual act). Certainly these two components relate to each other—the poet's concern with his marriage and its termination; the convert's concern with the appropriate understanding of sexuality. Yet, the extensiveness, the disproportion even, of this concern is suggestive.

In the course of his discussion of sexuality and its relation to the spiritual life, Antoninus refers to St. Augustine's decidedly negative attitude toward sexuality, and instances that venerable Doctor's Rule for the monastic order he had founded and which was read at regular intervals in the St. Albert's refectory:

> And you listen agreeably to his gentle admonitions, his sweetness, gravity, moderation and control; until at last he approaches his old compulsion [i.e., sexuality], and then his breath begins to thicken, the pitch rises, the language takes on a more electric urgency, and soon one sees the sweat upon that agitated brow.

One wonders if any of the other Dominicans sitting there saw "the sweat upon that agitated brow." More likely, the poet's acute imagination reflected the monk's unacknowledged fellow-feeling.

Is it too much to speculate that the extensive concern with sexuality had its source in the particular power sexuality exerted within Everson, but which Antoninus attempted to suppress? That his diverse discussions of sexuality within the doctrinal parameters—however honest his belief in those parameters, however valid those parameters might be—were a form of that "willed imposition" by which to stave off the threatening eroticism: a perpetuation of that "mask" he thought had been "demolished": his need to "contain the interior demon in the cage of verbal structure"—buttressed now by a doctrinal structure as well? Such questions provide the atmospherics. We need not speculate.

In mid-1954, Antoninus wrote "The Cross Tore a Hole," the last substantial poem before the poetic drought took hold. It was, as I mentioned earlier, patently violational, quite distinct from the sensitive use of sexual imagery in its predecessor, "A Savagery of Love," written two years earlier. Marked by a bold phallicizing of the crucified Christ, with the death-moment as orgasm, the poem's dark impress is heightened by the depiction of the profane crowd at Calvary and, especially, by a summary portrayal of some of the most lascivious and destructive women the pages of Scripture have to offer.

In effect, "The Cross Tore a Hole" had brought Antoninus to the brink of that deep interior realm inhabited by all the shadow-aspects of sexuality, where sexual *acts*, sexual *behavior*, are revealed as but the manifestations of the unconditioned, indiscriminate sexual *force*. Thus Antoninus' attempts to contain sexual behavior within the parameters of reason and doctrine were ultimately ineffective in terms of his personal situation. For a monk, as celibate and contemplative, Antoninus acknowledges that "no force is so disruptive to the serene interior life as the sexual force." And here lies the deepest configuration of his tension, the "underlying torsion" (to borrow from his later poem of that title) between the erotic and the mystical—in spite of his recognition of the "deep sympathy between erotic and religious mysticism." And we have his word on it when, writing of himself in the third person some twenty years later, he stated: "It is clear that Brother Antoninus's dark night was directly due to the repression of Eros which monasticism necessarily entails...."[19]

In her renowned *Mysticism*, Evelyn Underhill writes that mysticism "involves the organizing of the whole self, conscious and unconscious...a remaking of the whole character on high levels in the interest of the transcendental life."[20] The writing of *Prodigious Thrust* was the work of consciousness. In its re-visioning of the past and its delineation of the present, the book served to clear the ground for the future: refining, honing consciousness until only the thinnest of layers separated Antoninus from the deeper psyche of the unconscious. The more his mind sought to contain the sexual force by considering the manifestations of sexuality and retaining them within reason and doctrine, the greater that force became in the unconscious—the psychological counterpart to the law of physics: every action has an equal and opposite reaction. And then the book took him one step further.

His Preface, dated July 2, 1956, signalling the book's completion, the time for laying it aside, was premature. The episode of the impotence that disrupted the sexual union which he extolls (while acknowledging its wayward context) remained to be told. And its telling came at the center of a week of such psychic density that a brief recounting (drawn from the poet/monk's personal papers) of what transpired is necessary so that our purpose of regarding the book "within its original circumstances of composition and completion" will be fulfilled.[21]

As the result of a friend's dismissive attitude toward the poetry of the 1948 *The Residual Years*, Antoninus succumbed to a depressive mood—"a pattern that goes back to childhood," as he put it. Two days later [i.e., July 21], a close friend at St. Albert's, Fr. Blaise Schauer, visited him in his room and, in his concern for the troubled Brother, suggested that his propensity "for plunging into terrific moods showed some great interior [ir]resolution" and offered his advice that Antoninus be attentive to his dreams to "try to see some clue to the problem." The effect was dramatic:

> That set me to thinking. I had never associated my black moods to my interior situation, had seen them always in terms of concrete situations.

With this new awareness, Antoninus began to consider his emotional reactions in terms of the Freudian perspective.[22]

That evening he visited some married friends with whom he had developed a particularly close relationship. His notes give us a succinct account of what followed:

> We talked a bit about the castration complex, and the moments of impotences. Coming home on the bus I began to consider the impotence incident with Mary [i.e., his second wife]. I got home late that night, or rather early Sunday morning [July 22], and began to write the episode

> of the impotence scene for *Prodigious Thrust*. I wrote on it all day Sunday.
>
> ...
>
> Monday morning I had my great dream of Eric Gill and Fr. McNabb [which he entitled "The Destination Dream"], which gave me the clue to certain aspects of my vocation, and threw a whole new searchlight down the interior areas which Fr. Bla[i]se's talk with me had opened up.
>
> Then on Tuesday July 24, during Mass I perceived how yesterday's dream provided me with the opening and theme of my new book [i.e., the projected sequel to *Prodigious Thrust*].... I began to write the book, beginning with the dream, but at midday a letter came from a man who wants to publish my old war poem "The Raid" and asked for a few words on the genesis of the poem. As I considered what to say these "reductive" concerns of the last few days began to find form. Working down through level after level of the poem I saw that it was actually a kind of dream—an ideational form concealing a deeper meaning. And in this poem I saw the heart of my old guilt.

That "heart of my old guilt" was not other than the Oedipus Complex founded upon the incest wish. This was the immediate term of these few days, during which, as Antoninus comments, "the interior clarification has been going on at so fast a rate that I can hardly assimilate it."

The next day, July 25, he pursued his inner scrutiny by creating a narrative scenario meant to encapsulate his early adolescent situation under the Oedipal influence, an effort which led directly to the "breakthrough into the unconscious"—a descent into an incest phantasy of astounding and graphic dimensions, which played itself out in three successive occurrences.

This was his *initiation*, and nothing would be the same again. Looking back, three years later, Antoninus wrote: "In fact it was the writing of the impotence scene...which precipitated the new breakthrough, a breakthrough which began the total revamping of my life—I mean the reinterpretation of my past life and my place in the universe."[23]

Belatedly recounted, to be slipped in among the pages of his book at an appropriate juncture midway in Part Four, the impotence episode cuts across the momentum of Antoninus' effort in *Prodigious Thrust*. For the book is fundamentally masculine—its discursive process, its assertive tendentiousness. The very title, *Prodigious Thrust*, is so masculine, so phallic. Even Christianity's prime symbol partakes of this maleness:

> And who can ignore the intense phallic character of the Cross itself, the prodigious thrust transfixed by the prone line of the horizontal, male and female interlocked, pinned together by the compelling attraction each has for the other, Christ's passion purifying the basic generative symbol of the race?

This observation, a perfect gloss for the central imagery of "The Cross Tore a Hole," emphasizes the pervasive male sexuality at work within Antoninus during the composition of his book.

No wonder the episode had been nearly bypassed, this account of every man's nightmare: impotence. It provided a concretely specific correlative to the personal measure of his efforts gone awry: the *Psalter*'s abandonment, the poetic vacuum, the abortive attempt at the priesthood, the ineffectual "exterior observance." Antoninus says it himself in his Epilogue, a year before writing the account: "One thing I have discovered: imperfectly, confusedly, but still a discovery—that I am helpless, impotent." It was *Thanatos* given experiential embodiment as adversary to *Eros*, gladiators in the arena of the deeps of the psyche.

In effect, taking up the impotence episode was the final turn of the screw to bring that tension born of "the repression of Eros which monasticism entails" to its final pitch. Thus it was not the Preface which signaled the completion of *Prodigious Thrust*. It was the "Destination Dream"—pointing with its symbolic imagery toward a new direction for Antoninus. Referring again to those Bancroft papers, we find that, while napping after the completion of his early morning duties, Antoninus experienced the dream a second time, and, "as I come out of my dozing I realize that today [July 23, 1956] is the seventh anniversary of my Baptism [July 23, 1949]." With uncanny coincidence the day was also the tenth anniversary of his receipt on July 23, 1946, of the letter releasing him from his wartime conscription and into the circumstances that would culminate in his conversion. It was a closure.

Here we gain the recognition of how *Prodigious Thrust* takes its place in the trajectory delineated by Everson's penchant for writing his way through "life crises" and which, until now, has been tracked through the tripartite *Years* of his poetry—Residual, Veritable, Integral. *Prodigious Thrust* snaps into place, filling the hiatus between "The Cross Tore a Hole" and the psychological breakthrough which would resolve the restraining tension, dissolve at last the self-imposed "mask," and usher in the renewal of the poetic flow. However incomplete Antoninus chose to regard his book, the truth is that it had indeed been consummated: the work of *separation* accomplished, *initiation* at hand, and *return* in the offing.

\* \* \*

*And so much to be said. And so many better ways to say it.*

As we conclude this consideration of *Prodigious Thrust*, we realize that it could not be, after all, the book Antoninus set out to fashion: "essentially a book of poetry supported by an autobiographical context." The poetry is there, to be sure, reminding us that within the convert, within the monk, there was, as always, the poet. And certainly the book contains much of interest as to the inception and significance of the poems—as, indeed, there is much of interest and value in the book as autobiographical document, as elucidation of the ideas and practices at work within Everson's poetry, as a compendium of insightful ruminations, as an impressive example of the poet's way with prose, and much else. However, such interest as it bears in these and other aspects (and it is considerable) must be left to the reader's own inclination and to the commentaries of others.

As we have noted, conversion involves mystery, as does that assent to faith by which the process springs to life. Antoninus tells us that "the positive evidence in a man's life, the true line by which the intellect is led to its assent, is something extraordinarily subtle and complex, *and the very fabric of this book is meant to summon up the way the soul engages it in the context of the real*" [italics mine]. This his book does. *Prodigious Thrust* is not the exposition or the explication of conversion, of a man's assent to faith; it is, rather, the literary incarnation of that profound interior process. This fact is the book's particular, nearly unique excellence. In this also lies the reason why, in spite of the passing of so many years and the radical personal and institutional developments that took place, there was no revision.

For this we are properly grateful: anything other would have been *about* the convert; what we have *is* the convert, warts and all. In Antoninus' earnest effort to show us himself as convert, we experience the full-hearted honesty of the *man*, whether we name him Antoninus or Everson, and in this experience we find the personal reward of our reading. For however restive we might become at his convert's tenacity in pursuit of some doctrinal ratiocination, or however uncomfortable in the glare of his zealous tendentiousness, his own acknowledgment of the faults and deficiencies assures us of the genuineness out of which he writes.

Consequently, beyond the differences and discomforts that may attend the reading, we feel a kinship, seeing in his effort something like our own need and our own efforts to make some conclusive sense of our lives. Perhaps, too, this response will be enhanced by the consideration of the evolving tensions which formed a singular part of his experience and his writing. Nor should we overlook the real possibility that, within the orthodoxy he propounds, there reside undeniable values, genuine verities that doctrines are meant to preserve and which Everson himself never abandoned, for, according to his appraisal from 1963, "it is not that my faith has in any way lessened, but that my attitude toward its tenets has tempered and gained breadth."

In any event, contrary to his sense that *Prodigious Thrust* was incomplete, "a painful truncation," the book *is* complete, its story told, compelling and authentic. True enough, the projected second volume that would "narrate the search for vocation and the spiritual ascent" was never written—nothing more than an opening episode revolving around a dream, but sputtering away amidst several subsequent and unsuccessful attempts to mould a continuation out of the proliferation of material that accumulated as he added a monumental probe of the psyche's netherworld to the specifically spiritual concerns of the mystical life (if, indeed, one may make such a distinction). Everson's life had other uses, other labors.

Perhaps one day that second volume will be compiled by some doggedly dedicated Everson scholar sifting carefully through the trove of papers housed at the Bancroft Library. Perhaps not. It is no matter to us here (though in those days it aroused enough enthusiasm that a group of clerical novices at St. Albert's pooled what resources they could gather and presented Antoninus with a new typewriter—specifically for the purpose of writing that companion volume).

No, the only regret is that Bill Everson does not live here anymore and is not a party to his book's long-delayed publication.

I am reminded of Maritain's bittersweet question: "What are we all but men condemned to die, hastening strangely to pronounce our message before passing on to the place where all messages are useless and where all things are visible in their nakedness?" [24]

Strange, even incongruous as it may seem, *Prodigious Thrust* is part and parcel of William Everson's "message"—its scansion previously limited mainly to the *Years* of his poetry. Now, this book fills the gap with its publication (due, we should appreciatively acknowledge, to the judiciously vigorous stewardship of Bill Hotchkiss as Everson's literary executor). In that retrospective appraisal from 1963, Everson was moved to a sense of regret that his book had not been published in its own season, for "a great many things about my development would be made clear."

I would like to think that the approach I have taken and the observations I have offered contribute to that clarification my friend anticipated.

Allan Campo

January 21, 1995
Toledo, Ohio

## Notes:

1. Hermann Broch, *The Death of Virgil*, trans. Jean Starr Untermeyer (San Francisco: North Point Press, 1983), p. 315.
2. Victor White, O.P., S.T.B., *God and the Unconscious*, Foreword by C.G. Jung, Introduction by William Everson (Dallas: Spring Publications, 1982), p. ix. "Introduction" collected in William Everson, *On Writing the Waterbirds and Other Presentations*, ed. Lee Bartlett (Metuchen, N.J.: The Scarecrow Press, Inc., 1983), pp. 149-50.
3. Quoted and cited material not otherwise referenced is taken from *Prodigious Thrust* (with the exception of the phrase "breakthrough into the unconscious," a descriptive phrase Everson often used for his 1956 encounter with the unconscious).
4. Joseph Campbell, *The Hero with a Thousand Faces*, Bollingen Series XVII, "2nd ed." (Princeton: Princeton University Press, 1968), p. 30.
5. *Ibid.*, p. 51.
6  William James, *The Varieties of Religious Experience* (New York: The Modern Library, Random House, Inc., n.d.), p. 193.
7. Barbara Hannah, *Jung [:] His Life and Work [,] A Biographical Memoir* (New York: G.P. Putnam's Sons, 1976), p. 109.
8. Ruth Teiser, *Brother Antoninus: Poet, Printer, and Religious* [Interview] (Berkeley: University of California, Bancroft Library, 1966), pp. 76-77.
9. Martin D'Arcy, S.J., as quoted in William Everson, *Naked Heart; Talking on Poetry, Mysticism, and the Erotic* [Interviews] (Albuquerque: University of New Mexico, 1992), p. 17, n. 9.
10. *Ibid.* p. 11.
11. Antoninus Wall, O.P., Interview by Allan Campo, Nov. 6, 1975.
12. Everson, *On Writing the Waterbirds...*, pp. 36-37.
13. *Ibid.*, p. 37.
14. *Perspectives on William Everson*, ed. James B. Hall, Bill Hotchkiss, Judith Shears (Grants Pass, OR: Castle Peak Editions, 1992), p. 58.
15. Teiser, pp. 76-77.
16. Everson, *Naked Heart...*, p. 11.
17. "The Cross Tore a Hole," written in 1954, did not appear in print until it was published with "A Savagery of Love," in William Everson, *The Mate-Flight of Eagles; Two Poems on the Love-Death of the Cross*, Afterword by Allan Campo (Newcastle, CA: The Blue Oak Press, 1977). It was then included in William Everson, *The Veritable Years 1949-1966*, Afterword by Albert Gelpi (Santa Barbara, CA: Black Sparrow Press, 1978).
18. William Everson, *River-Root [:] A Syzygy for the Bicentennial of These States* (Berkeley: Oyez Press, 1976), p. 48. "Afterword" collected in *On Writing...*, p. 94.

19. *Ibid.*, p. 45. In *On Writing...*, p. 88.
20. Evelyn Underhill, *Mysticism* [:] *A Study in the Nature and Development of Man's Spiritual Consciousness* (New York: Meridian Books, Inc., 1955), p. 90.
21. The material from which the "brief recounting" is derived is in the collection of William Everson's papers maintained at the Bancroft Library of the University of California at Berkeley. The specific papers used here are journal pages contained in Carton 13.
22. Everson's use of Freudian concepts was based largely upon his then-recent reading of Herbert Marcuse, *Eros and Civilization; A Philosophical Inquiry into Freud* (Boston: The Beacon Press, 1955).
23. Brother Antoninus, Letter to Allan Campo, Sept. 11, 1959.
24. Jacques Maritain, *Existence and Existent*, trans. Lewis Galantiere and Gerald B. Phelan, "Vintage Books" (New York: Random House, Inc., 1966), pp. 145-46.

Photo: Ron Chamberlain

# WILLIAM EVERSON

### September 10, 1912-June 2, 1994

Throughout the course of his long life, William Everson passed through three distinct careers as a poet. Growing up in the heart of California's San Joaquin Valley (in the town of Selma, not far from Fresno), Everson discovered his true poetic vocation in his 1934 encounter with the poetry of Robinson Jeffers—an encounter that led Everson to aspire toward the creation of a body of poetry drawn from the material of his valley, as well as from his own personal experiences. His initial confessional sequences were twenty years in advance of the mode that ultimately gained currency from the late '50s onward. There in the Valley of the San Joaquin, the poet and his high school sweetheart, Edwa Poulson, were married following Edwa's graduation from Fresno State, and the young couple leased the old Wenty Ranch, where the poet tended grapevines and wrote. The Second World War interrupted this San Joaquin isolation when Everson was conscripted as a conscientious objector and spent over three years interned in federal work camps. At Waldport, Oregon (his primary place of internment), he was instrumental in the founding of the Untide Press and in the establishment of the Waldport Fine Arts Program—projects which were to contribute to the development of the San Francisco Renaissance of the 1950s. The War years saw the breakup of Everson's marriage to Edwa, and, after his release from "alternative service," the poet eventually settled in Berkeley with his second wife, poet and artist Mary Fabilli.

On Christmas Eve of 1948, Everson underwent a conversion from his proclaimed agnosticism to Catholicism; and, because the Church could not recognize their marriage, Bill and Mary were obliged to separate. In 1951, Everson became Brother Antoninus of the Dominican Order, at St. Albert's Priory, in Oakland, California, where he wrote *Prodigious Thrust*, a book destined to remain unpublished for forty years. Indeed, the post-conversion years gave birth to the second major division of his career. Through the publication of his three major collections of religious poetry and his readings throughout the country from 1958 on through the 1960s, Antoninus became known as "the Beat Friar" and achieved a measure of fame quite beyond that of the earlier period.

After eighteen and a half years, Antoninus' situation was, again, abruptly changed—this time by virtue of his leaving the Dominican Order in December, 1969 (a year short of his final vows), to marry Susanna Rickson.

Resuming his secular identity, William Everson, his new wife, and his adopted son, Jude, moved in 1971 to Kingfisher Flat, in Big Creek Canyon, some fourteen miles north of Santa Cruz. As poet-in-residence at Kresge College of the University of California at Santa Cruz, he spent ten years giving a series of meditative lectures and resurrecting the Lime Kiln Press. This latter project not only brought Everson new fame as a master printer but enabled him to nurture an entire generation of creative printers and artists. To match his earlier handpress printing of the *Psalter*, executed during his first years as a Dominican, Everson and his students at the Lime Kiln Press produced a series of acclaimed editions, including *Granite and Cypress*, a collection of Robinson Jeffers' poems in a volume that has been hailed as one of the masterworks of American fine-press printing—as, indeed, the *Psalter* had been twenty years earlier.

During these Santa Cruz years, Everson created more poetry, brought forth several handpress volumes, became a recognized first-rank critic and scholar of Jeffers' poetry, continued his public readings, and added further essays and interviews to his growing body of work—even as Parkinson's disease took its increasing toll on his physical capacity.

On the occasion of his eightieth birthday, Everson and his wife Susanna separated and were subsequently divorced. Struck down by pneumonia in the fall of 1993, the poet survived the nearly fatal attack and returned to his beloved Kingfisher Flat home where, a few months later, after an interval during which he was visited by a constant stream of friends, scholars, former students, and fellow poets, William Everson died in his own bed on June 2, 1994. Following a memorial mass and funeral services at St. Albert's Priory, he was buried in the Dominican Cemetery in Benicia, California.

Hailed by Albert Gelpi as "the most important religious poet of the second half of the twentieth century" and by Diane Wakoski as "one of the most essential and dynamic American poets of the mid-twentieth century," Everson received various honors and awards, from a Guggenheim Fellowship in 1949 to the silver medal of the Commonwealth Club of California, the Shelley Award from the Poetry Society of America, and the PEN Center West Body of Work

Award. Finally, and perhaps most heartwarming of all, Everson received the Santa Cruz County 1991 Artist of the Year Award.

William Everson has left us about fifty published volumes, including some thirty-five of his poetry, several books of Jeffers scholarship and criticism, and various volumes of superb handpress work. At the time of his death, he had completed half of his projected autobiographical poetic epic, *Dust Shall Be the Serpent's Food.*

## ALLAN CAMPO

Allan Campo was born in Los Angeles in 1934 and remained a resident there until he moved to Toledo, Ohio, at the end of 1993. Obtaining both a Bachelor's and a Master's degree from Loyola University (now Marymount), Campo taught high school for eight years before taking work with the Postal Service, from which he retired after nearly twenty-five years. He is the father of two sons and three daughters.

Campo's friendship with William Everson began in 1958—as a result of the poet's initial reading appearances in Los Angeles, his first readings outside the San Francisco Bay Area—and was sustained by numerous letters, phone conversations, and visits (including many to the poet's Kingfisher Flat home during the last twenty years of Everson's life); the friendship was accompanied by Campo's ongoing interest in the poet's work.

Allan Campo co-edited, with Lee Bartlett, *William Everson: A Descriptive Bibliography* and wrote an "Afterword" for Everson's *The Mate-Flight of Eagles*. Most substantial has been his long-time "work in progress"—*Soul and the Search: The Poetry of William Everson* ("finished several times," as Campo says, "but only now approaching completion")—from which substantial segments have been included in *Poet from the San Joaquin, Benchmark and Blaze*, and *Perspectives on William Everson*.

Currently, Campo and Bill Hotchkiss are heading up the preparation of an authoritative collection of Everson's *Complete Poems*—to be issued by Black Sparrow as a three-volume sequence under the individual titles of *The Residual Years, The Veritable Years,* and *The Integral Years.*

Printed April 1996 in Santa Barbara
& Ann Arbor for the Black Sparrow Press
by Mackintosh Typography & Edwards Brothers Inc.
Text set in Souvienne with University Ornate heads.
Design by Barbara Martin.  This edition
is published in paper wrappers;
there are 250 hardcover trade copies;
& 126 numbered deluxe copies have been
handbound in boards by Earle Gray.